ENGLISH POTTERY
AND PORCELAIN

ENGLISH POTTERY AND PORCELAIN

By

GEOFFREY WILLS

Guinness Superlatives Limited
2 Cecil Court, London Road, Enfield, Middlesex

ISBN 0 85112 145 4

First published in Great Britain by
Guinness Superlatives Limited
2 Cecil Court
London Road, Enfield, Middlesex

Colour Separations By
Newsele Litho Limited, London and Milan

Printed in Great Britain by
Redwood Burn Limited, Trowbridge, Wilts.

CONTENTS

POTTERY

PORCELAIN

INTRODUCTION

IN the following pages the reader will find described the history of the various pottery and porcelain manufactories, large and small, which were active in England between about 1600 and 1900. In addition, there are black-and-white illustrations and colour plates showing many hundreds of specimens of their output. The pieces shown are of all types and not confined to the rare and costly, but include many that are comparatively commonplace. A large proportion of them have been photographed especially, and give the book an added interest. In this connection, the writer is grateful to Robert Chapman of Plymouth for his skilful use of his cameras, and for his congenial company during many lengthy journeys to visit collectors and museums. No less, thanks are due to those who have so kindly allowed pieces in their ownership or their care to be handled and photographed, and to Roger Penhallurick for his line-drawings of maps and marks.

Continuing research adds much to our knowledge of the past. The keen collector assists in this no less than does the mechanical digger, and the fact that there must remain so much to explore and bring to light is a spur to further interest. It is hoped that this book will stimulate investigation of the subject, and will encourage collectors, old and new, to add their quota to the record of this important achievement of our forefathers.

Geoffrey Wills.

BIBLIOGRAPHY

T<small>HE</small> following is a list of the principal sources consulted in writing this volume:

Pottery and Porcelain—General

Llewellynn Jewitt
The Ceramic Art of Great Britain, 2 vols., 1878.

L. M. Solon
The Art of the Old English Potter, 2nd edition, 1885.

J. E. and E. Hodgkin
Examples of Early English Pottery, 1891.

W. B. Honey
English Pottery and Porcelain, 5th edition, 1952. *European Ceramic Art*, 1952.

W. Mankowitz and R. G. Haggar
Concise Encyclopaedia of English Pottery and Porcelain, 1957.
English Ceramic Circle, Transactions, 1933–.

Pottery—General

Bernard Rackham
Catalogue of the Glaisher Collection, 2 vols., Cambridge, 1934.

Ross E. Taggart
Catalogue of the Burnap Collection, 2nd edition, Kansas City, 1967.

Monographs—Red Clay Ware

Ronald C. Cooper
English Slipware Dishes, 1968.

Delftware

F. H. Garner
English Delftware, 1948.

Geoffrey Wills
English Pottery in 1696, in *Apollo*, June 1967.

Anthony Ray
English Delftware, 1968.

Cream Ware

Donald C. Towner
English Cream-coloured Earthenware, 1957. *The Leeds Pottery*, 1963.

Wedgwood

Elizabeth Meteyard
The Life of Josiah Wedgwood, 2 vols., 1865.

Alison Kelly
Decorative Wedgwood, 1965.

Edited by Ann Finer and George Savage
Selected Letters of Josiah Wedgwood, 1965
Wedgwood Society, Proceedings, 1956–.

Porcelain—General

J. E. Nightingale
Contributions Towards the History of Early English Porcelain, Salisbury, 1881.

Arthur Lane
English Porcelain Figures of the 18th Century, 1961.

Bernard Watney
English Blue and White Porcelain of the 18th Century, 1963.

Edited by R. J. Charleston
English Porcelain, 1965.
English Porcelain Circle, Transactions, 1928–1932.
(See also Pottery and Porcelain—General.)

Bow

British Museum
Catalogue of the Special Exhibition, 1959.

Hugh Tait
Some Consequences of the Bow Porcelain Special Exhibition, in *Apollo*, February, April and June, 1960.

Derby

John Haslem
The Old Derby China Factory, 1876.

Worcester

R. W. Binns
A Century of Potting in the City of Worcester, 1865 and 1877.

Cyril Cook
Life and Work of Robert Hancock, 1948. *Supplement to the Life and Work of Robert Hancock*, 1955.

H. Rissik Marshall
Coloured Worcester Porcelain, Newport, 1954.

Franklin A. Barrett
Worcester Porcelain and Lund's Bristol, 2nd edition, 1966.

Longton Hall

Bernard Watney
Longton Hall Porcelain, 1957.

Lowestoft

G. J. Levine
Inscribed Lowestoft Porcelain, Norwich, 1968.

Bristol

Hugh Owen
Two Centuries of Ceramic Art in Bristol, 1873.

Victorian

Geoffrey A. Godden
Victorian Porcelain, 1961.

Ernest Reynolds
Collecting Victorian Porcelain, 1966.

Elizabeth Aslin
The Rise and Progress of the Art Union of London, in *Apollo*, January 1967.

Shirley Bury
Felix Summerly's Art Manufactures, in *Apollo*, January 1967.

Marks on Pottery and Porcelain

Geoffrey A. Godden
Encyclopaedia of British Pottery and Porcelain Marks, 1964.
Handbook of British Pottery and Porcelain Marks, 1968.

J. P. Cushion and W. B. Honey
Handbook of Pottery and Porcelain Marks, 3rd edition, 1965.

J. P. Cushion
Pocket-book of English Ceramic Marks, 1965.

1 Red Clay Ware:
Part 1

WHILE pottery was made in England from very early times, such wares are more in the province of the archaeologist than in that of the collector. Medieval examples are almost equally as scarce as those of preceding centuries; most of them are now in museums and few appear on the open market. Survivors from the aptly-named Dark Ages rarely interest present-day collectors, because so few specimens are available and in most instances they are unsuited for display in modern surroundings. Nonetheless, they form part of the history of pottery, and the techniques employed in their making will be found to lead forward to the more familiar shapes and patterns of later times.

The earliest of the pottery, dating between the 12th and 14th centuries, took the form of jugs and other utilitarian articles. They were made mostly from red clay, although occasionally grey and brown ones were used, baked hard and sometimes embellished with ornament. The latter was of a simple nature, and the attraction of the ware lies principally in its shaping. The symmetry given by the potter's wheel and

Right, *Fig. 1: Jug of buff-coloured clay, formed as a man. 14th/15th century. Height 4¾ inches. (Burnap Collection, Nelson Gallery-Atkins Museum, Kansas City, Missouri.)*

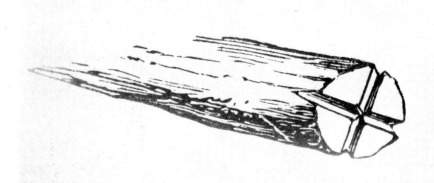

Above, *Fig. 2: Stick cut with notches for impressing a pattern in clay.* **Below,** *Fig. 3: Yellow-glazed tile moulded with the royal arms and initials of Edward VI (died 1553) or Elizabeth I (died 1603). Sixteenth century. 13½ by 10⅛ inches. (County Museum, Truro.)*

hands, and approved by his eye, resulted in vessels of plain but satisfying shapes.

It had been found at an early date that pottery vessels were porous unless treated in some way to make them watertight. To achieve this in a permanent way the makers dusted the dried clay surface with powdered lead ore, which melted in the heat of the kiln and combined with silica present in the clay. The effect was to give the article a coating of what was literally glass: known when on pottery as glaze.

In 1685, Dr Robert Plot published a *History of Staffordshire*, and included in it accounts of glazing, decorating and firing. These had not changed materially from earlier times, and his eye-witness descriptions apply to English red clay pottery at almost any date. Plot wrote thus of glazing:

> After the vessels are dry they lead them, with that sort of lead ore they call smithum, which is the smallest ore of all, beaten into a dust, finely sifted and strewed upon them; which gives them the gloss, but not the colour . . . But when they have a mind to show the utmost of their skill in giving their ware a fairer gloss than ordinary, they lead them with lead calcined into powder,

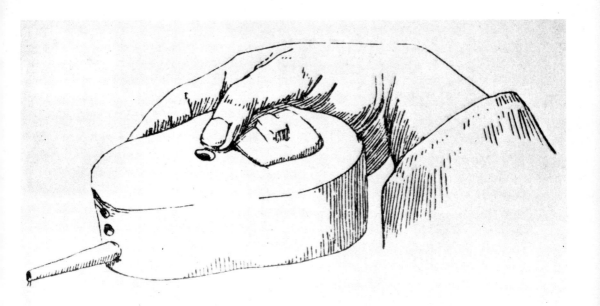

which they also sift fine and strew upon them as before, which not only gives them a higher gloss, but goes further into their work, than lead ore would have done.

While it was essential to glaze the interior of most vessels, it was soon discovered that an attractive finish was given by treating the outside in the same way. It was found, too, that the addition of certain oxides would give tinted glazes. Considerable use was made in this way of copper oxide which, when applied over a thin coating of white clay, gave the ware a greenish-yellow finish. On a red clay it produced a dark brown.

The clear lead glaze on its own did not give a perfectly colourless finish. Although glass-like in composition and as regards its glistening surface, it was never free from a brownish stain of varying intensity. This was due to impurities in the clay body of the article together with others in the lead, which in the heat of the kiln blended with the glaze. The effect is particularly noticeable where white clay is concerned, and it will be seen that this is invariably changed to a deep cream colour.

Almost as popular with the public as the

Above, Fig. 4: Slip trailer, drawn by M. L. Solon. Below, Fig. 5: Slip-decorated tyg, dated 1653 and initialled G.R. for George Richardson. Wrotham, Kent. Height about 6½ inches. (City Museum and Art Gallery, Hanley, Staffordshire.)

greenish-yellow glaze was one of a dark brown or black, made with the aid of manganese. In the course of excavations conducted at the end of the nineteenth century many fragments of thinly-potted red clay articles covered in glazes of these colours were found. As they were discovered on the sites of Cistercian Abbeys in Wales and Yorkshire it was supposed that the wares had been a speciality of that order. In more recent years similar examples have been recovered from secular sites, but all are usually grouped together and termed 'Cistercian'. The same name is used for them whether they came from the Abbeys (and are therefore pre-1540 when the order suffered dissolution) or from elsewhere, and are mostly later in date.

Some of the Cistercian pieces have on them small pads of white clay and these, together with strapwork of the same material as the body or in a contrasting colour, were sometimes used on other wares. Ornamentation also took the form of patterns made on the semi-finished article with a pointed or notched stick (Fig. 2), a

patterned wheel or a carved mould (Fig. 3). Alternatively, jugs were modelled in human (Fig. 1) or animal shapes; precursors of the eighteenth century Toby.

A further method of decorating was to brush, 'dribble' or inlay clay of a contrasting colour to that of the body of the piece; usually dark brown or white on red. Inlaying was employed frequently in the 13th century for tiles, which were impressed by means of a carved wood block. The recesses thus produced were filled with white clay, the surplus removed and the whole baked. Clay for painting with a brush, or for 'dribbling', was thinned with water to make what is named 'slip'; the liquid being made of a consistency to suit the work.

For this type of decoration, Dr Plot noted certain types of clay, which 'being of a looser and more friable nature; these, mixt with water, they make into a consistence thinner than a syrup, so that being put into a bucket it will run out through a quill'. The word 'bucket' probably meant a container of some kind that was not

15

necessarily the modern article with that name. A practical slip trailer is shown in Fig. 4. The flow from the nozzle was controlled by tipping the device and by putting the thumb over the air-hole in the top.

Although their decoration varied in detail, the different wares shared processes: the article was modelled in clay and allowed to dry and harden, decoration and glaze were applied if and where required, and lastly the piece was put, with others, into the kiln for baking.

Baking or firing the articles was described by Dr Plot as follows:

They are carried to the oven, which is ordinarily about eight feet high and about six feet wide, of a round copped forme, where they are placed one upon another from bottom to top; if they be ordinary ware such as cylindrical butter pots etc., they are exposed to the naked flame, and so is all of their flat ware though it be leaded [*lead-glazed*] having

only parting shards, i.e. thin bits of old pots between them, to keep them from sticking together. But if they be hollow leaded wares, they do not expose them to the naked fire, but put them in shraggers [*saggers: cases made of rough clay*] . . . In 24 hours an oven of pots will be burnt, then they let the fire goe out by degrees, which in 10 hours more will be perfectly done . . .

W ARES of the types described are of limited interest, and it is not until the reign of Queen Elizabeth I that pottery, like so many other arts and crafts, took a big step

Below, *Fig. 8: Cup of 'Metropolitan Ware'. Early 17th century. Height 4¾ inches. (County Museum, Truro.)* **Right, Plate 1:** *Dish with slip decoration, made and signed by Thomas Toft. Staffordshire. Circa 1680. Diameter 19 inches. (County Museum, Truro, Cornwall.)*

17

Plate 2 (Left) *Jug with a mottled glaze, excavated at Nottingham. Sixteenth century. Height 11 inches.* (Right) *Jug partly covered in a green glaze. Sixteenth century. Height 9½ inches. (County Museum, Truro.)*

Fig. 9: Slipware dish decorated with 'The Pelican in her Piety signed JOHN WRIGHT and dated 178 for 1708. Staffordshire. Diameter 17½ inches. (Phillips, Son & Neale, London; now in the City Museum and Art Gallery, Hanley.)

forward. From the early 1600's onwards it becomes possible to trace more easily the progress of ceramics in England, and more frequently leave the realms of speculation for surer ground.

The seventeenth century saw the establishment of a pottery at Wrotham, between Sevenoaks and Maidstone, Kent. A local red clay was used for making articles of all kinds, most of which have perished long ago. Survivors include a number of drinking-vessels, many of them of the type named 'tygs', which have three or more handles round the body. Ornament takes the form of shaped discs of white clay with patterns impressed on them, strands of white and red clay woven together like rope, and 'drips' of slip covering many of the remaining undecorated spaces. More rarely, the entire surface of a piece was covered with white clay and a design was scratched through this to reveal the red ground; a technique known as 'sgraffito' (see *Chapter* 2 page 23).

Dates on the surviving examples of Wrotham ware range between 1612 and 1739, and are usually accompanied by initials. These have been found to belong to members of local families connected with the pottery: the Livermores, Ifields, Richardsons and Hubbles, whose relations with the manufactory and with one another by marriage have been traced. A few pots and other pieces are inscribed WROTHAM, which has been of considerable help in research so that related items can be attributed to the common source. About sixty pieces of inscribed and dated Wrotham ware are known, and no doubt a few remain unrecognised and unrecorded and will come to light over the years.

Contemporary with the earlier Wrotham pieces was the manufacture of a type of pottery given the name of 'Metropolitan Ware', because much of it has been found in and about the city of London. The body is of a light red colour, and is decorated with white slip that appears cream (Fig. 8). Many specimens bear dates between 1630 and 1670, and a proportion are inscribed. The inscriptions often reflect the prevalent Puritanism of the country at the time,

Above left, *Fig. 10: Dish decorated in slip with the coronation of Charles II, and signed* WILLIAM TALOR. *Staffordshire.* Circa 1660. *Diameter 16½ inches. (Burnap Collection, Kansas City.)* **Above right,** *Fig. 11: Slip-decorated dish or charger signed by Ralph Toft.* **Opposite,** *Fig. 12: Jug with slip decoration, initialled W.S. for William Simpson and dated 1691. Staffordshire. Height 8¼ inches.*
(Sotheby's.)

Fig. 13: Slip-decorated posset pot inscribed 'The best is not too good for you', and dated 1679. Staffordshire. Height 5½ inches. (British Museum.)

with exhortations like *FEAR GOD, FAST AND PRAY* and *BE NOT HY MINDED BUT FEAR GOD.*

In recent years, preparations for the building of roads and houses at Harlow New Town, Essex, have led to the uncovering of the sites of some old kilns. They were at a place named Potter Street, where potters have been recorded as living from as early as 1254 down to the mid-seventeenth century. The many fragments found there were of 'Metropolitan' type, and clays for making it were in the area. As the potteries were situated only about 25 miles outside London, it is likely that they supplied much of the needs of the inhabitants.

Towards the close of the seventeenth century Staffordshire rose rapidly to become the centre of pottery manufacture in the country. It gained this status because

it was the site of ample supplies of suitable clay, as well as having large deposits of coal nearby. The latter was an important consideration, as the use of wood fuel for iron-founding and glass-making had depleted forests to such a degree that the Government encouraged alternative sources of heat. Transport was a further factor, and the location of coal and clay close together proved irresistible in the establishment and enduring supremacy of the district known familiarly as The Potteries.

The best-known of the wares surviving from the numerous potters in the area are the large-diameter chargers. Some of them measure as much as 22 inches across, and are heavily built in proportion. Their decoration in coloured slip is on the same scale, and has an attractive artlessness that has been long admired by successive generations of collectors and critics.

The chargers were not articles of everyday commerce, but were made to commemorate special events, to present to important local patrons and to give to relatives and friends. Their very size has given them a daunting magnificence which has doubtless ensured their preservation, while untold quantities of interesting, but purely utilitarian, ware has perished.

A number of the chargers bear names on them, many being of members of a family named Toft, and for that reason they are referred to sometimes as 'Toft' dishes. At one time it was thought they had been made for presentation to, or use by, Thomas Toft and the other named persons, but the finding of further inscribed examples made it not unreasonable to assume that the Tofts were actually potters. Evidence of this is now forthcoming, and a number of men bearing the surname have been noted as living in north Staffordshire and elsewhere in the county during the second half of the 17th century. The five children of a Thomas Toft, who died in 1689, were christened at Stoke-on-Trent.

In addition to the dishes, four other pieces bearing the name of Thomas Toft are known. They are a six-handled tyg, a three-handled posset pot, a jug, and a pot inscribed *Though neer so deep In me none peep*. Thomas Toft had a son of the same name, and it is thought that some of the forty or so pieces inscribed *THOMAS TOFT* may have been the work of Thomas junior. Others of the family who put their names to dishes similar to those of Thomas, were Ralph and James Toft.

The patterns on the Toft chargers cover a wide range, from representations of Charles II in the Boscobel Oak to massive renderings of the Royal arms complete with lion and unicorn supporters. Most of them have distinctive wide borders of criss-cross patterning of light and dark lines on a white ground, the latter of brushed-on slip, with a reserved space in which the name is written. Variants are a dish with a border of surprised-looking ladies' heads between floral motifs, another with a running loop pattern,

Fig. 14: Dish decorated with a formal pattern in slip. Staffordshire. Circa 1680. Diameter 14¼ inches. From Chirk Castle, Denbighshire. and now in the Burnap Collection, Kansas City.

and a third having tulip blooms alternating with bulbous shapes.

Dishes comparable in size and pattern to those of the Tofts were made by John and William Wright, William and George Taylor and Ralph Simpson, as well as by other potters who did not sign their work (Fig. 14) Those who did put their names on record were not always accurate in their spelling, and such oddities as *RALALPH TO* (for Ralph Toft) and William Talor and Tallor (for William Taylor) have been noted.

In 1907 Marc-Louis Solon, who was a French-born china-decorator working at Mintons's Staffordshire factory as well as being a keen student of early English pottery, wrote of a remarkable find of old chargers at Chirk Castle, Denbighshire. He recorded that some of them

> were standing on high shelves of the dark corridors of the castle; but the majority had been fixed, with heavy iron cramps, against the white-washed walls of a small dairy, elegantly equipped for the gratification of the Arcadian tastes entertained by one of the ladies of the family.

The dishes included examples signed by the Tofts and Ralph Simpson, and most of them are now in museums on both sides of the Atlantic. It is most improbable that a similar *cache* will ever again be brought to light, for the publicity attending the Chirk find caused a widespread search of attics, dairies, cellars and other likely places in the vain hope of comparable hauls (see Fig. 14).

In addition to dishes of all sizes, the Tofts and their contemporaries made many other articles (Figs. 12 & 13), but only a very small number of them still exist. Jugs and vessels for posset and other drinks popular at the time must have been very plentiful, and such things as fuddling-cups and puzzle-jugs will have existed in quantity. Both the latter challenge the drinker to empty the vessel, and most attempts to do so leave him with the contents in his lap or spilled down his shirt-front.

A former country custom was the giving of a miniature pottery cradle to a wedded couple. It was once said that such cradles were christening gifts, which some may well have been, but it is now suggested that they were fertility symbols presented at the time of marriage. Many surviving examples have slip decoration which records the names of the couple and the year of marriage. Dates on them cover about 150 years from 1670 onwards.

THE large dishes so far discussed were made by taking a lump ('bat') of kneaded clay and pressing it firmly over a simple domed mould. Often the finger- and thumb-marks of the potter remain at the back to prove how it was done. The edge of the dish was trimmed even with a knife, or patterned by pinching or by pressing on it a suitable object. The latter was sometimes a cockle-shell, which gave a neat fluted effect.

Fig. 16: Press-moulded dish with raised slip-filled decoration showing Charles II in the Boscobel Oak, initialled S.M. for Samuel Malkin of Burslem. Staffordshire. Circa 1720. *Diameter 13¾ inches. (Burnap Collection, Kansas City.)*

Alternatively, from early in the 18th century, the mould was given an incised pattern, and this would appear raised on the surface of the dish. The moulds used for this purpose were themselves made of clay, later baked, and two of them are now in museums. One, in the British Museum, has scratched on the back *William Bird made this mould in the year of our Lord* 1751. The front is cut with the figure of a man wearing a frock-coat and a tricorn hat, and a dish made from it is in Manchester City Art Gallery. The other surviving mould is in the Victoria and Albert Museum, has a geometric design on it and bears the name of a member of the Wedgwood family (perhaps Thomas Wedgwood, who died in 1737).

After being lifted from the mould, the dishes were further ornamented with coloured slip to fill the spaces between the raised lines of the design. Additional slip decoration applied in the ordinary manner was sometimes used on borders and to enhance the principal central pattern. While a greater number of dishes could be produced by this method than by the other, the effect of them is much stiffer with a noticeable loss of the earlier spontaniety.

The best-known exponent of this moulding technique was Samuel Malkin, who signed one dish with his name in full and several others with only his initials. He was perhaps born in 1668, lived and worked at Burslem, Staffordshire, and died in 1741. Dated specimens of Malkin's dishes range from 1712, their subjects are mostly religious or proverbial, and their diameter varies between 13¾ and 17 inches. All have rims finished with neat notches, and the raised outlines of the designs are usually milled with a series of narrow parallel lines, like the edge of a coin, made with a roulette.

2 Red Clay Ware:
Part 2

Fig. 17: Tickenhall, Derbyshire, dish decorated in slip with a fox hunt.

By the middle of the 18th century wares of red clay had become confined to the purely utilitarian, and the material was only rarely employed for show-pieces. It continued to be used for such essentials as jugs, mugs, baking-dishes and pocket-flasks, often quite plain, but also enhanced with slip ornament. They were made in a large number of places up and down the country wherever suitable clay and fuel were to be found, and the products were disposed of in local markets. The goods were only very occasionally marked, varied little from each other in appearance, and it is seldom possible to determine where they originated.

Mostly the wares have little appeal apart from their age, which entitles them to respect but not necessarily to admiration. A small proportion of specimens, however, has a wider interest because they bear dates, names or inscriptions. These not only give the pieces a personal association, but sometimes help in identifying the source of manufacture. This, in turn, can assist in allocating unmarked, but similar, examples.

Only a few of the potteries that once existed are now recorded; others live on in the names of streets and fields, and excavations occasionally bring to light remains of a kiln and its associated rubbish-tip. Unfortunately, it is seldom possible to allow sufficient time for full investigation, and archaeological work of this nature is usually conducted with a builder's foreman or clerk of works looking hard at his watch. Whatever little that can be done under such circumstances is better than nothing, but it is tantalizing, to say the least, to have to leave unsearched a suspected area that is going to be covered with buildings and remain inaccessible for an unknown time ahead.

The places where it is known that red clay pottery was made in the 18th and 19th centuries include the undermentioned, although it must be stressed that there were hundreds of others that came and went without leaving identifiable traces of their existence. The following list groups the potteries under counties, as it is found that many of the workshops in each area had characteristics in common with one another.

Buckinghamshire

Buckland. 'Thomas Brackley Potter' is inscribed on a jug covered in a dark brown glaze dated 1759, and a bottle of similar

Above, Fig. 18: Candlestick glazed in blue and yellow, dated 1649, marked in relief and inscribed made in Essex England. Castle Hedingham, late 19th century. Height 8½ inches. (Victoria and Albert Museum.)

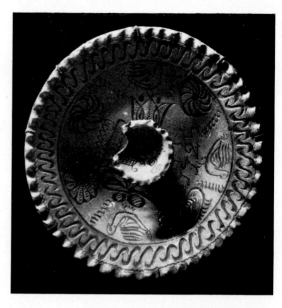

Above, Fig. 19: Dish of light red clay with incised ornament, initialled H. F. and dated 1725. Bideford, Devon. Diameter 14⅝ inches. (Now in Glashier Collection, Fitzwilliam, Museum, Cambridge.) **Right,** *Fig. 20: Salt kit of red clay inlaid with designs in white, initialled W.W. for William Woodward and dated 1749. Nottingham. Height 9½ inches. (Glaisher Collection.)*

Cumberland

Penrith. The Weatheriggs pottery was active in the nineteenth century, and made articles of red clay with white slip decoration.

Derbyshire

Bolsover. In 1895 fragments of slip-decorated ware, of buff body covered in a dark red slip, were excavated on the site of a pottery near the Market Square, Bolsover. Other pieces bore marbled patterns of red and white slip, made by carefully mingling together the two colours to produce a resemblance to stone or marble. The recovered fragments all have a yellowish glaze, and dishes and cups of a comparable greenish-yellow glaze and incised decoration.

type is inscribed 'Buckland Common 1793'. Another jug dated 1701 is linked with these two pieces, and points to a working-period lasting throughout the 18th century. The pottery was sited at Buckland, which is between Tring and Aylesbury.

Cambridgeshire

Ely. A pottery was owned by a family named Lucas, and closed in about 1840. The ware was decorated by inlaying white clay in the red body, and a typical example is a jug initialled *JL* (for Jabez Lucas) with the date 1796. A smaller establishment was that of Robert Sibley, which closed in 1861. Glazed pottery was made by Sibley 'only to order', and a specimen dated 1861 has a appearance have been recorded. One of the dishes is dated 1784.

Fig. 21: Tyg *and cover, initalled* W.D.
and dated 1677. Donyatt, Somerset.
Height 12½ inches. (Glaisher Collection.)

Tickenhall. There were potteries at Tickenhall (Ticknall), near Burton-on-Trent, from
mediaeval times, and a writer in 1650 noted
'earthen vessels, potts, and pancions (*pun-
cheons: large jars for holding liquids*),
at Tycknall, and carried all East England
through'. Nearly a century and a half
later the scene of prosperity had changed,
and it was recorded that

> Formerly a very large quantity of
> earthen ware was manufactured at this
> place; but lately business has much de-
> clined. It is said, that, since the land in
> the neighbourhood has been enclosed, it
> has been difficult to meet with proper
> clay.

Shallow baking-dishes of hard red clay with
simple slip decoration are attributed to
Tickenhall. They are covered with a yellowish glaze, but the backs of them are left
unglazed. Some examples with marbled slip
are also said to have been made there (see
Bolsover, above). Tickenhall wares do not
seem to have been marked or inscribed, and
it is only by comparison with well-authen-
ticated examples that attributions have
been made. One of the best-known pieces is
the dish in Fig. 17, in the City Art Gallery,
Manchester, which has been allocated to
the pottery for the past one hundred years.
However, such attributions, which rest on
honestly-held beliefs that do not always
withstand serious investigation, are always liable to be changed. Much that has
for long been labelled 'Tickenhall' is now
suspected as having originated in Staffordshire.

Devonshire

There have been, at one date and another,
numerous potteries in the vicinity of
Bideford, in the north of the county,
where the local white clay was available
for use in conjunction with the red clay of
Fremington. A popular speciality of the
area (and of Somerset, see below) was the
use of a type of decoration named sgraffito;
from the Italian, meaning scratched. The
red clay article was covered in white slip,
the pattern scratched in it with a pointed
instrument of wood or metal, and glazing
and firing then took place. The finished
effect is that the red underbody shows
through the incised places, and in most
instances the decorator achieved a rustic
simplicity comparable to that on Staffordshire slipware (Plate 3).

The motifs used were numerous, and
included coats of arms, flowers, birds and
the mariner's compass. Many pieces bear
names and dates, the latter ranging from
1700 onwards, and those with rhymes on
them usually rival in their theme and
spelling the efforts of potters elsewhere.
Harvest-jugs of generous capacity and
with the requisite sturdy handles have survived in some quantity. A verse on one of
them is typical in all respects of many
others, and runs:

> Harvis is cam all bissey
> Now in mackin of your
> Barly mow when men do
> Laber hard and swet good
> Ale is better far than meet
> Bideford   April 28
> 1775   M — W.

At Fremington, near Barnstaple, a pottery was established by George Fishley
towards the end of the 18th century, and
continued in the ownership of his descendants until 1912. The usual local-style
sgraffito-decorated wares were made, but in
addition to domestic articles there were
chimney ornaments in the form of figures
and watch-stands of red clay with applied
details in other colours under a deep yellow
glaze. An impressed mark *G. FISHLEY
FREMINGTON DEVON* was used in the
late 18th/early 19th centuries. From about
1839 the business was in the hands of
Edmund Fishley, and from about 1861 to
1906 the proprietor was Edwin Beer Fishley.
The names of these two are sometimes

found incised on their wares, and a jug inscribed 'R. Fishley jug' is recorded.

Essex

Castle Hedingham. A potter who had worked at Lambeth, named Edward Bingham, removed from London to Gestingthorpe (see below) in 1829, and six years later to Castle Hedingham, near Halstead. There, in the shadow of the ancient castle he built himself a pottery where he made flower pots and other domestic wares. His son of the same name eventually took over the business and in due course, after many vicissitudes, achieved success with his distinctive pseudo-archaic productions. He copied genuinely old pieces as well as creating his own 'antiques'. In the latter category is his 'Essex Jug', which is decorated with white clay reliefs showing historic local scenes, important buildings in the county, and the coats of arms of Essex and its bigger towns. It is glazed a dark brown and stands 14¾ inches high. The jug was produced in 1895, and there are examples of it at the Fitzwilliam Museum, Cambridge, and at the Colchester and Essex Museum, Colchester. In 1899 Bingham passed the business on to his son who was also named Edward, and two years later it was sold to become the Essex Art Pottery. The new firm did not endure for long and closed in 1905. In the following year Edward Bingham senior, then aged 77, went to the United States to join his family and shortly afterwards wrote to a friend: '. . . I feel and believe, my son Edward too, that we have done with pottery forever, He is working at a large store in the city as a china packer . . .'

Castle Hedingham ware has the maker's name and address incised beneath the base, together with a representation of the castle on an applied pad (see above).

Gestingthorpe. John Houghton, who recorded much that was happening in his lifetime, wrote in 1693:

> From my ingenious good friend, Mr Samuel Dale, of Braintree, in Essex, I am informed, that at Gestingthorpe, in that county, are made a sort of hard yellowish bricks and pavements, called white brick, and Walpet brick, from a town in Suffolk of that name, where they were first made; they are harder and more durable than common red brick, and therefore much used for pavement of floors in lower rooms, and also for fire-hearths, except where just they make their fires.

The tile and brick works closed at an unspecified date, and was followed, although not necessarily on the exact site, by a pottery making domestic wares. A jug of dark red clay with a brown-flecked yellow glaze is in the Glaisher Collection at the Fitzwilliam Museum, Cambridge. It is inscribed *Ritcherd Murrells Josuph Reppingel* and dated 1770. The second name links it with another jug (at Manchester City Art Gallery) which bears on it *Josuph Reppingell, Guesting Thorpe Essex*, and the date 1767. Each of these jugs is of a distinctive shape with a globular body, short neck, three ridged handles and a projecting spout.

Hampshire

Fareham. Although no marked pieces have been recorded, a particular type of ware is attributed to Fareham, situated to the

Fig. 24: Dish with a sgraffito design of two cocks, inscribed Thomas Berr, *and dated 1767. Probably Staffordshire. Diameter 13½ inches. (Phillips, Son and Neale.)*

Plate 3 *Harvest jug decorated with a sgraffito pattern and inscribed: 'The Potter fashioned me complete,| as plainly doth appear|for to supply the harvest men with| good strong English beer| Drink round my jolly reapers and| When the corn is cut we'll have| the other jug boys and cry A Neck A Neck Able Symons   1813'*
North Devonshire. Height 10¼ inches. (City Museum and Art Gallery, Plymouth, Devon.)

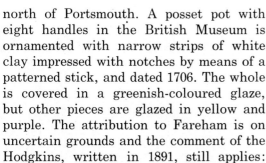

Left, Plate 4: *Dish decorated in coloured slips with a stag. Staffordshire, mid-18th century. Diameter 13½ inches. (City Museum and Art Gallery, Plymouth.)*

Right, *Fig. 25: Cup of cream-coloured clay with red slip decoration. Early 18th century. Height 3⅛ inches. (County Museum, Truro.)*

north of Portsmouth. A posset pot with eight handles in the British Museum is ornamented with narrow strips of white clay impressed with notches by means of a patterned stick, and dated 1706. The whole is covered in a greenish-coloured glaze, but other pieces are glazed in yellow and purple. The attribution to Fareham is on uncertain grounds and the comment of the Hodgkins, written in 1891, still applies:

> We confess that, although it satisfies on all grounds our requirements as to date and character, we can offer no information as to its real origin.

Nottingham

Two salt-kits are recorded; one in the Castle Museum, Nottingham, is inscribed with the initials W.W. and dated 1799, the other, at Cambridge (Fig. 20) is similarly initialled but dated 1749. The first-noted was acquired from a descendant of the maker, William Woodward and presumably bears this potter's initials. The interval of half-a-century between the two pieces assumes he was very long-lived, but it may have been that he had a son of the same name. This was not an uncommon happening, and still occurs today.

Somerset

A number of potteries existed near Il-minster, at Donyatt, Whitney Bottom and, as commemorated in its name, Crock Street. Local red clay was used, and white was obtained from Poole, Dorset. Sgraffito decoration was the commonest, as was general in the West (see Devon, above), but the designs were less ambitious than those of the Bideford area. Drinking vessels of various kinds were made, and there would seem to have been a strong preference for puzzle-jugs. An example dated 1794 is inscribed 'fill me full of liker that is swet for it is good when friends doo meet. fill me full of sider ann drink of me while you cann'; a harmless enough wish in spite of its erratic spelling. Such jugs present the drinker with alternative orifices from which to imbibe, but only one of them will supply him satisfactorily; the others result in a drenching. The pottery at Crock Street is said to have been in the possession of the Rogers family during three generations, and closed in 1906.

Sussex

There were numerous potteries active at various dates in the county. The earliest were probably situated at Rye, where excavations in 1931 brought to light fragments of tiles and other wares datable to the 14th century. While manufacturing activity doubtless continued there and elsewhere, there is little or no evidence to prove what types of ware were made. It is not until the later years of the 18th century that proof in the form of inscriptions and dates enables attributions to be made with confidence.

The distinctive feature of much of the later ware from the locality is the use of printers' type to stamp words, numerals and decorative features which were then filled-in with white clay. A yellowish glaze completed the making. All kinds of objects have survived, ranging from harvest-flasks to money-boxes, and when inscribed their wording is usually evocative of rustic pleasures. A typical example occurs on a small flask made at Herstmonceux in 1835, which runs:

Orcans of brandy, rivers of wine
Fountains of tea & a girl to my mind.

Other wares were decorated in a more conventional style with white slip on the red body, and occasionally a partly-blended mixture of red and white (agate ware) was employed. A few figures were made in the early 19th century.

During the course of the 19th century a factory at Cadborough, near Rye, made ordinary domestic wares under the ownership of families named Smith and Mitchell. In 1869 one of the Mitchells established a pottery at Rye where he used a clay that fired to make a noticeably light-weight ware which was given a rich brown glaze. At both places were made the so-called 'Sussex Pigs': jugs in the form of a pig, the removable head forming a drinking-cup

Below, *Fig. 26: Brown-glazed jug and cover, the latter forming a cup, in the shape of a pig. It stands as shown, or can be sat on its haunches when filled. Sussex, early 19th century. Length 10 inches.* (*County Museum, Truro.*)

Right, *Fig. 27: Spirit flask of red clay inlaid with white, inscribed with a rhyme, Made by John Siggery Herstmonˣ Sussex, and dated 1835. Height 4½ inches. (Glaisher Collection.)*

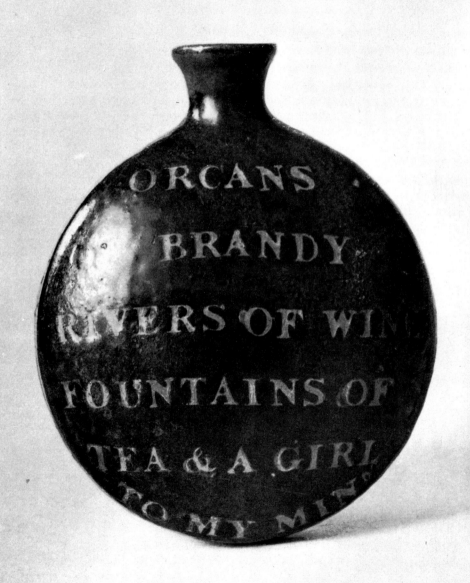

ORGANS
BRANDY
RIVERS OF WINE
FOUNTAINS OF
TEA & A GIRL
TO MY MIND

(Fig. 26). According to Llewellynn Jewitt, writing in 1878:

> In Sussex these pigs are used at weddings when each guest is invited to 'drink a hogshead of beer to the health of the bride'; and at other social and convivial meetings. On these occasions each person is expected to drink this cup — or hog's head — full of liquor.

Wiltshire

A group of wares is attributed to one or more potteries in the neighbourhood of Salisbury, in the west of the county. They take the form of goblets and puzzle-jugs of red clay decorated with patterns and inscriptions incised under a brown glaze. Many of the surviving pieces are dated between 1603 and 1799, and some of the earlier ones bear the initials *WZ*, which are said to be those of a potter named Zillwood. The spelling of inscriptions is, as elsewhere, often erratic although the sentiments expressed in them are laudable. A typical example is on a goblet dated 1710, which reads: *MERI MET AND MERI PART I DRINK TO V WITH ALL MI HART.*

Yorkshire

Blackburton. At Blackburton, about twelve miles from Lancaster, were some potteries using a dark red clay which was fired very hard, decorated with white slip, and covered in a glittering glaze (see Halifax, below). One of the establishments, named the Town End Pottery, is said to have been in the ownership of Thomas Bateson during the early years of the 18th century, and another belonged to a family named Baggaley from about 1750. Surviving dated pieces that were probably made in the area cover the years 1774 to 1865, and take the form of

Below, *Fig. 28: Staffordshire slipware miniature cradles. (Left) Red on white; dated 1839; length 10 inches. (Right) White on red; late 18th century; length 9 inches. (City Museum and Art Gallery, Hanley.)*

money-boxes, flasks and models of chests of drawers. The latter, for spices, would appear to have been a county speciality, as they were also made in Halifax.

Halifax. In the area of Halifax a number of potteries existed from at least the 18th century, from when dated examples have been preserved. All are made from red clay which has been described as being 'of quite exceptionally heavy weight', decorated with white slip and covered in a yellowish glaze. The latter is sometimes noticeably full of tiny glittering particles, as at Blackburton. The Halliday family had a pottery at Pot Howcans, which was in existence for many decades and closed finally in 1889. The Catheralls were at Swill Hill (or Soil Hill) for an undetermined length of time. The latter are supposed also to have had an establishment at Denholme between 1785 and 1907, while there was a further manufactory at Bradshaw which operated between 1805 and 1870.

Yearsley. Some of the Staffordshire Wedgwoods moved to Yorkshire in the seventeenth century, and established a pottery at Yearsley, in the North Riding. A few pieces attributed to them are distinguished by their brown-green glaze, and the fact that each is inscribed with a date and the name of a member of the family. Two puzzle-jugs, each incised *John Wedg Wood* and dated 1691, are known, one in the Victoria and Albert Museum and the other in the Fitzwilliam Museum. It has been argued whether they were the work of John Wedgwood who died in 1707, or his nephew Richard who leased the pottery from him.

Fig. 29: Posset pot and cover with a greenish-brown glaze, the body moulded with the names William *and* mary Goldsmith, *and the cover incised* June yᵉ 7th 1697. *South Wiltshire. Height 8¾ inches. (Glaisher Collection.)*

3 Delftware:
Part 1

Fig. 30: Jug of 'Malling' type decorated in powdered manganese-purple. Probably London, late 16th century. Height 5½ inches. (Sotheby's.)

AT some time in the 9th century A.D., or earlier, potters in the area of Mesopotamia were making wares of ordinary clay with the distinctive addition of an opaque glaze. The articles were exported to other countries bordering the Mediterranean, and by the next century were being copied in Spain. In due course, the Spaniards sent some of their productions to Italy, using for the purpose ships based on Majorca. For the latter reason, the Italians gave the pottery the name used in early times for the island: *maiolica*.

By at least the year 1454 an Italian potter named Piero, of Faenza, agreed to supply a service of what he described as *maiolicha biancha fina* (fine white majolica). Before long this type of ware was being made at several places in the country. Knowledge of its existence and of the secret of its making spread across Europe, and finally, towards the end of the 16th century its manufacture was begun in England.

The secret of majolica was the addition of some tin-oxide to the normally-transparent lead glaze. The opaque-white, or near-white, surface that resulted formed an ideal and novel background for painting, and allowed the potter a much wider range of expression than was possible with the co-existing unsophisticated red clay wares. In the course of time, the name 'majolica' has been assigned to Italian productions. English ones were once called 'gally-ware', but are now usually referred to as 'tin-glazed earthenware' or 'delftware'; the

Fig. 31: Tankard painted in blue with birds and flowers, and inscribed William and Elizabeth Bvrges. 24 Avgvst 1631. Dated below the handle 1632. Southwark. Height 4⅝ inches. (Victoria and Albert Museum.)

Fig. 32: Dish painted in colours with a view of buildings and the inscription THE. ROSE. IS. RED. THE. LEAVES. ARE. GRENE. GOD. SAVE. ELIZABETH. OVR. QVEENE. London, dated 1600. Diameter 10 inches. (London Museum.)

latter spelled with a small 'd' to distinguish it from the similar pottery made at Delft in Holland.

The oldest recorded pieces of English delftware are a number of jugs covered in an opaque glaze stained in various colours, including purple, turquoise-blue and black. The earliest of the jugs is datable from the silver mount on it, which is hall-marked for 1550, and another, decorated with orange, purple and red splashes, is hall-marked 1581. This last example was once in the church at West Malling, Kent, and as similar jugs have been found in the same county they are all sometimes described as 'Malling' jugs (Fig. 30).

The earliest information about the manufacture of delftware in England is to be found in John Stow's *Survey of London*, a book first published in 1603. It was republished at various later dates, and one of its editors and enlargers was John Strype, who had in his possession a petition relating to two Flemish potters. Strype wrote as follows:

About the year 1567, Jasper Andries and Jacob Janson, Potters, came away from Antwerp, to avoid the Persecution there, & settled themselves in Norwich; where they followed their Trade, making Gally Paving Tiles [*glazed floor tiles*], and Vessels for Apothecaries and others, very artificially. Anno 1570 they removed to London, with the testimonial of Isbrand Balckius, the Minister, and the rest of the Elders, and Deacons of that Church; & desired by petition, from Queen Elizabeth, that they might have Liberty to follow their Trade in that City without Interruption; and presented her with a Chest of their Handywork. They set forth in their Petition, that they were the first which brought in & exercised the said Sciences in this Realm, and were at great Charges, before they could find the Materials in this Realm. And that the same Science was so acceptable to King Henry VIII, that he offered the same Jasper's Father good Wages & House-room, to come and exercise the same here; which then came to no Effect. They beseeched her, in Recompense of their great Cost & Charges, that she would grant them House-room in or without the Liberties

Fig. 33: Charger painted in colours with the 'Mary', the royal yacht of Charles II, initialled W.A.H. *and dated 1668. The initials are probably those of Willoughby Hannam who married his wife Anne in 1668. Lambeth. Diameter 16½ inches. (Burnap Collection, Nelson Gallery-Atkins Museum, Kansas City, Missouri.)*

of London, by the Water-side; and Privilege for the Time of twenty Years, that none but they, their Wives & Children, and Assigns, might exercise the same Science in this Realm; and to sell & transport the same, as well outward as inward, to all Men, free of all Custom.

Andries was in East Anglia during 1571 and 1572, but then disappears from record. On the other hand, his colleague Janson, who anglicised his name and called himself Jacob Johnson, is known to have settled in Aldgate and to have died in 1593. Other Flemish potters were living in the same parish in 1571, and possibly, in view of the wording of the petition, they worked for Johnson.

In spite of the very great number of fragments of late 16th century delftware unearthed in the city of London, none has been identified as having been made by Johnson who, it is assumed, established his pottery near his dwelling-house in Aldgate. As he and his men were foreign-born it is probable that their products would have closely matched wares from abroad, and with which they competed on the London market. Any differences there may have been between the goods made here and those from Flanders would have been slight, and at present we do not know enough about their characteristics to tell them apart.

A dish in the London Museum (Fig. 32) is dated 1600, shortly after Johnson's death, and seems likely to have been made in London. The motto on it is in good English, allowing for the vagaries of spelling common at the time, although it is always possible that details were sent across the Channel and copied painstakingly. The same applies to the odd-looking buildings depicted in the centre of the dish, which may

or may not represent the Tower of London. Present-day opinion favours a London origin for the piece, and as there is no positive evidence of its source it seems pointless to dispute this reasonable attribution.

Another pottery was established in or about 1617 at Southwark, across the river Thames and not a great distance due south of Aldgate. It was owned by a man of German-Dutch origin, Christian Wilhelm, who had come to England twelve years earlier and followed the trade of a vinegar-maker and distiller of spirits. In 1628 he petitioned as 'Gallipot-maker to the King' (Charles I) and was granted the privilege of being the 'sole manufacturer of gallyware in England for 14 years, he being the inventor thereof . . .' Wilhelm endeavoured also to gain the exclusive right to make smalt; a preparation of cobalt essential in painting in the popular colour of blue. He does not appear to have been successful in obtaining this latter concession, and he died sometime after 1640.

Wilhelm tried twice to possess the smalt privilege, which can indicate that he needed it for his work. That being so, it may be concluded that his output was mainly of blue-and-white, and it would have been imitating as closely as possible in pattern the Chinese wares then arriving from the East.

A quantity of pieces fulfilling these conditions have been attributed to Wilhelm. All have blue decoration in the late 16th/ early 17th century Ming style, showing birds and foliage and a few bear dates of the 1620-40 decades (Fig. 31).

Southwark continued to be the location of one or more potteries that were active until the late 18th century. On 16th September 1693 the *London Gazette* printed an advertisement reading:

Any gentlemen that are desirous to be concerned in the Art of Pot-making, and Painting of Earthen Ware, curiously imitating the Holland Ware & are willing to set up a Pot-house, may hear of artificers (that will perfect the same

on reasonable Terms) at Mr Downing's, at the Plume of Feathers, at St. Mary Overies, Southwark.

It is known that men named William Bellamy, William Constable and Thomas Harper were potters in the area, and it is possible that Bellamy carried on Wilhelm's establishment after the death of the latter. Research is made difficult because of the possibility of confusion between men who made delftware, stoneware and ordinary red clay ware; in many cases they were all referred to simply as 'potters'. A typical instance occurs in an advertisement in the *Post Boy* of 8th January 1723, which stated:

> To be lett, an old accustomed working Pott House in STONEY Lane SOUTH-WARK, late in the occupation of Messrs. GROVES & ROBINS.

THE next area of London to come into prominence is Lambeth; a name commonly used to designate all tin-glazed earthenware of types made in the capital. This is a long-standing attribution, probably a relic of 18th century times when the factories of the district were the most important ones actively making delftware. It would seem that little or no pottery was made there until the reign of Charles II, when, by 1676, a man named James Barston had established a manufactory. He was prominent among those who protested loud and long against the importing of foreign earthenware, stating that '. . . unless a more effective Prohibition be established, the consumption of English manufactures will cease . . .'

In opposition to Barston and his fellows, the Company of Glass Sellers, whose members profited greatly by the trade, countered by saying that the pot-makers '. . . never did, neither can they, make such painted earthen ware as is imported . . . Adding: 'There are but 6 or 7 of the said Pot makers in England who may imploy 50 families or thereabouts . . . some have had patents for the sole making of Fine Earthen Wares here after the manner of Holland . . . but could never make such Ware. . .' The Company concluded their indictment with the cynical argument: 'The importing of foreign Earthen Ware has been a great example to the very Pot-makers themselves, by making their wares after Foreign Patterns to their great interest'.

This last sentence is a reminder that the close resemblance between home-made and imported articles is no accident. It was done deliberately at the time, and many pieces must remain unallocated at the present day and probably forever.

A large factory was started early in the 18th century in Fore Street, Lambeth, and during the past twenty years its site has yielded many fragments. The death of its owner was reported in the *Public Ledger* of 1st April 1761:

> Saturday evening [29 March] died at Lambeth Mr. GRIFFITHS, said to have been the most considerable potter in England.

His widow, Abigail Griffiths carried on the business until 1773, and the firm then traded as Griffiths & Morgan. In 1840 it came into the possession of James Stiff, and then manufactured stoneware. The old premises were demolished and rebuilt in 1860, and until that date the premises bore on the outside a signboard of delftware tiles.

Finally, there was a pottery at Vauxhall, adjoining Lambeth. There are records of potters living in the district, but nothing is known for certain about their lives or what types of earthenware they made. John Houghton, who published a series of 'Letters' relating to trade and other matters at the end of the 17th century, recorded on 13th March 1695-6 that in 1694 imports of teapots were only ten in number, 'and those from Holland. To our credit be it spoken, we have about Faux-Hall (as I have been informed) made a great many, and I cannot gainsay but they are as good as any come from abroad'.

These particular teapots may have been made of red stoneware, but an eyewitness account of some years later refers without

Below left, Fig. 37: Plate painted in blue with a lady and a gallant, initialled and dated 1696. Lambeth. Diameter 9 inches. (Sotheby's.) **Below,** *Fig. 38: Money-box painted in blue and yellow with sprays of flowers, initialled and dated 1692. Lambeth. Height 7¾ inches. (Sotheby's, now at Colonial Williamsburg, Va.)*

doubt to delftware. The Yorkshire antiquary Ralph Thoresby wrote in 1714 that he 'went by water to Fox-Hall and the Spring-Gardens. After dinner we viewed the pottery and various apartments there. Was most pleased with that where they were painting divers colours, which yet appear more beautiful and of divers colours when baked'.

Another visitor out of the many who must have inspected the pottery over the years, also made notes of what he saw. He was a German, Zacharias Conrad von Uffenbach, and his brief, but censorious, record reads:

> 1710. On 21 July, Monday morning, we first went to see the porcelain sheds at Foxhall. The articles made here are very coarse and heavy, not near as fine as those from Frankfurt or Hanau. The work is no different from what I saw in Berlin and Delft, excepting that here the clay is washed in great vats in the yard, dried in the sun, and then prepared for manufacture.

The use by von Uffenbach of the word 'porcelain' to describe what can only have been pottery was not unusual at that date, and later, and followed Continental practice. In Holland the earthenware made at Delft was known as 'Hollandsche porselein' (Dutch porcelain), and in Germany the site of the big pottery in Frankfurt remains the *Porzellanhofstrasse* (Porcelain-high-street). References in old books and documents are sometimes misleading in this respect, and many an attractive theory has been founded on a mistaken belief that such mentions were to true porcelain and not pottery.

In 1695 the Government decided that the makers of glass and earthenware, who were treated as a single trade, should contribute their share towards the expense of the current war against the French. For the purpose, a Duty of 20% was placed on pottery (and the like amount on most glass), and not unexpectedly the makers protested that it would ruin them. A number of them gave evidence to the effect before a com-

Fig. 39: Mug painted in blue with a bust of Charles II and dated 1660. Lambeth. Height 4½ inches. (Burnap Collection, Kansas City.)

mittee of the House of Commons, and eventually it was agreed that they, and the glass manufacturers, had proved their case. The Duty was halved in 1698, and a year afterwards was abolished altogether.

A document prepared in 1696 in connection with the Duty gives an interesting insight into the range of articles then on the market, and the prices at which they were supplied. The 'Fine Painted Ware' included:

Fine large rib'd Jars　　pr. pair £3 to 5s.
Ditto round and Painted　　do. £3 to 5s.
Fine small rib'd Jarrs
　　　　　　　　2s. 8d. to 6s. pr. Doz.
Fine Large Beakers　　　do. 15s. to 4d.
Fine large Dishes painted
　　　　　　　　24s. to 20d. pr. Doz.
Fine large Basons and Punch-bowles
　　pr. piece　　　　　　　4s. to 3s.
Fine painted Chamber Pots
　　　　　　　　do. 12d. to 4d.
Fine pots and drinking Cups
　　　　　　　　6s. to 2s. pr. Doz.
Apothecaries Potts　　　9s. to 8s. do.
Porringers　　　　　　　at 20d. do.
Mugs　　　　　　　　10s. to 2s. do.

THE work of the painter-potters of Deruta, Castel Durante and elsewhere in Italy during the first decades of the 16th century was never equalled, but was adapted in other lands to meet their less exacting standards. Quantity triumphed over quality and what had been reserved for display and use by the wealthy was amended to provide everyday necessities for the mass of the people. In the words of an early 18th century writer: 'if there were but a hundred Men in the World, ninety of them wou'd eat off earthen Ware'.

Having been formed, either on the wheel or in moulds, the articles were then put aside to dry and become sufficiently hard to be handled. Then they were given a first baking in the kiln, from which they emerged in the so-called 'biscuit' state and were clay-coloured and porous. After cooling, each piece was dipped into the liquid glaze mixture, which quickly dried to leave a smooth and powdery surface.

The next operation was painting, and the skill of the artist was directed to quick and accurate work. The surface of the ware had the property of blotting-paper, so that

Below, Fig. 40: Plate painted in blue with an Oriental scene, initialled and dated 1697. Lambeth. Diameter 8½ inches. (Colonial Williamsburg, Va.)

Plate 5 *Charger painted with the coats of arms and crest of the Weavers' Company, of London, initialled and dated 1670. Lambeth. Diameter 16 inches. Cotehele House, Cornwall. (The National Trust.)*

Plate 6 *Group of tin-glazed earthenware, mid 17th-century. Vase and candlestick, Lambeth, heights 8 and 7 inches. Dish, Netherlands, diameter 12½ inches.*

Fig. 41: Jug painted in blue with farming scenes, and a coat of arms incorporating implements, with a bull and a saddled horse as supporters. Initialled, and dated 1699. Lambeth. Height 9½ inches. (Sotheby's.)

Left, *Fig. 42: Barber's bowl painted in blue with a surgeon-barber leading his horse and with the tools of his trade. Initialled and dated 1706. Lambeth. Width 12¼ inches. (Sotheby's.)*

Below, *Fig. 43: Dish painted in blue within outlines of manganese-purple with* Christ and the Woman taken in Adultery, *initialled and dated 1698. Lambeth. Diameter 18⅞ inches. (British Museum.)*

Fig. 43a: Wet drug pot (for holding a liquid medicine) painted in blue and inscribed S. DE ROS. SICC:. *Lambeth late 17th century. Height 7¼ inches. (County Museum, Truro.) The jar was for holding Syrup of Rose-Juice, of which it was said: 'It strengthens the heart, comforts the spirits, bindeth the body, helps fluxes and Corrosions or gnawing of the guts, it strengthens the stomach, and staies vomiting'.*

the contents from direct contact with the flames, and to equalise the heat, more or less, inside the kiln. It was of the greatest importance that no two objects should be touching during firing, or the molten glaze might run from one to another and both would be spoiled. After cooling they would be found stuck together and useless.

Large articles each had a sagger to themselves, but plates and dishes were fired in quantity, and for them there were alternative methods of separation: use could be made of either spurs or pegs. The former were three-pronged pieces of baked clay, which were placed between the six or seven items in each sagger. They resulted in a set of three small marks on the front and back of most of the contents, although the top dish or plate would be unblemished. Alternatively, pegs were inserted in holes in the side of the sagger, and the rims of the dishes rested on them. In this case, too, signs are visible on the finished articles, but as they are only on the edges of the undersides they are much less noticeable.

Tin-glazed earthenware is completely opaque to transmitted light, and the foot-rim of a piece nearly always shows the underbody of clay which forms its substance. Another feature of most specimens is its deplorable tendency to chip at the edges. This has often been the result of using wire frames for displaying plates and dishes in cabinets and on walls. The modern plastic-covered type of frame is less damaging in this respect, but most of the irreparable chipping on old delftware was done before these came on the market.

each brush-stroke soaked in and could not be corrected. This fact accounts for the attractive spontaniety of the work on better examples, and a shortage of first-class craftsmen is the reason why the majority of the output is no more than mediocre.

The principal colour employed was blue, obtained from cobalt, but the palette included also a purple-brown from manganese, yellow from antimony and red from iron-oxide, all of them usable singly or in mixture. In order to assist the fusing of the colours with the glaze, they were mixed with a little clear lead glaze; i.e. without any tin-oxide in it. This was known to the Dutch as '*kwaart*', and was applied by them over the whole surface after the article had had its final baking. It necessitated a further firing, and resulted in a brilliant finish approaching that of true porcelain. Once thought to be a distinguishing feature of Dutch Delftware, it is now known to have been employed in England and is another reason why differentiation between the' productions of the two countries is a matter of argument.

The painted wares were made ready for their baking or firing by putting them in covered containers of baked clay, known as 'saggers'. Their purpose was to protect

4 Delftware:
Part 2

BRISTOL and nearby Brislington, in the west of England, were important centres for the manufacture of delftware from the mid-17th century onwards. Both enjoyed local supplies of clay and of timber from the neighbourhood and Wales, and were able to take advantage of the facilities provided by the busy port. Much of their output went by water to the Indies, America and other places overseas, but a proportion was shipped to London and much was sold in the district.

Below, *Fig. 44: Back of plate with bianco sopra bianco border, on the right in Plate 8. Note the three marks near the rim, where the plate rested on supports while being fired.*

The origins of pot-making in the area are unknown, but two men, John Bissicke and Robert Bennet, who were recorded as gally-pot makers at Brislington in 1650-60, are thought either to have come from Southwark or to have been connected with families there. Bennet was a Quaker, and possibly Bissicke was also one; and another potter, Robert Wastfield, married Bennet's daughter in 1672.

This mention of a link between the Society of Friends and ceramics continued for many decades and is to be discovered not only in the history of pottery, but includes a number of men prominently connected with porcelain manufactories. It is perhaps not of particular significance, but is a recurring feature revealed by research. Members of the Society largely shared their activities with their fellow-believers, and much of the success achieved by the early makers of pottery and porcelain is due to their industry.

Excavations at Brislington in 1913-16 resulted in the unearthing of many fragments of delftware, of which the earliest dated piece is of 1649. Others dated 1652 and 1653 were also found. There is no evidence, however, by which it is possible to decide whether any particular pieces were made there or at Bristol. From about 1720 it is known that the pottery was perhaps managed by Thomas Taylor, who leased the premises from Thomas Dixon. In February 1743 the *Gentleman's Magazine* recorded that 'Tho. Taylor, of Bussleton, Somerset, Gallipot Maker' was bankrupt, and three years later the premises were

put up for sale. It is concluded that delft-ware ceased to be made there after that date.

In 1683, a Brislington potter, Edward Ward, bought a pottery in Bristol, presumably one making ordinary red clay wares, and established a delftware manufactory. It was known as the Temple Back or Water Lane Pottery, and continued in operation until 1746. In April of that year an announcement in the *Bristol Oracle* stated:

Notice is hereby given.

That the Pot House in Water Lane, Temple Street, late Ward's is now occupied and the Work carried on by Thomas Cantle junior and Company, by whom all persons may be supplied with all sorts of Earthenware, on most reasonable Terms.

The mention of 'all sorts of Earthenware' did not necessarily mean that everything sold by the firm was manufactured on the premises. It was normal practice for potters to supply wares from sources other than their own kilns, and in 1784, when the pottery changed hands once again, an Inventory of the stock-in-trade included black ware, red china ware, Nottingham

Above, *Fig. 48: Plate alleged to have been painted by Joseph Flower of Bristol; and* (**right**) *Fig. 49: the initials and date on the back of the plate.*

ware, and brown stoneware. The values of the various types ranged from 18s. for tortoiseshell ware up to £159 16s. 11d. for brown stone ware; the latter being the principal output at that date.

It is advisable that the terms 'Staffordshire ware' and 'Nottingham ware' should not be taken literally, as when such origins are named they were no more than generic. No doubt goods were being made in Bristol in Staffordshire and Nottingham styles, although in this instance they may not have been made by the pottery offering them for sale. A similar instance occurs in the numerous English country towns which used to boast a 'Manchester Warehouse', which did not really mean that everything on the premises had been made in Lancashire.

There were numerous other potteries in Bristol during the course of the 18th century. Their owners came and went, and many of them intermarried resulting in amalgamations of the firms concerned. One of the most important, and at present the best documented, is that at Redcliff Backs, belonging to the Frank family who were originally at Brislington. It was discovered recently that between at least 1757 and 1767, during the ownership of Richard Frank and Son, a Swede named Magnus Lundberg worked there.

Lundberg had served his apprenticeship at the Rörstrand factory in Sweden, where in 1745 they were introducing a new type of decoration known as *bianco sopra bianco:* literally, white upon white. It takes the form of white painting against a bluish-white or greyish-white background, and is found confined to the borders of plates and bowls (Plate 8). It is most likely that Lundberg was responsible for bringing *bianco sopra bianco* to England; not only to Bristol, but perhaps also, while on his way

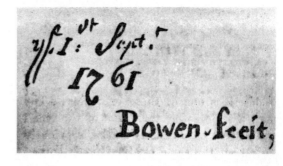

Left and above, *Figs. 50 and 51: Plate painted by John Bowen of Bristol, and his signature on the back.*

westwards, to London. The earliest known English-made examples of pottery with the decoration are dated 1747, and the same border pattern was found on fragments excavated at Lambeth a few years ago.

A most interesting contemporary account of the Bristol factory, contributed anonymously, appeared in the *Göteborgska Spionen* in May 1767. The writer mentioned that Lundberg 'has an interest, but also is in charge as master. There are forty-two persons at work here, whose different tasks we watched . . .' He went on to describe the processes employed, mentioned that local clay was mixed with a proportion imported from Ireland, and that the wood used in the kilns came from Wales; 'coal is unserviceable'.

One of the painters working for the Frank pottery was Michael Edkins, better known perhaps for his alleged work on glass (see *English & Irish Glass, Signature 12*). Hugh Owen, author of a book on Bristol pottery and porcelain published in 1873, wrote that in 1859

> . . . the author had a conversation with Mr Edkins [*William Edkins, grandson of Michael*] . . . He stated that his grandfather had been a delft-ware painter in his youth, and had worked at the manufactory of Richd. Frank, on Redcliffe Back; and, in proof, exhibited

half-a-dozen dinner plates bearing the initials of the painter and his wife — Michael and Betty Edkins, with the date 1760 . . . These plates were painted by Michael Edkins as a labour of love, just previous to his leaving the works.

One of the plates is now in the Victoria and Albert Museum, and another is in the British Museum (Figs. 46 and 47).

One other of the Frank pottery apprentices has achieved a long-enduring renown as a decorator, and has also been inflated over the years to an unmerited importance. On 17th August 1736, Joseph Flower, 'crate-maker to the glass-house and pot-house', bound his son, also named Joseph, to Richard Frank. A few pieces of blue-painted delftware were preserved in the hands of his descendants, together with the oral tradition that Joseph junior had decorated them.

The fact that some of the alleged Flower-decorated articles bear initials including the letters *J* and *F* has been put forward as strong evidence in favour of his having done the work. In fact, the initials are more probably those of ownership, rather than those of an artist. However, a large bowl in the Warren Hall Collection, at the Ashmolean Museum, Oxford, is signed clearly *Joseph Flower sculp*, with a less legible date which is probably 1743. As this is the

year in which his apprenticeship terminated the bowl may have been his 'masterpiece', but there is no explanation of why he wrote 'sculp' in place of the more usual 'pinx'.

It is quite possible that Flower painted the other articles as well as the bowl, but his career has been embroidered by successive writers who have stated that he owned a pottery. There seems to be no real basis for the suggestion, which has been given credence because directories and newspapers of the time described him as 'Joseph Flower, potter'. It was common practice in the 18th century for a man to be given the name of a trade, whether he was a manufacturer in it or only a retailer of its products. His wife's decease was noticed in *Felix Farley's Journal* on 25th April 1767, which stated that 'on Wednesday Mrs Flower wife of Joseph Flower who keeps the earthenware house at the side of the quay'. There are other references to his having kept a shop, and it would appear without doubt that following his apprenticeship to Frank he traded as a retailer until his death in 1785.

A comparable tradition surrounds the name of John Niglett, who is recorded as having been apprenticed to a Brislington potter in 1714. At one time it was supposed

that he specialised in Chinese-style painting, and as a result a large quantity of surviving ware with such decoration was assumed to have been executed by him. The foundation of the story is a dish dated 1733 with the initials *J N E* arranged triangularly on the back, and stated to be those of John Niglett and his wife, Esther. Adherents to the theory ignored the fact that Mrs Niglett's first name was Hester, and that her husband, like Joseph Flower, appeared in contemporary records as 'potter'.

Another man, John Bowen, has also had attributed to him a large quantity of delftware. A plate, 'decorated in clear blue with figures in the peculiar manganese colour that is characteristic of the Bristol pottery', has been recorded. On the back it was signed 'Ye 1st Septr. 1761 Bowen fecit', but it has vanished since a woodcut of it (Fig. 50) was published in 1873. However, as it depicts figures seen against a landscape background every piece of old delftware with more or less similar decoration has since been attributed to the same overworked artist.

Wincanton

THE Somerset town of Wincanton was the home of a delftware pottery supposedly established by a man named Nathaniel Ireson in about 1730. Ireson was also a builder and a sculptor, and left his native Warwickshire to build Stourhead, the mansion situated some five miles from Wincanton. A jug bearing Ireson's name is in the Glaisher Collection, at the Fitzwilliam Museum, Cambridge, and half-a-dozen dated examples, some with the word 'Wincanton' on them have been recorded. His activities as a sculptor included the carving of his own monument, now in Wincanton churchyard, which 'he executed in his lifetime and kept it ready to be erected after his death'.

Nathaniel Ireson is known to have bought land in Wincanton, and to have built a house there. A quarry on his property yielded good clay, and it is not improbable that he established a pottery to use it. He has been described as 'a skilled potter', but there is no proof of this statement.

Excavations on the site of the pottery have revealed fragments in quantity, and many are noticeably poorly painted. The surviving marked examples show decoration in both blue and manganese, sometimes employed as a 'powdered' ground. Copied from the Chinese, this cannot be said to be peculiar to Wincanton, and most of the surviving output cannot be distinguished from that made elsewhere (Fig. 57).

Liverpool

DELFTWARE made in Liverpool dates from at least the year 1710, when the London *Post Boy* reported:

> The Corporation of Liverpool in Lancashire have encouraged there a manufactory of all sorts of fine and painted pots and other vessels and tiles in imitation of China both for Inland and Outland trade, which will be speedily ready and sold at reasonable prices.

In August of the same year there was proof in the same newspaper that the establishment was in production:

> A large Pot-house, lately set up in Liverpool, and now making all sorts of White and Painted Wares in imitation of China. The owners, on Notice sent 'em, would buy any parcels of Firewood,

Below, *Fig. 53: Bowl painted in blue with figures in a landscape. Bristol, circa 1760. Diameter 10½ inches.*

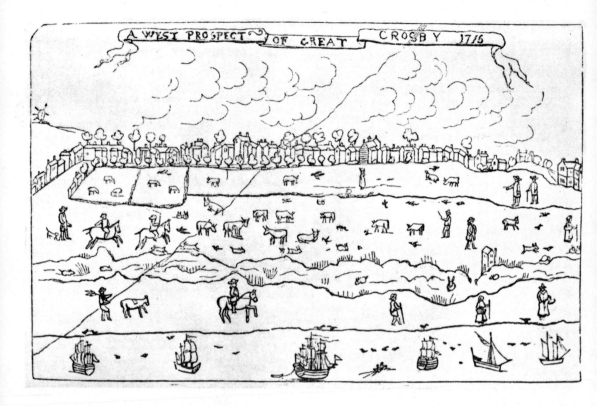

which lye any where convenient for Land or Water-Carriage; or if brought to 'em, will give the full value.

A large plaque, 31 inches wide and 20 inches high, formerly in Liverpool Museum and destroyed by bombing in 1941, showed a view of Great Crosby across the river Mersey, dated 1716. There are some other pieces of about the same time in existence, and all may have been made at a pottery in Lord Street owned by Alderman Josiah Poole.

In about 1724 a pottery was started near Dale Street by another Alderman, named Shaw. It has been suggested that he gave his name to the area known as Shaw's Brow (site of the present Liverpool Museum),

a rising piece of ground on the east side of the rivulet that ran at the bottom of Dale Street. Here the early pot-works were established, and here in after years they increased, until the whole 'Brow' became one mass of potter's banks, with houses for workmen on both sides of the street; and so numerous were they that,

according to the census taken in 1790, there were as many as 74 houses, occupied by 437 persons, the whole of whom were connected with the potteries.

There are records of other manufactories of delftware in the city, and it is assumed that altogether they had a large output. Much of it doubtless was sent overseas, as at Bristol, where the increasing populations provided a ready market.

The best-known name connected with the history of Liverpool delft is that of Thomas Fazackerley. He was neither a potter nor a painter, but the recipient in 1757 of a quart mug said to have been made for him by a friend at Shaw's pottery. The piece bears

If this be
the wager
that you
before th

his initials, and a year later, following his marriage, the same friend made another mug, this time of a smaller and more lady-like pint size, with the initials, C.F, of his wife. Both mugs were painted with flowers in colours that are now accepted as exclusive to the district: the so-called 'Fazackerley colours'. They have been described as 'lemon yellow, orange yellow, sage green, French blue, pale manganese and a very distinctive clear red, with drawing in black'.

The mugs were lost with much else in Liverpool Museum, in the air-raids of 1941, but a large quantity of ware with the characteristic colouring remains (Plate 7). Their origin is confirmed by the finding in the city of fragments similarly painted. The ware is recognisable not only by the combination of colours used on it, but also by the marked assymetry of much of the decoration. One or more of the painters strongly favoured Chinese-inspired floral groups incorporating a fence, and the example in Plate 7 is typical of the style.

Scotland

A FACTORY was established at Glasgow under the managership of a London potter, John Bird. It opened in 1748, but news of the event would appear to have been slow in filtering back to the capital. The *General Evening Post*, published in London, reported as late as January 1752:

We hear from Glasgow, that a Manu-

factory is set on Foot there for making all Sorts and Kinds of Delft or Lime Ware, viz. Plates, Bowls, Tea Pots, Tea and Coffee Cups and Sawcers, Flower Pots of all Kinds, Bottles and Basons, Water Pots, Chimney Tiles, Gally Pots of all Sizes, &c. and 'tis said they outrival the Dutch.

Later in the same year the sixth Duke of Hamilton married the famous beauty, Elizabeth Gunning. The couple took up residence at Hamilton Palace in May, 1752, and it was reported that on the 16th of the month they went to Glasgow where they were 'waited on by the Magistrates' and visited the delft manufactory. Apparently it was by then a sufficiently established concern to form one of the sights of the city.

Although it was started for the purpose of using clay from land belonging to the owner of the pottery, Robert Dinwoodie, this apparently did not prove suitable. Recourse had to be had to imported Irish clay from Carrickfergus, with successful results. Much of the ware was exported, and none has been positively identified. A bowl painted in blue with devices taken from the arms of the city and the words 'Success to the town of Glasgow' is recorded and may have been made there.

Ireland

IN Belfast there was probably a delftware pottery in operation during the late 17th century. A visitor in 1708 noted:

Here we saw a very good manufacture

Right, *Fig. 57: Plate painted in blue with the arms of the Masons' Company, the name* Gs: Clewett *and the date 1737. Inscribed* Wincanton *on the back. Diameter 8¾ inches.* (*Sotheby's.*)

Below, *Fig. 58: Bowl painted in blue with Chinese patterns, and inscribed under the base:* june the 27th 1758. *Perhaps Dublin. Diameter 9 inches.*

of earthenware, which comes nearest to Delft of any made in Ireland, and really is not much short of it; it is very clean and pretty, and universally used in the North.

The only known piece that may have been made there is a model of a shoe inscribed with initials, the word 'Belfast' and the date 1724.

At Dublin, John Chambers operated the 'Pot-house on the Strand' from about 1730, and some plates dated 1735, each painted with the arms of the Duke of Dorset, Lord-Lieutenant of Ireland, were probably made by him (Fig. 59). A succession of owners led to Captain Henry Delamain, who had been a partner in the short-lived enamel works at Battersea, outside London. In 1752 he began petitioning the Dublin Society and the Irish Parliament for financial assistance and two years later petitioned Parliament in London to the same end. He told the latter that he had discovered a way of constructing a kiln so that firing could be done with coal, 'in less time and in larger quantities than the method now practiced by burning with wood, and at one third part of the expense . . .'

A bowl, sixteen inches in diameter, in the British Museum is inscribed beneath the base with the words 'Clay got over the Primate's Coals — Dublin 1753'. It alludes to the fact that the fuel had come from land owned by the Archbishop of Armagh, and is convincing proof of the success of the pottery. In 1754 Delamain began to re-build his manufactory with the future intention of employing two or three hundred workpeople, but he died in 1757, before his big plans could come to fruition. The pottery carried on under the ownership of his widow and others, and apparently closed by 1771.

The few pieces of Dublin delftware that have been identified are of high quality as regards both potting and painting.

The *Dublin Journal* of 10th April 1742 mentioned a pottery at Rostrevor, Co. Down, which produced blue-painted wares. They included punch-bowls, basins and other domestic articles, but none have been identified.

In the south of the country there was a manufactory at Limerick. In 1762, John Stritch and Christopher Bridson were awarded a premium by the Dublin Society, a Government-aided forerunner of the Society for the Encouragement of Arts and Manufactures (now the Royal Society of Arts) in London. The sum of £30 was given to the two men 'for erecting a manufactory of earthenware in imitation of delft or white ware'.

Three matching plates are recorded. All are inscribed on the back 'Made by John Stritch Limerick 1761', and one of them bears the date 4th June 1761 in full. On the

Plate 7 (Left) *Lambeth, circa 1750: diameter 9 inches.* (Right) *Liverpool, circa 1760; diameter 8¾ inches.*

Plate 8 (Left) *Lambeth, circa 1720; diameter 8⅞ inches.* (Right) *Lambeth, dated 1747 see Fig. 44; diameter 8¾ inches.*

Plate 9 *Tankard painted with the arms of the Blacksmiths' Company, and dated 1752. Inscribed* 'Brother Vilckin Let Us Drink Whilst Wee Have Breath For There's No Drinking After Death: Joseph Piper.' *Lambeth. Height 7¼ inches.*

Above, *Fig. 60: Cup painted in 'Fazacker-ley' colours. Liverpool, circa 1760. Height 2½ inches. (City Museum and Art Gallery, Plymouth.)* **Above right,** *Fig. 61: Plate decorated with a hand-coloured purple-brown transfer-print of the coat of arms and name of Edmond Sexton Pery, elected member of Parliament for Limerick in 1760. Inscribed on the back in blue 'Made by John Stritch, Limerick, 1761'. Diameter 8⅝ inches. (British Museum.)*

front of each is the coat of arms of Edmond Sexton Pery, member of Parliament for Limerick at the time, within a border showing three small branches of flowers and leaves. The decoration is not painted in the normal manner, but printed from engraved copperplates in a purple-brown colour and with tints added by hand. The style of decoration is very similar to that of Chinese porcelain made for export to Europe, and it is possible Stritch copied it deliberately to demonstrate how closely he could imitate the esteemed Oriental product (Fig. 61).

SURVIVING articles of delftware are varied in form, although because of the larger quantities that were made there is a predominance of plates and dishes. Teapots and cups are among the rarer articles, because of the tendency of the ware to chip in use and to crack when in contact with hot water; which are good reasons for discarding it. Other pieces, such as coffee pots, jugs, tankards, salts, tea-caddies, puzzle-jugs, candlesticks and vases were made of the pottery but have endured in larger numbers in more satisfactory materials. Punch bowls and bowls of small size were also made, and the same remarks apply to them.

Specimens of all these domestic articles that have been preserved are in many instances inscribed and dated ones, and the majority of ordinary pottery in daily use had a short life before being discarded. Coats of arms of individuals and of the city Companies are found on a proportion of pieces, and the latter, especially, seem to have been popular. Examples date from the mid-17th century onwards, often with the addition of the name or initials of the original owner (Fig. 57 and Plate 9).

While much research has been directed towards identifying the output of the various centres and individual potteries, more remains to be done in this direction. In the meantime, the words 'or' and 'perhaps' must continue to make frequent appearances in descriptions.

5 Stoneware:
Part 1

By the 15th century German potters were firing certain types of clay to a high temperature, and making a very hard, waterproof pottery which they named *Steinzeug:* stoneware. In addition to the clays it was essential for the makers to have ample supplies of wood fuel, and the manufacture centred in the heavily-forested area of the Rhineland. In particular Cologne, Frechen, Siegburg and Raeren were important sites of numerous potteries that exported the ware all over Europe.

A proportion of the stoneware was sold in an unglazed state: greyish in colour and with a matt surface. Most surviving examples, however, are found to have been given an all-over glaze. The glazing was performed in a remarkably simple manner by throwing a quantity of common salt into the kiln during firing, which deposited a thin, uniform coating over the contents of the kiln.

Salt-glazed stoneware is a noticeably hard product, and can be recognised by its orange-peel surface, and by the thinness of the covering gloss. Unlike the glaze on other kinds of pottery and on porcelain it does not collect in pools, but is spread evenly. Older readers may recall it in the shape of ginger-beer bottles, and it remains in production today for such unromantic but essential objects as drain pipes. Both of these commercial products will be found

Below, Fig. 62: Cologne 'tiger-ware' (glazed stoneware) jug with silver lid, collar and foot added in England. Jug, late 16th century; silver, hallmarked 1587. Height, 8½ inches. (County Museum, Truro.)

Left, *Fig. 63: Saltglazed stoneware cup with silver rim mount. Fulham,* circa *1685. Height, 4 inches. (E. N. Stretton, Esq.)*

to have the same features as the stoneware of earlier times.

In some instances stoneware articles were given a wash of slip made with clay containing iron, which gave them a brown-coloured finish. After salt-glazing they emerged with a mottled surface ranging in tone from light to dark brown, named because of its resemblance to the animal's skin: 'tiger-ware' (see Fig. 62). In the later 16th century, Cologne tiger-ware jugs were sometimes mounted in English silver, often found to be stamped with Exeter hall-marks. Why the West-country should have apparently specialised in such work has not been explained.

The manufacture of stoneware in England may possibly have been begun soon after the first quarter of the 17th century. In 1626 a patent was granted by Charles I to Thomas Rous and Abraham Cullyn of London, which gave them 'The sole making of stone potts, stone juggs, and stone bottells . . . for the tearme of fowerteene yeares'. For this privilege they agreed to pay annually the sum of five pounds.

At one time it was thought that the two men were only importers of foreign-made articles, and attention was drawn to the fact that the name Cullyn might have been an anglicisation of Cologne.

It has been found that Rous (Ruys) was born in Holland, and Cullyn or Cullen, the son of a Dutch hosier, Richard van Ceulen, was born in Norwich. They married sisters, Judith and Elizabeth Moone, daughters of Martin Moone of Norwich, 'formerly a resident of Brabant', and each had a daughter, amongst other children, who married a Lord Mayor of London.

While much has been discovered about the genealogy of the two families, it remains problematical whether the men in question actually did make any stoneware. Support for the possibility occurs in a paragraph printed in William Maitland's *History of London*, published in 1756, which mentions the discovery in the mid-18th century of 'an arched room, ten feet square, and eight feet deep, with several arched Doors around it, stopped up with earth'. The 'room' was found just north

Right, *Fig. 64: Lydia, daughter of John Dwight, who died in her seventh year on 3rd March, 1673. Engraving by M. L. Solon of the Fulham stoneware effigy now in the Victoria and Albert Museum.*

of Fenchurch Street on the site of the old Mansion House, near the church of St. Dionis Backchurch. Rous was buried at the latter in 1640, and not very far away, at St. Helen's, Bishopsgate, Cullen was laid to rest in 1658.

While ordinary red clay pottery and delftware were fired in tall conical kilns, stoneware was placed for the purpose in square arched buildings. It has been suggested that the so-called room mentioned casually by Maitland was none other than the kiln used by Rous and Cullen. There is no record of stoneware fragments or kiln wasters being picked up on the spot, nor were any noticed during a further rebuilding operation in the present century. It is possible, however, that they would have been disregarded unless someone there at the time was particularly interested in such things.

The most popular type of stoneware article in use in 17th century London would seem to have been the fat-bellied jugs known as 'greybeards' or 'Bellarmines': the latter name attaching to them in contemptuous reference to an Italian cleric, Cardinal Roberto Bellarmine. The Cardinal was looked upon by Protestants as a champion of the papacy, and known to Englishmen for his criticism of James I after the latter's legislation against Catholics following the failure of the Gunpowder Plot.

Hundreds of old Bellarmines have been found in and around the City of London, some of them with a bearded head alone stamped on them, and others with devices embodying tavern signs and initials. Some bear the coat of arms and initials (E.R.) of Queen Elizabeth I, and they range in colour from an even brown to the mottled tiger-ware marking.

A mould for stamping the royal arms of Elizabeth was found on the site of a kiln at Raeren, so it is not by any means unlikely that the other devices also were impressed there. Some of the tavern signs and initials have been identified and dated, but there are no visible differences between known imported ewers and supposed London-made ones. Thus, the queries

Above, *Fig. 66: Saltglazed stoneware Bellarmine found in a vault at the Fulham Pottery in 1864. Fulham, late 17th century. Height, 8⅛ inches. (British Museum.)*

Left, *Fig. 65: Bust of Prince Rupert of the Rhine (1619-1682), grandson of James I and a famous leader of Royalist cavalry in the English Civil War. Fulham, circa 1680. Height, 24 inches. (British Museum.)*

concerning Rous and Cullen remain un-answered, at any rate at the present time.

THE first positively identified English stoneware dates from the last decades of the 17th century, and the man responsible for it was John Dwight. He was born in about 1636, and his early years were spent at Chester and Wigan in the service of the Bishops of Chester. In 1671 he was granted a patent by Charles II, following a petition in which Dwight stated that he had discovered

> The Mistery of Transparent Earthen-ware, commonly knowne by the Names of Porcelaine of China, and Persian Ware, as alsoe the Misterie of the Stone Ware vulgarly called Cologne Ware; and that he designed to introduce a Manufacture of the said Wares . . . . where they have not hitherto bene wrought or made.

Like all such claims it was probably somewhat exaggerated, but there is no doubt that he did know how to make stoneware. That it had not 'hitherto bene wrought or made' was open to argument, but a statement of this kind was more a matter of form than of fact and appeared on many similar documents. The patent was for the usual term of fourteen years, and in return Dwight was to pay the sum of twenty shillings annually to the King. He estab-lished his manufactory at Fulham, south-west of the City of London and near the river Thames.

There are a number of interesting con-temporary references to the potter and his activities, and they leave it quite beyond doubt that he was engaged in making stoneware. He was acquainted with Robert Hooke, the inventive member of the Royal Society, who recorded in his diary on 20th September 1673, that he 'met Dwight, he told me he used to throw salt into his fire as the Dutch'. A few months later the potter gave evidence before the House of

Lords and it was stated that 'Mr. Dwite saith he can make as good and as much Collen [Cologne] ware as will supply England'.

Robert Plot, in his *History of Oxfordshire*, published in 1677, wrote several lengthy paragraphs which refer to the potter. One of them reads, in part:

. . the ingenious John Dwight, formerly M.A. of Christ Church College, Oxon, hath discovered the mystery of the stone or Cologne wares (such as d'Alva bottles [*an alternative name for Bellarmines*], jugs, noggins) heretofore made only in Germany, and by the Dutch brought over into England in great quantities; and hath set up a manufacture of the same, which (by methods and contrivances of his own, altogether unlike those used by the Germans), in three or four years' time, he hath brought it to greater perfection than it has attained where it hath been used for many ages, insomuch that the Company of Glass-Sellers of London, who are the dealers

for that commodity, have contracted with the inventor to buy only of his manufacture, and refuse the foreign.

The contract for exclusive supply to the Company was made on 25th March 1676, and specified the quantities and prices of the goods as well as safeguarding their consistent quality. The Company had gained its charter only a few years previously, in 1664, and its coat of arms showed a glass cup, a looking-glass, and a 'laver-pot of white wair': a ewer of white pottery. They were empowered to control the trade in glassware and looking-glasses, and in 'hourglasses, stone pots, or earthen bottles . . . or any other white or galley ware'.

Hooke recorded also in his diary that he had been shown some figures made by

Fig. 67: Red stoneware teapot decorated with panels of Oriental trees and birds in relief on a gilt ground. Elers, circa 1690. Height, 4 inches. (Victoria and Albert Museum.)

Plate 10 (Centre and right) *Two brown-red stoneware mugs with stamped decoration. Elers, Staffordshire, circa 1690. Height, 3½ inches.* (Left) *Brown-glazed stoneware mug with 'carved' ornament. Nottingham, circa 1700. Height, 4 inches.* (*County Museum, Truro.*)

Plate 11 *Brown-glazed stoneware tankard with relief ornament, inscribed below the rim:* 'Drink to the Pious Memory of Good Queen Ann, July ye 25: 1729'. *Fulham. Height, 8¼ inches.*

Dwight, and was lent one by him. This he exhibited to members of the Royal Society on 25th February 1674/5, where the event was duly noted:

> Mr. Hooke brought in an artificial head resembling china, made in England, of English clay, so hard and solid, that he said, nothing would fasten on it, except a diamond; and that it received its polish in the fire.

A number of Dwight's figures have been preserved, and are remarkable for their outstanding craftsmanship and finish: far in advance of anything of the kind produced at the time or for several decades to come. The figures comprise a total of seventeen statues and include classical and other personages, busts of notabilities of the time (Fig. 65), and a striking half-length figure

Fig. 68: Reverse side of a teapot similar to that shown in Fig. 67, but without the gilt ground in the panels. Elers, circa 1690. Height, 4 inches. (E. N. Stretton, Esq.)

of a child. Inscribed on the back of the latter, which represents the potter's daughter, is: *Lydia Dwight, died March 3 1673* (Fig. 64).

The figures had remained in the possession of descendants of the potter, and were purchased in about 1862 by a Mr. Baylis who announced his important acquisition in the *Art Journal* for October of that year. Later they were bought by a prominent collector of the time, Mr. C. W. Reynolds, and following his death were sold at Christie's on 30th May 1871. Most of them are now in museums in London and Liverpool.

Over the years there has been continual argument about the figures. It has not been disputed that they came from the Fulham pottery, but their actual authorship has been debated. They are obviously the work of a most skilful modeller, each being made individually and not cast from a mould. There is no record of John Dwight having

Above, *Fig. 69: Red stoneware mug with moulded bands and stamped ornament, the latter comprising a wyvern, a Merry Andrew, and prunus blossom; the last is not visible here, but cf. Figs. 70 and 72. Elers, late 17th century. Height, 3¼ inches. (Victoria and Albert Museum.)*

Opposite, *Fig. 70: Red stoneware mug of unusually tall shape, with moulded bands and stamped ornament. Elers, late 17th century. Height, 6⅞ inches. (E. N. Stretton, Esq.)*

done any modelling himself, and there have been suggestions that the figures might have been the work of the best known carver and sculptor of the day, Grinling Gibbons. As it is, their authorship remains a mystery.

Preserved with the figures in the possession of Dwight's descendants were four jugs of Bellarmine type. Their number was increased in 1864 when workmen broke into an unsuspected 'walled-up arched chamber' at the pottery. They were said also to have found a pot containing some engraved brass stamps, bearing patterns of the kinds used in ornamenting pottery and which are now in the British Museum.

Probably made at Fulham are some small-sized stoneware pots with ribbed short necks. A number of the surviving examples bear silver neck mounts, like the one illustrated in Fig. 63, and two in the Victoria and Albert Museum are engraved with initials and the date 1682. All are very neatly and thinly potted, so much so that they are translucent in places. This may well have led Dwight and others at the time to think they were indeed 'Transparent Earthenware . . . . Porcelaine of China'.

In 1869 a visit to the still-functioning Fulham manufactory by two well-known collectors, Mr. Charles and Lady Charlotte Schreiber, resulted in the finding of two of John Dwight's note-books. They contained numerous entries covering the years 1689 to 1698, with recipes for different types of ware as well as a lengthy list of places where the potter had concealed sums of money on the premises. A typical entry reads:

> To make Transparent Porcelane or China Cley—Take fine white thirty pounds. Best cley sifted twenty pounds. Mingle and tread. This works strong and may be wrought thin upon the wheel.

There are also recipes for 'Mouse coloured cley to endure boiling water', 'for marbling stone-pots', 'A Mouse colour'd Por-

cellane with white specks', 'To make a deep red Cley of the Staffordshire red Cley', and 'Another good red of the same Cley'.

Dwight's patent expired in 1684, and in the same year he was granted another. The document opened as follows:

> Whereas John Dwight, Gentl., hath represented unto us that by his owne industry and at his owne proper costs and charges, hee hath invented and sett up at Fulham in our County of Middx., Severall New Manufactures of Earthenware, called by the Names of White Gorges, Marbled Porcellane Vessells, Statues, and Figures, and Fine Stone Gorges and Vessels, never before made in England or elsewhere, and alsoe discovered the Mistery of Transparent Porcellane, and Opacous, Redd, and Darke-coloured Porcellane or China and Persian Wares, and the Mistery of the Cologne or Stone Wares . . .

Right, *Fig. 72: Enlarged view of a red stoneware mug by Elers; compare stamped ornament with Figs. 69 and 70. Late 17th century. Height, 4 inches. (Victoria and Albert Museum.)*

Below, *Fig. 71: Red stoneware teapot with stamped ornament, in the centre a Royal couple with initials 'G.R.'. Staffordshire, mid-18th century. Height, 4½ inches. (County Museum, Truro.)*

The mention of 'Redd, and Darke-coloured Porcellane' is a reference to a type of red stoneware made at Yi-hsing, near Soochow, and imported in the shape of teapots. They were brought into the country along with consignments of the leaf, and it was widely believed not only that tea brewed in them was superior to any other but that they were made of a variety of porcelain. In fact, they were stoneware, and the possibility that Dwight made some is arguable. The evidence in favour is an entry in one of his note-books, with a recipe for glaze, which reads:

October 1695
. . . The little furnace where the last Red Teapots were burnt I take to be a convenient one for this use.

On 14th February 1695, the *London Gazette* printed a small advertisement announcing:

At the Marine Coffee-House in Birchin Lane will be exposed to sale fine red figured and flavered [? *a misprint for 'flowered'*] Teapots, Chocolate Cups. and other Curiosities.

These may perhaps have been of Dwight's manufacture, but equally they could have been imported or have been made in this country by two brothers, David and John

Fig. 74: Stoneware cup, streaked in black and brown, labelled 'Mr. Francis Place's China', formerly in the collection of the Hon. Horace Walpole and now in the Victoria and Albert Museum. From a woodcut.

Philip Elers, who came to England from Holland in about 1686.

D AVID Elers was making pottery at Fulham from about 1690, and in 1693 was taken to court by Dwight for infringing the latter's second patent. He then moved to Vauxhall and carried on a manufactory of 'brown ware and theapotts'. The other brother made similar wares in Staffordshire during the same period.

John Philip Elers's fame must have spread, because a visitor to the district in 1698 noted:

> I went to this Newcastle in Staffordshire [Newcastle-under-Lyme] to see the making of the fine tea potts. Cups and saucers of the fine red Earth in imitation and as Curious as that which Comes from China, but was defeated in my design, they Comeing to an End of their Clay they made use of for that sort of ware, and therefore was remov'd to some other place where they were not settled at their work so Could not see it . . . .

In December 1700 both men were declared bankrupt and ceased to be active potters.

The wares attributed to the Elers brothers are distinguished by their careful finish, and range in colour from dark to light red. Decoration is sometimes in the form of raised small branches of prunus blossom or of other patterns in relief. There has been much argument from time to time about impressed Chinese-looking marks beneath the bases of teapots and other pieces, but they are not by any means confined to the Elers's productions. Many such marks are on pieces of much later date, for their manufacture continued until well into the 18th century.

O NE other early maker of stoneware-cum-porcelain deserves a mention: Francis Place, of York. He was a talented amateur artist, engraver and potter, who made a stoneware cup that has survived, together with an impeccable pedigree, from the years 1683-93. The cup, which is now in the Victoria & Albert Museum, was once owned by the 18th century collector, Horace Walpole. In his *Anecdotes of Painting* Walpole recorded some facts about Place's life and work, noting: 'I have a coffee cup of his ware; it is of grey earth, with streaks of black, and not superior to common earthenware' (Fig. 74).

A portrait of Place which remains in the hands of his descendants, shows him holding in his left hand a cup of similar pattern to the one illustrated. At one time a number of examples of his stoneware had accompanied the picture down the centuries, but these have been dispersed at some time. Now they have vanished, like so much else of their kind, and it may be hoped that some or all of these links in ceramic history will come to light again one day.

6 Stoneware: Part 2

Plate 12 *Salt-glazed stoneware jug, painted in colours and inscribed with the initials* D.S. *and* A.M., *and* One lugg more and then 1766. *Staffordshire, Height, 7¾ inches. (City Museum and Art Gallery, Plymouth.)*

Plate 13 *Teapot of buff-coloured stoneware with reliefs in white and blue-grey. Staffordshire, mid-18th century. Height, 4¼ inches. Teapot of salt-glazed stoneware painted in colours with a portrait of Frederick the Great, King of Prussia. Staffordshire, circa 1760. Height, 3¾ inches. (County Museum, Truro.)*

Plate 14 *'Brick' for holding cut flowers, of salt-glazed stoneware with 'scratch blue' decoration. Staffordshire, mid-18th century. Length, 6¾ inches. (County Museum, Truro.)*

THE Fulham factory started by John Dwight continued in production throughout the 18th century. Surviving from the first decades are some quart-sized tankards, made of salt-glazed stoneware, partly dipped in coloured brown and ornamented with small stamped reliefs. The subjects of the reliefs include heads of Royalty, components of the hunt and figures of Beefeaters (see Plate 11). Many are inscribed with ill-spelt legends, like an example in the Victoria and Albert Museum which runs: 'On Banse downs a hair wee found thatt led uss all a Smoking Round 1729'. This is presumably a reference to Banstead Downs in Surrey; and while possibly commemorating an actual hare-hunt may equally refer to some forgotten political event.

Similar tankards bear names, which suggests they were made either for visitors to the pottery or in response to orders from customers. Typical of them is a large-sized example with the words 'The Lord Blefs us All, Henly, 1740'. Most often the names are those of innkeepers like 'Henry Bacon att Cock in Henham, 1719', or 'Jsm Nash, Woods Close; Cheyne; Aleman'. They are sturdy articles, suitable for everyday use and with few signs remaining of the delicate modelling and careful finish of the earlier wares.

In 1795 it was recorded that:

The Works are still carried on at Fulham by Mr. White, a descendant in the female line of the first proprietor. Mr. White's father, who married John Dwight's Granddaughter, obtained a premium in 1761 from the Society for the Encouragement of Arts, &c., for the making of crucibles of British materials.

The White family continued to own the Fulham pottery until 1862, and following a

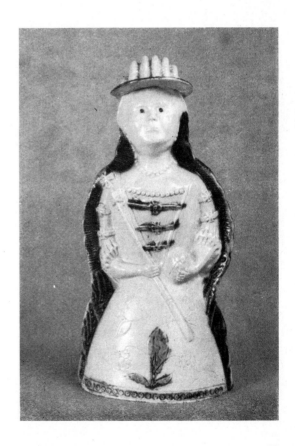

Right, Fig. 75: Half-length figure of Queen Anne, with details coloured blue. Staffordshire, early 18th century. Height, 7 5⁄16 inches. (Burnap Collection, Nelson Gallery-Atkins Museum, Kansas City.)

Fig. 76: Two cups with patterns in relief. Staffordshire, circa 1745. Heights, 1¾ and 2⅜ inches. (City Museum and Art Gallery, Plymouth.)

short interval it was bought by a Mr. C. J. C. Bailey. It was the latter, inaugurating changes to modernise the premises and manufacturing methods, who was responsible for finding the cache of Dwight figures and other pieces. A few years later he came upon two of the potter's original note-books, which he gave to the eminent collectors, Mr. Charles and Lady Charlotte Schreiber (see page 84). It may be added that the note-books have since disappeared, but fortunately their contents were transcribed and the copies are safely in the British Museum.

Elsewhere in the London area, at Lambeth, stoneware was made from the end of the 17th century. Giving evidence before a committee of the House of Commons in 1698, James Marriner described himself as a 'workman for Stone Bottles about London', which indicates that Dwight's innovation had gained imitators. No doubt most or all of the ware being made was of negligible artistic importance, and would have comprised pots and jars of various kinds.

Contemporary references to actual potters and potteries are not plentiful, but one of them makes two appearances in the press of the time. On 2nd June 1720 the *Daily Post* advertised:

> To let, Carlile Pot-House, near Lambeth Marsh, with two very good White Kilns and two Stone Kilns. The said House was formerly made use of for linen manufacture.

Six years later, on 25th June 1726, the same journal printed:

> CARLILE POTHOUSE now in trade, completely fix'd with KILNS and all other Utensils for the carrying on a large trade in the WHITE and STONE Way, will admit of a partner that has £500 or upwards to bring in Stock, one of the present partners will quit the business: if not willing to be concerned in Partnership may have the whole. Enquire at the POTHOUSE in LAMBETH MARSH and know further.

Later in the century there is some confirmation that production of stoneware in the district included the utilitarian, although we can only guess what might have been being made by others. The *London*

Gazette of 2nd April 1774 printed an advertisement by John Lawrence 'water pipe and crucible manufacturer, Lambeth', and the very lack of announcements by potters in the area could mean that they had nothing out of the ordinary to offer. It can be assumed, perhaps, that the makers of stoneware concentrated on useful pieces, while their colleagues in the delftware trade turned their attention to the more decorative.

Much the same thing occurred at Bristol, although stoneware does not seem to have been made in quantity until the second half of the 18th century. An advertisement in *Felix Farley's Journal* on 17th March 1764 would appear to be an early reference to such activity, and reads:

> At Read and Co's Pothouse at Counterslip near Temple Cross, Bristol, Merchants and others may be supplied with all Sorts of Stone Bottles as cheap as imported. Also pickling Jars, &c. 30 per cent. under common selling Price in this city. Also all Sorts of Muggs &c. at Lowest Price.

A Victorian writer noted an amusing anecdote perhaps referring to a predecessor of the above. He reported:

> It is said that the delft-ware potteries were preceded by a maker of Salt-glazed stone-ware, a German named Wrede or Reed, and a curious story is told in connection with him, and the difficulty he had in establishing his works. It appears that the people, being surprised at the glaze he produced on his ware, and the secrecy he endeavoured to preserve regarding his pottery, and noticing the dense cloud of vapour which every now and then arose from his kiln (caused of course by the throwing of salt upon the heated ware), believed he called in supernatural aid, and that the fumes which ascended were caused by visits of the devil. He was mobbed by the people, his place injured, and was forced to fly the town.

If the German did precede in date the delftware makers he must have set up his pottery in the late 17th century, but the above story is the only evidence we have of his existence. It may well have a basis in fact, and if he was indeed chased out of the city soon after he had established himself it is not unlikely that he disappeared without any further trace. A similar lack of references surrounds any other makers of stoneware who may have been active in Bristol at the time, and because of such a vacuum it cannot be assumed that there were none.

In 1777 Richard Frank & Son removed their 'Earthen and Stone Pot Works' from Redcliffe Backs to Water Lane, and a few years later the proprietor sold the pottery to his son-in-law, Joseph Ring. The latter announced that he was continuing to make 'Bristol Stone Ware', and listed some examples on his trade-card. They included bottles ranging in capacity from 1 gallon to 3 gallons, and pickling pots.

Fig. 77: Group of a monkey with young. Staffordshire, mid-18th century. Height, 7½ inches. (Victoria and Albert Museum.)

Above, Fig. 78: Brown-glazed bowl, inscribed Mr. A. F. 1725. Nottingham. *Diameter, 10¼ inches. (E. N. Stretton, Esq.)* **Right,** *Fig. 79: Dish of exceptionally large size, commemorating the victories of Frederick, King of Prussia.* Staffordshire, *circa 1760. Diameter, 15⅞ inches.*

I**T** is known that a considerable quantity of stoneware was made farther north, in Nottingham. It is of a distinctive rich brown colour, made by washing the finished article with a slip of clay containing iron, is thinly potted and often has a slight metallic sheen. Many of the wares were decorated with incised patterns, and a proportion bear names and dates, of which the earliest recorded so far is 1700. This is on a large posset-pot, now in the Castle Museum, Nottingham, which bears the names of Samuel and Sarah Watkinson, mayor and mayoress of the city in that year.

The posset-pot exhibits a feature that is found on other pieces from the same pottery: part of the body is double-skinned, and the outer surface is pierced. A number of small-sized drinking cups with similar decoration have survived, and one of them in the Victoria and Albert Museum is dated 1703. A cup of the type is featured on an advertisement sheet, in the Bodleian Library, Oxford, issued by James Morley (see Plate 10).

The sheet is an interesting and unique scrap of paper that has somehow escaped destruction during the past two and a half centuries. It shows a half-dozen articles

and in addition to the cup, which is described as *A Carved Jug*, shows: *A Decantor* (a tall jug), *A Mogg* (a mug), *A Flower-Pot* (a jardinière), *A Carved Teapot*, and *A Capuchine* (a tall cup with a handle). Beneath the illustrations the advertiser announced:

> Such as have Occation for these Sorts of Pots commonly called Stone-Ware, or for such as are of any other Shape not here Represented may be furnished with them by the Maker James Morley at ye Pot-House in Nottingham.

Morley, along with the Elers brothers and some others, was one of the men taken to court in 1696 by John Dwight, who alleged they had infringed his second patent of 1684. The Nottingham potter, who is recorded as having served his apprenticeship in London, admitted selling 'brown mugs'. Dwight won his case, and obtained an injunction restraining the defendants from continuing their action. This, however, does not seem to have restrained Morley, unless he and Dwight came to terms.

The Morley family continued to make stoneware of similar appearance throughout the 18th century, but the city gradually ceased production in favour of nearby factories in the Chesterfield area. At these, stoneware of the same brown colour was made, and much of it is barely distinguishable from that of Nottingham.

Although it is known that James Morley and his descendants owned the pottery, no pieces bearing their names have been recorded. Attributions are based on the clear evidence of the advertisement sheet. However, a few pieces of Nottingham ware bear the signatures of their makers, who have been traced in documents of the period to have been employed as potters. William Lockett (*c.* 1740) and John Asquith (*c.* 1760) appear on a handful of articles, and a

tea-caddy is signed *M C maker at Nottm.* 1771; which probably refers to Moses Colclough listed three years later as a pot-maker.

On 12th June 1751 Dr. Richard Pococke, archdeacon of Dublin and a tireless traveller, was in the north of England. In one of the numerous letters, ostensibly addressed to his mother but probably with an alert eye to their eventual publication, he wrote:

> I went on [*from Ormskirk*] to Prescot, a little town most delightfully situated on a hill, its steeple, windmill, glass-houses, and earthenware-houses render it a very beautiful point of view at two or three miles distance. . . . they have two or three houses for coarse earthen ware and work it as they say higher with the fire than at Lambeth. They make it of a mixture of two sorts of clay which they find here.

Below, *Fig. 80: Teapot with 'scratch blue' decoration, inscribed on one side* Henry Muskett 1760 *and on the other,* Mary Sampson 1760. *Liverpool. Height, 5 inches. (County Museum, Truro.)*

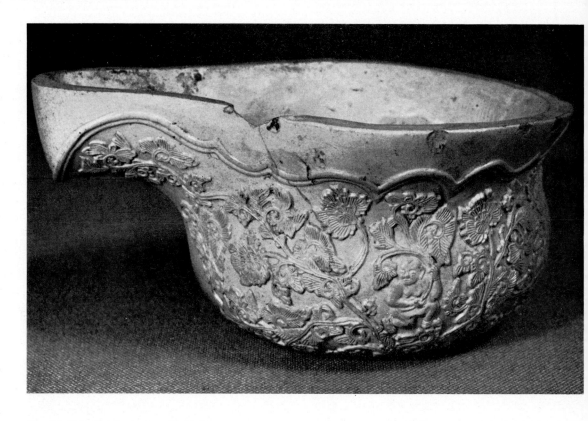

Fig. 81: Salt-glazed stoneware block for making moulds for a sauceboat. Staffordshire, mid-18th century. Length, 7¼ inches. (City Museum and Art Gallery, Hanley.)

No piece of high-fired earthenware, i.e. stoneware, has been found which can be attributed to the 'two or three houses' at Prescot, but a few pieces are known that came from the nearby city of Liverpool. One is a mug inscribed *Ser William a Plumper*, which was made to encourage supporters of Sir William Meredith in the election of 1761. The incised wording was emphasised by dusting it, before firing and glazing, with powdered cobalt-blue; a type of decoration, simple but effective, known as 'scratch blue' (Plate 14).

At the corner of Flint Street and Parliament Street in Liverpool stood the Flint Pot-Works, built at an unrecorded date by a timber-merchant and shipowner, John Okill. It was known that ordinary types of

earthenware were manufactured there from the early 1770's, but it is now clear that saltglazed stoneware was made at an earlier date.

Two pieces of ware are attributed to Okill's pottery: a four-sided tea caddy and a tea pot. The former is inscribed on one side *Henrey Muskit* 1760 *L* and on another *Elizabeth Cannon* 1760 *Liver*, and in both instances the colouring is such that the term 'scratch black' would be appropriate. The teapot has the more usual scratch-blue decoration which takes the form of conventional flowers, and in addition it is incised: *Henry Muskett* 1760 and *Mary Sampson* 1760 (Fig. 80).

The Liverpool Town Books contain an entry dated 27th November 1767 stating that Henry Muskett, a potter, had served his seven-year apprenticeship with John Okill & Company, and that he was duly given his freedom on paying 6/8d. Nothing

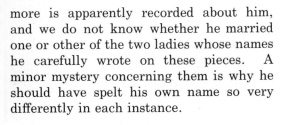

Left, *Fig. 82: Pew group in white and brown salt-glazed stoneware. Staffordshire, circa 1745. Height, 6½ inches. (Burnap Collection, Kansas City.)* **Above,** *Fig. 83: Teapot moulded with designs adapted from engravings in a book published in 1669; above the equestrian figure in the centre panel is the inscription* Young Vice Roy of Canton. *Staffordshire, circa 1745. Height, 4 inches. (E. N. Stretton, Esq.)*

more is apparently recorded about him, and we do not know whether he married one or other of the two ladies whose names he carefully wrote on these pieces. A minor mystery concerning them is why he should have spelt his own name so very differently in each instance.

WHILE there was considerable activity in stoneware-making in various parts of the country, it was in Staffordshire that the principal developments took place. A few potters in the county made it from about 1710, but there is no reason to suppose that any difference could be discerned between the products of one region and another. Although there were probably attempts to whiten the body so that it would more closely resemble Chinese porcelain, the majority of the output was greyish in colour and speckled with tiny impurities.

Within a decade, after numerous experiments with clay obtained from Derbyshire, it was found that Dorset and Devonshire white clays provided part of the answer. The other introduction was the addition of powdered flints, said to have been the result of an accident. A local man is said to have noticed how white was the powder produced when a flint was burned, and trials

were made with burned and ground flints to see if they would whiten the ware. They did, and with the addition of the clay imported from the south a greatly improved stoneware was the result.

At first the whiter pottery was made by squeezing it into patterned metal moulds, or by pressing it between a pair of moulds so that it could be stamped extremely thinly. The moulds were oiled to prevent the clay from sticking. Some of the old moulds have been preserved, and when they are compared with specimens made from them and fired it is noticeable how much the latter have shrunk in the heat of the kiln. This occurs not only with stoneware, but with all other types of pottery as well as porcelain.

There have also been preserved a number of pottery 'blocks' or master-models, from which it would have been a simple matter to make any number of clay moulds (Fig. 81).

THE next change was the bringing into the country from France of the process of casting. It is supposed to have taken place in the decade 1740-50, and to have been introduced by Ralph Daniel of Cobridge. The mould for an article was made of plaster or of lightly-fired clay (the latter known by the potters as 'pitcher'). It was filled with slip, and the porous nature of the mould allowed it to soak up water from the mixture near it. It thus became coated with a layer of clay, and as soon as the worker thought this was sufficiently thick, he poured out the surplus slip. The mould and its contents were put aside for a stated interval, and as it dried the clay shrank so it could be removed without difficulty. While articles of simple outline, like cups and bowls, with patterns raised on their sides, could be made easily, more complicated items had to be moulded in separate parts. These were assembled when hard, being stuck together with slip and the surplus carefully removed.

The process resulted in a ware of most attractive thinness, and with details of the patterned mould rendered sharply. The sharpness was not lost under salt-glazing, for the covering was so even that nothing

Below, *Fig. 84: Pair of figures of hawks, with details in brown and blue, copied from prototypes in Chinese porcelain. Staffordshire, mid-18th century. Height, 8⅞ inches. (Burnap Collection, Kansas City.)* **Right,** *Fig. 85: Mounted hussar. Staffordshire, mid-18th century. Height, 8 inches. (City Museum and Art Gallery, Hanley.)*

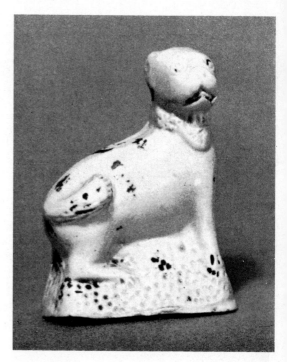

was obscured by it. The best saltglaze of the eighteenth century has a quality of its own and, although it challenged the supremacy of porcelain and failed, it was the material that first gave The Potteries the place it still holds after more than two hundred years.

The majority of surviving examples are pieces of tea-ware: teapots, cream or milk jugs, cups and saucers and small trays for spoons. The pots and jugs remain in the greatest quantity; no doubt the others had more usage and were quickly broken. The shapes varied greatly and are often surprising in their ingenuity, and their employment of motifs from unexpected sources.

Teapots can be found in the form of a seated camel with a square 'howdah' on its back, a squirrel holding a nut, or in the shape of a heart. Other teapots in the form of a fully-rigged ship commemorate the capture of Porto Bello in 1739, dishes encourage the King of Prussia some twenty years later, and a few articles have been recorded which are decorated with

panels in relief copied from engravings in a book published in 1669 (Fig. 83).

The material was used also for making ornaments of various types. Of these, the best-known and rarest are the so-called 'pew groups': two or more figures seated in a tall-backed settle or pew. They are modelled conventionally, rather in the manner of 'pin men', with eyes and other details rendered in brown or black slip. All of them are expressions of a pleasing rustic humour, and are far more representative of 18th century England than the more polished wares of Chelsea and Worcester.

Above left, Fig. 86: Two agateware figures of women. Staffordshire, circa 1730. Heights, 7⅛ and 6¼ inches. (Burnap Collection, Kansas City.) **Above**, *Fig. 87: Figure of a pug dog with traces of unfired oil-paint decoration. Staffordshire, mid-18th century. Height, 2⅜ inches. (City Museum and Art Gallery, Plymouth.)* **Right**, *Fig. 88: Jug and cover in the shape of a bear gripping a dog. Staffordshire, mid-18th century. Height, 9¾ inches. (Victoria and Albert Museum.)*

Equally appealing are single figures of soldiers, on horseback and on foot, crinolined ladies, and animals (Figs. 86, 87). Direct copies were made of Oriental pieces such as birds, lions and, occasionally, human figures.

Especially popular in Staffordshire and the Midlands generally were jugs and covers in the shape of bears; both bull- and bear- baiting were highly appreciated at the time as entertainments. Most of the bears are represented seated holding a dog between their paws, the removable head, which forms a drinking-cup, having a loose chain through the nose. The fur of the animal was rendered realistically by sprinkling the wet unfired body with small shreds of clay. They were made at many of the numerous Staffordshire stoneware potteries and also at Nottingham, but there are no grounds for allocating any particular example to one source or another.

Coloured or stained clays were used sometimes in combination and were moulded into articles. The clays, blue, brown and white, were carefully blended together to form an effect somewhat like marble, the resulting products being known as 'agate ware'. Pressing into moulds had to be done skilfully or the veining would be blurred or lost.

Surface decoration, in addition to the 'scratch blue' mentioned above, was employed from about 1745-50. Much of the colour and design was owed to imported Chinese *famille rose*, with its preponderance of pink. The painting was usually executed with a certain delicacy, but often without much pretension to good draughtsmanship

Below, *Fig. 89: Sauceboat moulded with a scroll and diaper pattern, probably copied from a silver prototype. Staffordshire, mid-18th century. Length, 7¾ inches. (City Museum and Art Gallery, Plymouth.)*

and regardless of the surface. Thus, a moulded piece was often decorated with designs that ignored both its shaping and pattern. The few surviving examples with careful painting are outstanding, and show the fine results that could be achieved by a really good artist.

Many surviving pieces are undecorated, except for moulded ornament, but were probably once 'cold painted': i.e. painted with ordinary enamels, which were not fired and have since worn away. An example is the pug dog in Fig. 87, which retains traces of the oil-paint that once coloured it.

An unusual blue was employed sometimes as an all-over glaze and is known as 'Littler's Blue', because it is supposed to have been invented by William Littler, who was connected later with the Longton Hall porcelain manufactory. The blue was applied in the form of finely-sieved slip stained with cobalt into which the article was dipped. Some pieces were left plain, but others were painted effectively with white enamel and a few were embellished with designs in gold leaf.

Fig. 90: Teapot of white stoneware covered in a bright blue ('Littler's Blue') glaze and painted in white. Staffordshire, mid-18th century. Height, 4½ inches. (City Museum and Art Gallery, Plymouth.)

7   Cream Ware

A TOMBSTONE in Stoke Parish churchyard is inscribed 'John Astbury the elder, of Shelton, Potter, who departed this life March the 3rd, 1743, age 55'. It records the major part of what is known for certain of the life of Astbury, who has been credited at one time and another with many of the innovations in potting.

The authority for attributing so much to this one man, and for similar details as regards many others, is a Manchester-born writer, Simeon Shaw. He was the principal of two Academies for Young Gentlemen in Hanley and Tunstall between 1818 and 1851, and published a *History of the Staffordshire Potteries* in 1829 (reprinted in 1891). He

was in a good position, geographically and socially to get the necessary information, and was writing at a time when there were still many men living who could give first-hand information of what had occurred in the past. Unfortunately, Shaw has been proved to be inaccurate in many of the statements he made, and this has thrown doubt on some of the others. Whatever his merits, he remains the chief published source of information about the Stafford-shire potteries.

John Astbury was stated by Simeon Shaw to have introduced into The Potteries two ingredients that led to immense improvements in the ware: Devonshire white clay and ground flints. In addition, he was supposed to have acquired and made use of the methods of the Elers brothers (see *Chapter* 5, page 89). How this came about is related by Shaw as follows:

Head of page, Fig. 91: Unglazed 'wasters' excavated in the vicinity of Thomas Astbury's pottery, Shelton, in 1965. (City Museum and Art Gallery, Hanley.)

Fig. 92: Brown and white clay figure of Dr. Henry Sacheverell (? 1674-1724). Staffordshire, circa 1730. Height, 6⅜ inches. (Burnap Collection, Nelson Gallery-Atkins Museum, Kansas City.)

Having assumed the garb and appearance of an idiot, with all proper vacancy of countenance, he presented himself before the manufactory at Bradwell, and submitted to the cuffs, kicks and unkind treatment of masters and workmen, with a ludicrous grimace, as the proof of the extent of his mental ability. When some food was offered to him he only used his fingers to convey it to his mouth, and only when helped by other persons could he understand how to perform any of the labours to which he was directed. He next was employed to move the treadle of an Engine Lathe, a very different machine from those of this day, and by perseverance in his assumed character he had opportunity of witnessing every process, and examining every utensil they employed. On returning home each evening he formed models of the several kinds of implements, and made memoranda of the processes, which practice he continued a considerable time (near two years is mentioned), until he ascertained that no further information was likely to be obtained, when he availed himself of a fit of sickness to continue at home, and this was represented as most malignant, to prevent any person visiting him. After his recovery he was found so *sane* that Messrs Elers deemed him unfit longer to remain in their service, and he was discharged, without suspicion that he possessed a knowledge of all their manipulations.

In spite of a lack of corroborative evidence, certain types of lead-glazed earthenware have for long been attributed to Astbury. They are tea-wares and ornaments made of red clay with white clay embellishments, sometimes covered in clear glaze but on other occasions roughly blotched with colours. Some confirmation of the long-standing tradition came to light in the summer of 1965, when excavations in the vicinity of where his pottery once stood, not far from Shelton Church,

Plate 15 *Red clay teapot and cover with white clay reliefs; height, 4 inches. Spoontray, mottled with white rim; length, 6½ inches. Staffordshire, circa 1740. (City Museum and Art Gallery, Plymouth.)*

Plate 16 *Agateware teapot and cream jug. Staffordshire, circa 1740. Height, 4 inches. (City Museum and Art Gallery Plymouth.)*

revealed some 'wasters': unfinished and malformed pieces, in this instance also unglazed, rejected by the maker as unsuitable for sale (Fig. 91).

The most attractive of the Astbury wares are the small figures which, like the Stoneware 'pew groups' (*Chapter* 6, Fig. 82), have an appealing vitality. The little statuette illustrated in Fig. 92 depicts Dr. Henry Sacheverell, a well-known divine whose sermons were politically biased and earned him suspension from preaching. As a result he was the subject of popular acclaim, and the Government that had impeached him fell from power. He died in 1724, so the figure might be dated to about that year, but no doubt it was a stock model and served to represent any preacher after Sacheverell had been forgotten.

Typical of Astbury-type pieces are the figures of musicians (Fig. 93). They have their bodies modelled in white clay, with hats, bases and instruments in red,' the whole coated in a glaze streaked with colours. In some instances the basic clays are employed in a different manner, and

redware faces have been used to represent negroes. They are usually equipped with drums, while their fellow-musicians play a variety of instruments including bagpipes, violins, and horns.

The figures excited interest particularly in the twenties of this century, and their financial value rose accordingly. It inevitably induced some potters to try their hands at making reproductions, which were accepted unsuspectingly as genuine for a short while. As soon as the impositions were detected, experts were on their guard and points of difference between old and new were detected. It was noticed that the modelling of the copies was less accomplished, but in most instances the modern pieces were much heavier in the hand than eighteenth century ones.

The next development was to cease using the red clay and employ only the white, which when glazed appeared creamy in colour. The man whose name is linked most closely with its successful exploitation is Thomas Whieldon, who was born in 1719 and died at the age of 76 after having acquired a fortune estimated at £10,000. The term 'Whieldon' is applied nowadays to a very wide range of wares basically cream-coloured and covered in transparent lead glaze tinted in blue, green, manganese-brown, yellow and grey. In fact, as so many of the makers are now forgotten, and their

Above, left, *Fig. 94: Lady and gentleman in an arbour, covered in mottled glazes of manganese, green, grey and yellow. Staffordshire, mid-18th century. Height, 5⅞ inches. (Sotheby's.)* **Above,** *Fig. 95: Bull-baiting group; examples are recorded bearing the impressed mark of Ralph Wood. Staffordshire, circa 1770. Height, 5¾ inches. (City Museum and Art Gallery, Hanley.)* **Right,** *Fig. 96: Shepherdess with a shepherd playing a flute, the glazes stained green, blue, yellow and brown. Staffordshire, circa 1770. Height, 9¾ inches.*

particular specialities unidentifiable, it is customary and convenient to apply the name of one or other of the outstanding potters of the time to almost every kind of ware produced between 1750 and 1850.

While the colour-glazed wares, noted above, are particularly characteristic of the day, the earlier pieces were often of plain glazed clay with reliefs applied in a contratinsgly coloured clay. In former days such relief moulding had been executed by sticking pads of clay to the articles and then stamping them. By 1750 a much neater result was being achieved by what is known to potters as 'sprigging'.

'Sprigging' was done by using a patterned mould made of plaster. The soft clay was pressed into it and the surplus scraped carefully away, and after a short interval for drying and shrinking the relief was removed. The back was wetted

and it was placed where required on the object. A popular decoration consisted of raised leaves and grapes, copied from the Chinese, and these were linked by hand-rolled realistic stems and tendrils.

The coloured glazes were sometimes splashed or sponged on to produce the effect of tortoiseshell, or to imitate agate-ware. The latter was also made as it was in salt-glazed stoneware, of mixed coloured clays (Plate 16).

Excavations during the 19th century on the site of the Overhouse Works, belonging to one of the Wedgwood family, revealed many fragments of solid agate-ware.

Fig. 97: Toby jug in the form of an officer, drawing his sword with his right hand while raising a goblet with the other; glazed in green, yellow and brown, and incised on the base J. MARSH JOLLEY. Staffordshire, circa 1765. Height, 11½ inches. (Sotheby's.)

Commenting on them, Marc-Louis Solon, a practical potter himself, described the process in these words:

> The laminae of yellow and red clay were laid alternately upon each other until they formed a thick mass; from that mass thin slices were transversely cut with a wire, making thin bats which showed the veining produced by the superimposed layers of clays; these slices were then used to press the piece, the neatest being placed against the mould . . . as a rule, the bat required careful handling, as a pressure sideways in the wedging [*kneading*] in, or a too rough pressing in the mould destroyed the fineness in the marbling.

Thomas Whieldon is remembered also for the training he gave to a number of young men. His apprentices included Josiah Spode, who founded a firm still prominent in The Potteries, William Greatbach, who duly set up on his own, and Aaron Wood, member of a famous potting family who became the best-known modeller in the county and worked for many of the leading makers. Above all, Whieldon had as partner between 1754 and 1759 the most famous of all Staffordshire potters, Josiah Wedgwood.

Spode was taken on in 1749, and Whieldon's note-book records the event:

> April 9. Hired Siah Spoade, to give him from this time to Martlemas next 2s. 3d., or 2s. 6d. if he Deserves it.
> 2d. year   0. 2. 9d
> 3d. year   0. 3. 3d
> Pd. full earnest   0. 1. 0d

In 1752 Spode received 7s. a week with 5s. paid in earnest: i.e. to bind the bargain. Two years later his wage had increased to 7s. 6d. a week with an earnest of 31s. 6d.

There is also a record of goods ordered from Whieldon by a Mr. Green, of Aylsham, Norfolk. The list included:

> 4 tortoiseshell teapots, 4 coffee pots,
> 4 slop bowls, 4 ewers,
> 4 sugar boxes, 4 mustard pots,
> 8 salts, high feet, 2 dozen piggins,
> 3 quart coffee pots, 6 pint coffee pots.

In addition there were plates and dishes of

various sizes, which were with and without ribbed edges.

Another Staffordshire potter who achieved a lasting renown was Ralph Wood. He was succeeded confusingly by a son and a grandson of the same name, and the three generations span almost the whole of the 18th century. The first Ralph, who lived from 1715 to 1772, was the son of a miller and elder brother of Aaron Wood, the modeller and maker of moulds. He was perhaps himself a modeller, but less debatably he made saltglazed stoneware and colour-glazed creamware of the same type as Whieldon.

Some of the first Ralph Wood's glazed creamware figures are marked with Ra. Wood, R. WOOD, or Ra. Wood Burslem, impressed, and a few have a small relief of a group of trees: a rebus on the surname. Most of the pieces will be found to be free of glaze beneath the base, which is dry like plaster.

THE best-known of wares attributed to Ralph Wood are the early colour-glazed Toby jugs, so-named after Toby Fillpot, who was commemorated in a popular song, *The Brown Jug*, published in 1761. The three stanzas are an extended version of the ominous line found sometimes inscribed on tin-glazed earthenware, 'You and i are Earth', and run:

Dear Tom, this brown Jug that now foams with mild Ale,
(In which I will drink to sweet Nan of the Vale)
Was once Toby Fillpot, a thirsty old Soul,
As e'er drank a Bottle, or fathom'd a Bowl;
In boozing about 'twas his praise to excell,
And among Jolly Topers he bore off the Bell.

It chanc'd as in Dog-days he sat at his ease
In Flow'r-woven Arbour as gay as you please,
With a Friend and a Pipe puffing Sorrow away,
And with honest old Stingo was soaking his Clay,
His breath Doors of life on a sudden were shut,
And he died full as big as a Dorchester Butt.

His Body, when long in the Ground it had lain,
And time into Clay had resolv'd it again,
A Potter found out in its Covert so snug,
And with part of fat Toby he form'd this brown Jug,
Now sacred to Friendship, and Mirth, and mild Ale,
So here's to my lovely sweet Nan of the Vale.

The words appear engraved beneath the ample figure of a jovial tricorn-hatted man, holding aloft a foaming brown stoneware jug in his right hand and a smoking pipe in his left. It is in mezzotint, and was issued by the firm of Bowles & Carver, of St. Paul's Churchyard, London. The verses were written by the Reverend Francis Fawkes, who was more usually engaged on translations from the classics, but it has been pointed out that their theme was owed to the Latin of a noted Italian physician, Geronimo Amalteo, who died in 1574. Thus, it would seem that they were less out of character than might be guessed.

Fig. 98: Toby jug, perhaps representing Admiral of the Fleet Lord Howe, glazed in green and light brown with dark brown hat and boots. Staffordshire, circa 1770. Height, 9¾ inches. (Phillips, Son and Neale.)

Fig. 101: Figure of a bagpiper glazed in
green, grey and brown. Staffordshire,
circa 1770. Height, 7¾ inches.

Numerous real-life and fictional characters have been suggested as assisting in the
conception of the bibulous Toby, ranging
from Shakespeare's Sir Toby Belch to a
Yorkshireman, Henry Elwes, 'who drank
2,000 gallons from a brown jug and was
nicknamed Toby Fillpot'. This last feat,
it may be added, was not performed at a
single sitting but during a thirsty lifetime.

The Toby jug has a long ancestry which
can be traced back in this country to
medieval red clay jugs modelled with
grotesque human faces (*Chapter* 1, Fig.
1), and to 17th century stoneware Bellarmines (*Chapter* 5, Fig. 66). The 18th century
creamware counterparts take numerous
forms, but are most familiar as a seated
bluff-looking man with a brimming pint-pot
in his hand, and invariably wearing a tricorn hat, of which the crown is removable
(although frequently missing) to form an
inadequate drinking cup.

The forms in which Toby was made from
the 18th century onwards were numerous.
In distinguishing early from later it is
important to remember that the former used
transparent glazes, whereas after about
1790 opaque enamel colours were employed.
All types have been reproduced, and one
should be on one's guard with examples
that exhibit obvious crazing (a network of
brown cracks) and are heavy in weight.

Figures made by Ralph Wood include
some large-sized examples like the shepherd
and the shepherdess shown in Fig. 96;
Hudibras, adapted from William Hogarth's
engraved illustration to the poem by
Samuel Butler, showing an elderly man on
horseback drawing his sword from its
scabbard; and St. George and the Dragon,
normally with a mounted Saint lancing
the monster, but of which an example has
been recorded with a young lady riding
pillion behind him.

Other figures depict a gardener and his
companion, a Dutch boy and girl, actors
and actresses, soldiers, and a sailor and

his lass. The list is a long one, and covers the varied likes of English country inhabitants of the time, leaving the more exacting tastes of the town to be catered for by porcelain makers. It is no easier to state whether many of them were made by Wood or Whieldon or by anyone else, than to be certain of their original modeller. The originators of these rustic ornaments, known to the potters as 'Image Toys' (ornamental trifles, in modern language), are mostly unrecorded.

Much of the credit for them is accorded to Aaron Wood, in spite of the fact that his surviving work comprises block models for a dish at Burslem and a spittoon in the British Museum. His grandson wrote of Aaron: 'I have heard my father say, he was never heard to swear, chew tobacco, take snuff or whistle or sing in his life, and was considered the most lively, pleasant and merriest man in the country, and was known to everyone in the county'. Although these attributes do their owner great credit, they give no clue to his abilities as a figure-modeller. Nonetheless, in spite of the lack of positive evidence in support of the suggestion, Aaron's name has been mentioned frequently in connection with the statuette of an elderly man walking with the aid of two sticks, known as 'Old Age', and with several other models.

A well-known figure of a boy standing with crossed arms and with a bag, presumably containing soot, at his feet, named 'A Sweep', was adapted from a similarly-posed lad modelled by a Frenchman, Paul-Louis Cyfflé. The original was created for a factory established by the latter in 1766 at Lunéville, and which closed in 1780. A pair of Cyfflé's figures, 'The Stocking-Mender' and 'The Cobbler', the latter seated at his last and whistling to his caged bird, were copied at a later date and made in opaque-enamelled Staffordshire ware. How or why these particular pieces came to be selected for use in England is not known.

Fig. 102: Figure of the goddess Minerva glazed in blue-grey and green. Staffordshire, circa 1770. Height, 8½ inches. (City Museum and Art Gallery, Hanley.)

119

Attributed to one of the Ralph Woods because of their transparent glazing, are some jugs modelled with figures around a tree-trunk and named 'Fair Hebe' jugs because those words are inscribed on them (Figs. 99, 100). Examples bear the signature of J. Voyez and the date 1788, and some writers have suggested other Wood figures may have been the work of the same man.

John (or Jean) Voyez was of French origin, is said to have been trained as a jeweller, and when he came to London assisted in making a wax model of George III's State coach. In March 1768 Josiah Wedgwood wrote to his partner Thomas Bentley about him:

> I have hired a Modeler for three years, the best I am told in London, he served his time with a silversmith, has work'd several years at a China work, has been two or three years carving in wood and marble for Mr. Adam the famous Architect, is a perfect Master of the Antique stile in ornaments, Vases, &c., & works with equal facility in Clay, wax, wood, Metal or stone.

As a result, Voyez went to the Wedgwood factory and was paid six shillings a day for his services. However, his career there was a short one, for in the sping of 1769 he was sentenced at Stafford Assizes to three months' imprisonment and to be whipped. There appears to be no sure knowledge of what he did to deserve this punishment,

Above, Fig. 103: A squirrel, two hawks and an owl, glazed brown, green, and other colours. Staffordshire, circa 1765. Heights, 7¼ and 8 inches. (Phillips, Son and Neale.)

and in his correspondence with Bentley his employer only makes veiled references to the affair. He mentions Voyez only by the initial of his surname, explaining that '. . . all my feelings are up in Arms against even so much as naming him'.

When he left prison Voyez worked in Staffordshire and London making articles in imitation of Wedgwood's, and went so far as to forge the latter's name on them. By 1776 he had apparently ceased doing this, but there seems once again to be a gap in the record as it is uncertain how he was employed between that year and the date, 1788, on the 'Fair Hebe' jugs. The career of Voyez has excited great interest from time to time, perhaps more than it merits, and much has been surmised and printed about him.

Above left, *Fig. 104: Figure of a water buffalo with a man on its back, glazed in mottled brown, and blue. Staffordshire, circa 1750. Height, 6¾ inches. (City Museum and Art Gallery, Hanley.)*

Above right, *Fig. 105: Group of the Vicar and Moses (the clerk taking the service while the vicar dozes) glazed in blue-grey and brown. Staffordshire, circa 1770. Height, 9½ inches. (County Museum, Truro.)*

A series of figures of mythological gods and goddesses may point to Wood attempting to invade the more literate sections of the market, who demanded something other than purely rustic subjects (Fig. 102). Again, the modeller remains anonymous, but some of the pieces bear the trees rebus, which indicates their maker beyond doubt.

Probably the most popular at the time and now are the various models of animals and birds. Some were clearly copied from Chinese originals, others from those created by Johann Joachim Kändler at Meissen (Dresden), and others again were designed locally. In most instances, the coloured glazes do little or nothing to make the pieces attractive, and succeed only in obscuring whatever detail there may be. However, this criticism applies mainly to the earlier examples, for in time the workers grew more careful or more skilful and applied the various colours more or less where they were needed. Instead of just drenching the article in a thick covering, of which the glossy surface is perhaps the most admirable effect, they attempted to control the tints to accentuate the shape of the clay beneath.

8 Wedgwood:
Part 1

Born in 1730, Josiah Wedgwood was the thirteenth child of a potter who died when the boy was nine years of age. Josiah then went to work in the family business, the Churchyard Pottery, Burslem, where he was apprenticed in 1744 for five years to his eldest brother, who had inherited the pottery. Little is known of his early days beyond the facts that his schoolmaster, Thomas Blunt of Newcastle-under-Lyme, reported him to be 'a fair mathematician and master of a capital hand', and that during his apprenticeship he contracted smallpox.

In 1752 he entered into partnership with two potters at Stoke, but this venture did not endure. Two years later came a further partnership, one which was more productive and about which more is known, with the most prominent potter of the area: Thomas Whieldon. The joint venture was for five years, and towards the end Josiah Wedgwood recorded notes of his experiments and experiences. The first paragraphs give a somewhat pessimistic picture of what was being done at the time:

> White stoneware (*viz.* with saltglaze) was the principal article of our manufacture, and the prices were now reduced so low that the potters could not afford to bestow much expense upon it, or make it so good in any respect as the ware would otherwise admit of; and with

regard to elegance of form, that was an object very little attended to.

The next article in consequence to stoneware was an imitation of tortoiseshell, but as no improvement had been made in this branch for several years, the consumer had grown nearly tired of it; and though the price had been lowered from time to time in order to increase the sale, the expedient did not answer, and something new was wanted to give a little spirit to the business.

I had already made an imitation of agate, which was esteemed beautiful, and made a considerable improvement, but people were surfeited with wares of these various colours. These considerations induced me to try for some more solid improvement, as well in the

Fig. 106: Portrait of Josiah Wedgwood (1730-1795) painted in fired colours on a Wedgwood plaque by George Stubbs. Signed and dated 1780. 20 by 16 inches. (Josiah Wedgwood and Sons, Ltd., Barlaston, Staffordshire.)

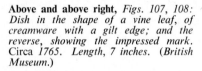

Above and above right, *Figs. 107, 108:*
Dish in the shape of a vine leaf, of
creamware with a gilt edge; and the
reverse, showing the impressed mark.
Circa *1765. Length, 7 inches. (British*
Museum.)

body as the glazes, the colours, and the forms of the articles of our manufacture. I saw the field was spacious, and the soil so good as to promise ample recompense to any one who should labour diligently in its cultivation.

Little is known for certain as to what Wedgwood and Whieldon made during the years they worked together, nor precisely what part was played by the former. From the evidence of his surviving memoranda it is certain that he made many trials to perfect coloured glazes, and it appears he made 'a new green earthenware, having the smoothness and brilliant appearance of glass'. Rich green and yellow glazes are found on some domestic wares, teapots, coffee-pots, etc., taking their form from cauliflowers and pineapples (Plate 18). These, along with some other well-finished pieces of comparable type are usually attributed to the partnership, or to very soon after it terminated.

In 1759 or 1760 Wedgwood leased from his cousins a pottery in Burslem, The Ivy House, so-called because the front was covered in a profusion of ivy, for which he paid a rental of £10 a year (Fig. 111). Again, there is little positive information about what he manufactured, nothing bore

marks of identification and each potter copied the successes of his rivals. Llewellynn Jewitt wrote in 1865, about a century after the event, that 'he turned his attention not to the making of the ordinary classes of wares which then formed the staple manufactures of the district'. Then he contradicted himself by adding: 'though, he still, to some degree, produced them, and to no small extent made the tortoiseshell and marble plates which had already gained much celebrity'.

Jewitt continued:

His principal products at this time were ornamental flower and other vases, with gilt or coloured foliage, mouldings, and handles; jardinières; white-ware medallions, and other goods of a similar kind. He also made much green-glazed earthenware, and designed and produced some tea-services, in which the different vessels were formed and coloured to represent various fruits and vegetables . . . and these novelties took so well that they soon had an abundant sale.

Not long after he had taken on the Ivy House, Wedgwood removed to larger premises, the Brick House Works, also in Burslem. By this time he had evolved not only better glazes and better clay mixtures, but he had begun to divide the labour among his workpeople. He ensured that as his staff increased in numbers and were beyond his immediate supervision, each man or women had a definite task and performed it well. In return, Wedgwood attended to their welfare and treated them with commendable fairness. As he rose to be in the forefront of the manufacturers of his time, he strove to attain the perfection of small-scale hand working, and at the same time keep his employees contented. One of his innovations was to place a bell above the building so that the men could be summoned to work, an improvement on the local use of a horn for the purpose, and his pottery was soon dubbed the Bell House.

Conditions in the industry at the time were made clear when in 1763, a petition to Parliament was presented by Burslem traders attempting to get the local roads improved. Part of the document read:

In Burslem and its neighbourhood are near 150 separate Potteries for making various kinds of stone and earthenware, which, together find constant employment and support for near 7,000 people. The ware of these Potteries is exported in vast quantities from London, Bristol, Liverpool, Hull and other seaports to our several colonies in America and the West Indies, as well as to every port in Europe. Great quantities of flint stones are used in making some of the ware which are brought by sea from different parts of the coast of Liverpool and Hull; and the clay for making the white ware is brought by water up the rivers Mersey and Weaver to Winsford in Cheshire; those from Hull up the Trent to Willington; and from Winsford and Willington the whole are brought by land carriage

Fig. 109: Salt-glazed stonweware 'blocks' used for making moulds for teapots (see Plate 18). Circa 1760-65. (Josiah Wedgwood and Sons, Ltd.)

to Burslem. The ware when made is conveyed to Liverpool and Hull in the same manner as the materials are brought from these places.

Josiah Wedgwood was in favour of the proposed new turnpike, and travelled to London to solicit support for it there. It was the first of many occasions on which he worked hard to further the interests of the locality, the industry in general and his own manufactory.

By 1763, too, the Bell Works was sufficiently important and productive to demand a London representative. Josiah's elder brother John lived there, and was apparently out of employment and seeking just such a task. He lived at the sign of the Artichoke, Cateaton Street, near Guildhall but now part of Gresham Street, in the City. To him were addressed all the questions depending for their answer on the understanding and experience of an agent in the capital.

It was in June 1765 that a letter from Josiah reached Cateaton Street, announcing no less than an order from Queen Charlotte, 'about which I want to ask a hundred questions, and have never a mouth but yours in town worth opening upon the subject'.

The order came from Miss Deborah alias Deb. Chetwynd, sempstress and Laundress to the Queen, to Mr. Smallwood of Newcastle [*under Lyme*], who brought it to me (I believe because

nobody else would undertake it) and is as follows.

A complete sett of tea things, with a gold ground and raised flowers upon it in green, in the same manner of the green flowers that are raised upon the *mehons*, so it is wrote but I suppose it should be melons. The articles are 12 cups for Tea and 12 Saucers, a slop basin, sugar dish with cover and stand, spoon-tray, Coffeepot, 12 Coffee cups, 6 pair of hand candlesticks and 6 mellons with leaves [*stands*], 6 green fruit baskets and Stands edged with gold.

A postscript to the letter opens with the sentence: 'Pray put on *the best suit of Cloaths you ever had in your life* and take the first opportunity of going to Court'. It then lists a number of queries arising from the order, which John is requested to get settled.

The Queen's tea service was finished by September 1765, and it is thought that Josiah took it himself to London and delivered it. Two years later his bill-heads bore the legend 'Potter to Her Majesty', and he was referring to his product as 'creamcolour, alias Queensware'. While the earliest creamware made by Wedgwood tended to vary between deep cream and yellow in colour, the perfected product was a pale cream. It was not only neatly potted and made into well-designed shapes, but took a bright and smooth glaze that did not hide a pattern moulded on it. In

Plate 19 *Plate from the service made for Catherine II, Empress of Russia. 1774. Diameter, 9 inches. (The Trustees of the Wedgwood Museum, Barlaston, Stoke-on-Trent.)*

addition, it was light in weight, and it could be sold at a price to compete with anything else then on the market.

The ware quickly appealed to the public in this country and, duly, overseas. In this it was aided by its maker, whose personality was such that he made just as pleasing and memorable an impression on others as did his products. By 1765 Josiah was in correspondence with Sir William Meredith, M.P. for Liverpool, who sent him patterns to copy, as well as clients to purchase the finished articles. Doubtless, too, the latter encouraged the go-ahead Wedgwood, who was by then spokesman for the district, as a trader using Liverpool and adding to

the prosperity of his constituents.

Wedgwood realised that to increase the sales of his ware it was important to make it "fashionable" in the accepted manner. Having obtained Royal patronage, this did not prove difficult. In July 1765 he mentioned to John (in London) that:

> Dr. Swan dined with Lord Gower this week; after dinner your Brother Josiah's Pottworks were the subject of conversation for some time, the Cream colour Table services in particular. I believe it was his Lordship said that nothing of the sort could exceed them for a fine glaze &c.

While a few days later he wrote that he had just received a visit from the Duke of Marlborough, Lord Gower and Lord Spencer, adding:

> The gentlemen above mentioned . . . . wonder I have not a Warehouse in

Below, *Fig. 111: The Ivy House, Burslem, the pottery which Wedgwood leased in 1759 or 1760 at a rental of £10 a year. An old woodcut.*

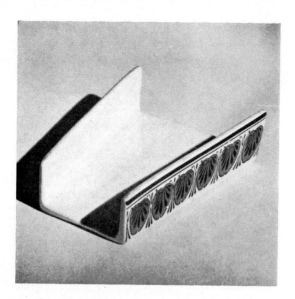

Above, *Fig. 112: 'Asparagus shell', for serving asparagus at the dining-table, painted with an anthemion pattern in red and black. Marked.* Circa 1780. *Length, 3⅝ inches. (Buten Museum of Wedgwood, Merion, Pa.)* **Below,** *Fig. 113: Plate painted in colours with a crest in the border and a central coat of arms; the latter that of Sir William Honeywood, Bt., and Frances, daughter of the second Viscount Courtenay, who were married in 1778. Marked. 1778. Diameter, 9½ inches. (Formerly in the collection of the late G. Duff-Dunbar, Esq.)*

London where patterns of all sorts I make may be seen . . . .

Later in the same year, Wedgwood was again prominent in local affairs. The Earl of Bridgewater was extending his system of canals by proposing to link the rivers Trent and Mersey, and public interest in the project was stimulated by petitions, pamphlets and subscriptions. The group of men organising this vital aspect of the scheme appointed Wedgwood as their treasurer, and he added this duty to the daily conduct of his factory.

In 1768, when in London, Wedgwood acted on the advice of his influential patrons; that he should open a showroom in the capital. For £105 a year he leased a house at the corner of Newport Street and St. Martin's Lane, 'where carriages may come to it either from Westminster or the City without being incommoded . . . . .'. During the visit he had an interview with the British Ambassador to Russia, Lord Cathcart, and also arranged to employ John Voyez (see *Chapter* 7 page 120).

Wedgwood had been acquainted with Lord Cathcart for some time and not only supplied him with a crested dinner and dessert service for use at the Embassy, but prevailed upon him to act as unofficial agent. As he wrote at the time: 'I have spent several hours with Ld. Cathcart, our Ambassador to Russia, & we are to do great things for each other'. Not long after, orders began to reach Wedgwood, one of which was from the Empress, Catherine the Great.

It was in 1773 that Catherine, referred to by Josiah as 'my Great Patroness of the North' and by Horace Walpole as 'the devil of St. Petersburg', ordered a very large service for La Grenouillière, at Tsarskoe Selo, outside the capital. It was

an important order from an important client, and Wedgwood gave the matter typically careful consideration. He wrote: 'I think we should have some assurance that no revolution in the North should affect the validity of the Consul's order to us . . . One would on the other hand avoid giving offence by over-much caution'.

Fig. 115: Supper-set of four open dishes and a covered central dish, painted with borders in blue and brown. Marked. Circa 1790. (Buten Museum of Wedgwood.)

The service was to be of creamware, each piece painted with a named view of a building or scene in England and the border containing the crest of a frog within a shield (*grenouille*—frog; Plate 19). There has been much discussion about the number of pieces actually supplied, the number of views painted on them, and other points relating to the order. The figures given by Wedgwood in 1774 were 952 pieces bearing 1,244 scenes, but both are debatable because the service was not fully completed when they were announced. The last items were finished in about August 1774, and soon afterwards the whole was packed and sent to Russia.

Prior to this, however, much of the service was exhibited in London. In 1769 Wedgwood had taken premises off the King's Road, Chelsea, whence plain ware was sent from Staffordshire to be decorated by

between twenty and thirty men and women painters. Together with a showroom in the West End, supervision proved difficult, and he was anxious to unite both premises under one roof. After rejecting the idea of leasing a portion of the Adam brothers' newly-built Adelphi, in the Strand, and toying with the proposition of taking the notorious Mrs. Cornelys's Society masquerade-rooms in Soho Square, he settled finally on No. 13 Greek Street. Early in June 1774 the new premises held an exhibition of the service, of which a visitor recorded: '. . . there are three rooms below and two above filled with it, laid out on tables, everything that can be wanted to serve a dinner . . .'

Much speculation has centred on the cost of the Catherine service, and what profit, if any, Wedgwood eventually made on it. No records have been preserved,

and guesses have ranged that the Empress paid a sum ranging from £2,000 to £3,500 for it, and that the manufacturer's cost was in the region of £2,500. A very large amount of work was involved, the views had to be obtained (a camera obscura was used to expedite the process), and each had to be adapted to suit the article on which it was painted. Extra hands were hired to do much of the work, and there must have been considerable wastage in preparing

Fig. 116: Jelly mould and cover; in use, the cover was filled with jelly and the wedge-shaped section lowered into it. When set, the cover was removed and the contents placed on the table with the painted decoration showing through the jelly. Marked. Circa 1790. Height of inner section, 5 inches. (Buten Museum of Wedgwood.)

trial pieces and rejecting unsatisfactory finished ones. Whatever the financial profit may have been, the publicity gained went a long way towards giving recompense for the labour involved.

The service was seen at Tsarskoe Selo in 1779 by the British Ambassador, Sir James Harris, but after that it seems to have vanished for 130 years. In 1909, Dr. G. C. Williamson, an expert on ceramics and other objects of art, was responsible for rediscovering it, and the Czar, Nicholas II, allowed 34 pieces of it to be exhibited in London. After that there was again an interval during which the whereabouts of the service was unknown, and in 1930 it was reported to have been purchased by a film star and to be in Hollywood. In fact, it had never left the country, and it has been on view for the past decade to visitors to the Chapel of the Old Winter Palace, Leningrad.

*　　*　　*

THE creamware improved and manufactured by Josiah Wedgwood from about 1759 was greatly enhanced after 1775. In that year he led the opposition of the Staffordshire potters to a renewal of the patent granted earlier to William Cookworthy of Plymouth. This had given the latter the monopoly of using Cornish china-clay and -stone, and the spirited arguments put forward by Wedgwood resulted in

Fig. 117: Perforated skimmer for separating cream from milk, painted with a crest and HALDON DAIRY. Originally in the dairy at Haldon House, near Exeter; seat of the Palk family, this large mansion was demolished in 1926. Marked. Circa 1790. Width, 7¾ inches. (Buten Museum of Wedgwood.)

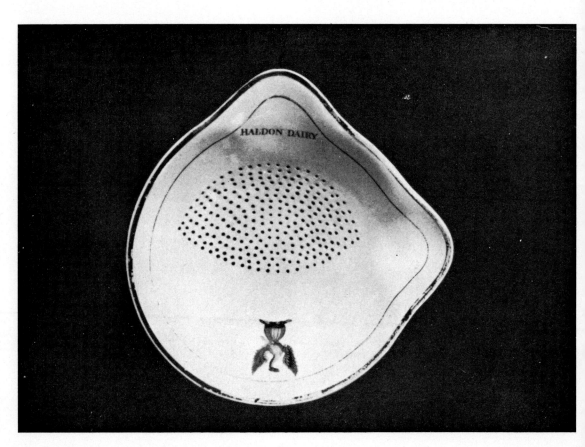

Cookworthy's successor, Richard Champion, retaining the monopoly only with regard to manufacturing porcelain. The clay and stone were thus freed for use in pottery, and creamware immediately benefited. It gave it a stronger body with greater resonance, and a strength approaching that of porcelain.

Pandering to public taste ('you know what Lady Dartmouth told us, that she and her friends were tired of creamcolor') Wedgwood devised in 1779 a near-white ware. He made it by slightly changing the clay and flint mixture of the cream-colour body, and adding a little cobalt to neutralise the normal yellow tint. The result, named Pearlware, set a fashion that was soon copied by other makers.

While, as has been mentioned, creamware was much employed by Wedgwood for useful domestic wares, he did occasionally use it for ornamental pieces. The vases and covers in Fig. 119 are of the rich creamy tone associated with his early work, and the engine-turned ornament is distinctive enough to be attributable to his pottery. It is known that Josiah owned a copy of a book on turning, Plumier's *L'art de tourner*, and that he had devoted time to discovering how to use the machine on semi-hard clay articles. In 1765 he proposed sending the Queen 'two setts of Vases, Creamcolour, engine-turned . . . ', which were probably similar in appearance to the vases illustrated. An original lathe for engine-turning, dating to the time of

Fig. 118: Fish slice with a perforated blade and a shaped handle. Marked. Circa 1800. Length, 11¾ inches. (Buten Museum of Wedgwood.)

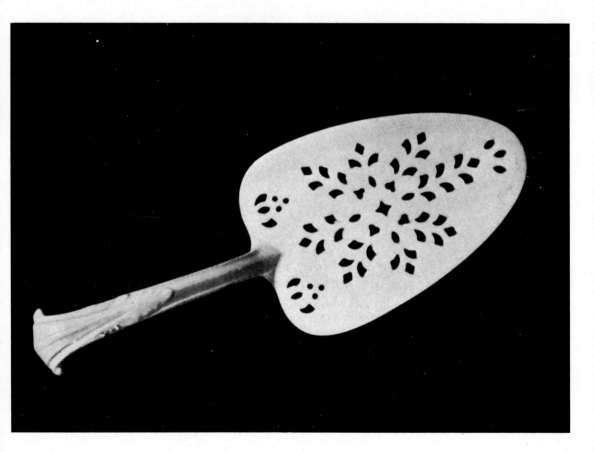

Josiah, is at the present Wedgwood manufactory, at Barlaston, and still capable of
turning out good work.

The difficulty of deciding whether some
of the early wares came from Wedgwood's
pottery or from elsewhere is accentuated
because they are unmarked. A mark was
not used consistently until sometime about
1770-71, and took the form of the impressed
name: Wedgwood or WEDGWOOD. It was
stamped by hand with a metal punch,
sometimes hurriedly and with a deeper
imprint in one portion than in another
(Fig.108). It is possible to overlook the mark
altogether in instances where it has been
impressed lightly and glaze has filled the
shallow lettering.

Below, *Fig. 119: Set of three vases and
covers, creamware decorated with turning
and gilding. Circa 1765. Heights, 13
and 11 inches. (Saltram, Devon: The
National Trust.)*

Much of the creamware was sold undecorated, but much was painted in colours, either at the factory or, from 1769, at Chelsea. From at least 1761 Wedgwood was sending increasing quantities weekly to Liverpool, where it was ornamented with transfer-printed designs by Sadler and Green (see *Signature* 16). Apart from the service made for Catherine II, which may be considered unrepresentative, painted ornament was usually sparse and with neo-classical motives predominating.

Josiah Wedgwood's early pattern-books, which have been preserved, show a restrained use of honeysuckle flowers and vine and other leaves in the form of running borders, leaving untouched the major portions of the articles on which they were used. Both the potter and his clients realised that the good shapes and careful finish of the chaste creamware required a minimum of embellishment. The taste with which the majority was applied has ensured the admiration of later generations.

Fig. 120: Plate with a pierced and moulded rim, the centre printed in lilac at Liverpool with classical ruins and figures. Marked. Circa 1770. Diameter, 9 inches. (British Museum.)

9 Wedgwood: Part 2

JOSIAH Wedgwood lived in times when the use of pottery had been largely confined to the poorer sections of the populace, and porcelain, either home-produced or imported, was the favoured choice of all who could afford it. He improved the existing earthenware, stimulated and satisfied demand for it and made it acceptable to all classes. His outstanding capacities for organisation and publicity were employed to the full, and his product was deservedly acclaimed throughout Europe and farther afield.

Wedgwood's early success was founded on the attractive and practical table-wares made from his cream-coloured pottery. Once he had firmly established this domestic side of his business he began to turn his attention to making vases and purely ornamental items. At first he made use of the creamware, relying on the lathe for engine-turning, together with modest gilding, for embellishment as on the vases shown in Fig. 119. It may be remarked that these early essays are so unlike in appearance the vases on which his fame rests that they are scarcely recognisable as his work.

Early in the second half of the 18th century there came a big change in the design of buildings and their contents. In 1758 James Stuart (nick-named 'Athenian' Stuart as a result of a visit to the Greek city) was building a small classical-style ornamental temple in Worcestershire, and at about the same date Robert Adam,

Fig. 121: Basaltes bust of Francis Bacon (1561-1626), marked Wedgwood and Bentley. *Circa 1780. Height, 18 inches. (Sotheby's.)*

newly-returned from Rome, was establishing himself in London. These two men were the apostles of the neo-classical style that rapidly replaced the rococo and *chinoiserie* of the mid-century.

A steady flow of illustrated books on classical antiquities culminated in the publication in 1766-67 of some imposing folios describing the renowned collection of ancient vases belonging to Sir William Hamilton. The latter was British representative at the Court of Naples from 1764 to 1800, and during all this time was able to take advantage of many of the excavations taking place. He formed a large collection of vases for himself, sold what he could not afford to keep (or did not want) and was a respected fount of knowledge on the subject. Sir William's sister was married to Lord Cathcart, with whom

Wedgwood was on good terms, and he passed on to the potter the illustrations to Sir William's book prior to its publication.

The interest of the scholarly world, as well as that of the less well-informed, was additionally focused on the subject by the excavations which had taken place at Herculaneum, near Pompeii, since about 1740. The results were largely unknown until, in the early 1760's a German, the Abbé Winckelmann, gave the world accurate information about the treasures for the first time.

The vases which formed the Hamilton and other collections were excavated from tombs sited mainly in northern Italy; a part of the country once inhabited by the Etruscans and known as Etruria. In the third century B.C. it was merged with the State of Rome, and its separate existence

Fig. 122: Agateware vase, marked Wedgwood and Bentley *and dating from* circa *1770. Height, 11¼ inches. (Nottingham Castle Museum and Art Gallery.)*

Fig. 123: Basaltes lamp and cover, the figures round the pedestal copied from those on the base of a silver crucifix given to St. Peter's, Rome in 1582 and possibly after Michelangelo. Circa 1770. Height, 14¼ inches. (Nottingham Castle Museum and Art Gallery.)

ended. Not unnaturally, it was thought in the 18th century that the vases were of local manufacture, and that the Etruscans had therefore been the foremost potters of classical times. Subsequently it has been discovered, and accepted, that although they were indeed potters, the finer examples found in the country had been imported from Greece and their own productions comprised inferior copies of these foreign wares.

The Greek vases discovered in Etruria were made from red clay coated with a black glaze, and designs were drawn on them using the latter as a medium. Three types were made: those with designs appearing red on a black ground; with designs in black on a red ground; and with designs in various colours.

By adding iron and manganese to the clay, Staffordshire potters since about 1740 had been making a ware known as 'Black Egyptian'. In 1768 Wedgwood seized on this as a suitable basis for making copies of the so-called Etruscan vases. He altered the traditional composition of the mixture so that it resulted in a dense, hard and evenly-toned deep black ware. In due

course, because of its resemblance to the natural stone of the name, he called it 'Basaltes'.

In order to imitate as closely as possible the dull surface appearance of the multicoloured vases, Wedgwood developed suitable matt enamels. For the first and only time in his career he took out a patent, which was granted to him on 16th November 1769. It was for 'The Purpose of Ornamenting Earthen and Porcelain Ware with an Encaustic Gold Bronze, together with a peculiar species of Encaustic Painting in Various Colours in Imitation of the Antient Etruscan and Roman Earthenware' (see Plate 20).

*   *   *

WHILE on a visit to Liverpool in 1762 Josiah Wedgwood injured his knee, which had been weakened by his earlier attack of smallpox. He was forced to postpone his return to Burslem and, on doctor's advice, remain in bed. During the course of the stay, his doctor introduced him to a local merchant, Thomas Bentley, thinking the two men might have much in common and the bed-ridden one would be

cheered. As it turned out, the two men quickly formed a lasting friendship. At first social, the acquaintance shortly became a commercial one, and in 1767 Bentley agreed to become Wedgwood's partner in the manufacture of ornamental wares.

There seems to be little doubt that it was Thomas Bentley's influence that encouraged Wedgwood to espouse the neo-classical style, and once the course had been taken it was pursued with characteristic vigour. By the date of Bentley's death, in 1780 at the age of fifty, its success was well-assured, and it remained only to continue its exploitation.

In 1766, Wedgwood purchased an estate of 350 acres lying between Burslem, Hanley and Newcastle-under-Lyme, and on it he proceeded to erect a pottery as well as a mansion for himself, his wife and his family. The new manufactory was to be solely for vases and other decorative pieces, while the 'useful' domestic articles of creamware, with which Bentley had no concern, would continue to be made at the Bell House, Burslem, until it was vacated in 1772.

The pottery was opened on 13th June 1769 and named Etruria, mistakenly in honour of the country whose products were thought to be so admirable. The event was commemorated by the making of six basaltes vases, turned by Wedgwood on a wheel worked by Bentley, painted with figures copied from those on one of Sir William Hamilton's vases of the fifth century B.C. (Plate 20).

Bentley gave up his connections in Liverpool, and while it was first thought that he also should have a house on the Etruria estate, it was decided that he would be employed more profitably in supervising the London end of the business. At first he lived on the premises in Newport Street, but soon a move was made to Chelsea.

At the former establishment there was probably a small-scale decorating department, but at Chelsea painting was done by a score or more of men and women. By early in September sales of the black vases were plentiful, and Wedgwood wrote to London:

> You want plain Etruscan Vases for painting immediately. I am glad you are beginning to paint and will supply you with some as soon as possible. . . . On receipt therefore of your letter on Saturday I sent Moreton immediately to the Wheel for Black Vases though it was near six, and made him stay and throw a quantity. We have dryed them this good Sunday ready for the Lathe tomorrow morning and I hope to have some dozens fired this week.

Three days later he had to amend his hopeful estimate:

> I hope to send you some plain ones [*vases*] Per Haywood as I mentioned in my last, a few to be doing with for they are much more tedious making than I

Fig. 128: Blue and white jasperware portrait plaque of Sir Isaac Newton (1642-1727), marked Wedgewood and Bentley. *Circa 1778. Height, 11¹³⁄₁₆ inches; depth from tip of nose to background, 2 inches. (British Museum).*

Plate 20 *Basaltes vase decorated in encaustic enamel, inscribed:* June XIII, M.DCC.LXIX. One of the first Day's Productions at Etruria in Staffordshire by Wedgwood and Bentley. Artes Etruriae Renascuntur [*The arts of Etruria are reborn*] *Height, 10 inches.* (*The Trustees of the Wedgwood Museum.*)

imagined, instead of four or five doz. as I expected. I shall not have two doz. I fear with our working night and day . . .

As well as Etruscan or Basaltes vases, Wedgwood was also making them in various types of agate-ware. His early years with Whieldon stood him in good stead over this, but the fine pieces he was now producing were very different from the simple tea-wares of twelve or so years earlier (Fig. 122). Again, classical shapes were employed, and Bentley was informed in September 1769:

> I would propose then for this winters Sale of Vases *four species* only Viz. *Blue Pebble, Variegated Pebble, Black Etruscan,* and *Etruscan Encaustic*— These with the variations of sizes, forms and Ornaments, Gilding, veining, Bass reliefs, &c. &c, will produce business enough for all the hands we

can possibly get together, and, I think, variety enough for all our *reasonable* customers.

In fact, the agate ware was made in several varieties, including the following:

Serpentine	..	Grey and green
Agate ..	..	Brown and yellow, sometimes with grey and white
Verde antico	..	Dark green, grey and black
Green jasper	..	Green and grey
Grey granite	..	White and black
Red porphyry	..	White on red.

Wedgwood also produced two others which he termed 'Holy Door' and 'Jaune Antique'. It has been thought that the first-named is a mixture of mauve and puce with gold and white, and the second a rich yellow with black.

JOSIAH Wedgwood's next essay was again an attempt to reproduce works of classical times. On this occasion it was carved gems and cameos; the originals being semi-precious and other stones minutely and laboriously chiselled with mythological scenes and portraits. They were cut either

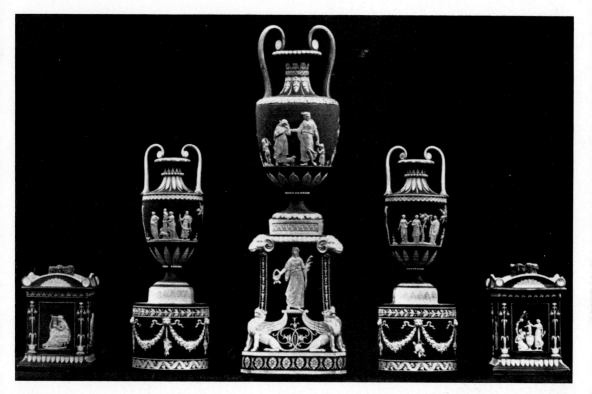

Left, *Fig. 130: Vase and cover of white, blue and olive-green jasperware, on the side a portrait medallion of George, Prince of Wales, later George IV, beneath his coronet, plumes, and motto. Circa 1785. Height, 14¼ inches. (Nottingham Castle Museum and Art Gallery.)*
Above, *Fig. 131: Sea-green and white jasperware vases and pedestals and a pair of flower pots. Circa 1785. Height of central vase and pedestal, 21¾ inches. Formerly in the Falcke collection.*

with the subject raised above the surface (in *basso relievo*) or sunken and in reverse for use as a seal (in *intaglio*). All were eagerly collected by wealthy connoisseurs, and as each was unique there was considerable competition for the best specimens.

For their making, Josiah devised white and coloured compositions that would stand up to the heat of the kiln without becoming mis-shapen, were extremely hard, and did not 'bleed' their colour when in contact. In 1774, in the second edition of the catalogue of his productions, he announced 'A fine white terra-cotta of great beauty and delicacy, proper for cameos, portraits and bas-reliefs'. Within a year this had been developed into a pure white material with all the desired qualities, together with 'a beautiful Sea Green, and several other colours, for grounds to Cameos, Intaglios, etc.'. It was named 'Jasper', and shortly was available in tints of light and dark blue, pink-lilac, brownish-green, sage-green, yellow and black.

While the intaglios were comparatively simple to make, the essential requirement being that they remained free of distortion after firing, the bas reliefs were more difficult. In some instances the relief and the base were fired separately, the latter ground smooth, and the two fixed together. Soon, however, recourse was had to the local method known as 'sprigging', and the article went into the kiln already assembled (see page 112).

At first the ground of the cameos was made entirely from coloured jasperware, but in April 1777 Wedgwood sent some portraits to Bentley, noting:

Left, *Fig. 132: The bedroom of Catherine II, Empress of Russia, at Tsarskoye Selo (near Leningrad) now named Pushkin. Designed by Charles Cameron,* circa *1780. A photograph taken in about 1935, reproduced by courtesy of Miss Alison Kelly.* **Above,** *Fig. 133:* *White and coloured jasperware teawares made for displaying in a cabinet rather than for daily use. Marked* Wedgwood. *Late 18th century. Formerly in the Sanderson collection.*

Although initially making cameos of comparatively small size Wedgwood was soon using his new material for making large ones; referred to in the letter above as 'tablets'. They could be used for insertion in chimney-pieces and walls, as decoration in place of modelled plaster or carved wood. This was but a short step to making vases and other ornaments of the same ware (Figs. 126 to 132).

Probably the 18th century mansion which contained the largest number of Wedgwood plaques in its decoration was the palace of Catherine the Great, Empress of Russia, at Tsarskoye Selo. The building was destroyed in the seige of Leningrad and the place has been re-named Pushkin, but photographic and documentary records of it remain (Fig. 132). Catherine's bedroom was probably ornamented with between fifty and sixty cameos of various sizes, and other apartments were similarly embellished to the designs of the Scottish-born architect, Charles Cameron.

From 1769 Wedgwood had employed a clever modeller, William Hackwood, who eventually took charge of the department. In 1775 Josiah mentioned in a letter to Bentley that he was glad 'Flaxman is so valuable as artist'. Within a few months this young man (he was aged twenty at the time) was modelling vases and bas reliefs, which he continued to do for many years. In 1782 another modeller, Henry Webber, was given employment, and five years later both he and John Flaxman, the latter financed wholly or partly by Wedgwood, went to Rome. There, with the assistance of a number of local artists, they copied and adapted classical works duly to be translated into jasperware.

In the box are two heads with exquisite blue grounds. I wish I may be able to make you some tablets in this way. They are coloured with the cobalt at 36/s.p. lb., which being too dear to mix with clay of the whole grounds we have washed them over, & I think them by far the finest ground we have ever made.

This, and other advances were made during the ensuing years, but shortly after the above was penned, Wedgwood had achieved sufficient success to write: 'I have tried my new mixing of Jasper, & find it very good . . . I am now *absolute* in this precious article . . . '.

The colour-coated ground, which was not only less expensive to make and proved easier to manage in the kiln, had an additional attraction. By grinding the edges of plaques made from it, the white interior was revealed and forms a neat frame. 'Jasper dip', as it was named, was in general use at Etruria from shortly after 1777, but solid jasper was re-introduced at a later date.

THE crowning achievement in jasperware was the long-famed copying of the Portland Vase; a vase of blue glass overlaid with white and cut with a mythological scene. The original was made in Italy in the late first century B.C. or early first century A.D., and had been in the possession of the Barberini family, in their Palace in Rome, since at least 1642. In 1780 it was sold, and three years later was in the ownership of Sir William Hamilton who brought it to England. He, in turn, sold it to the Duchess of Portland ('a simple woman, but perfectly sober, and intoxicated only by *empty* vases' said Horace Walpole), who enjoyed her purchase for about eighteen months before she died.

It was auctioned with the remainder of her collection, bought by her son, and on 10th June 1786 was loaned by him to Wedgwood so that he might copy it. In due course, after continual experiment lasting almost four years, success was achieved and about twenty copies have survived of the thirty or so assumed to have been made (Plate 21).

The first issue of the Vases, unlike other jasperware pieces made at the same period, was unmarked, except sometimes for one or more pencilled numerals just inside the mouth. These earliest Wedgwood copies are distinguished by the high finish of the white reliefs and by the colour of the specially-compounded jasperware ground, which varies between blue-black and a slaty-blue. Some less carefully-made examples were produced at about the same time at Etruria, but on the normal blue-coloured ground, and were sold at a lower price than the thirty-two guineas (£33.60) charged for the finer ones.

Mention may be made of a variant edition of the vases made by Wedgwood's successors from 1839 when, in conformity with the taste of the day, the male figures were discreetly draped. Finally, a short paragraph written in 1865 by the ceramic historian, Llewellynn Jewitt, will not be out of place:

> It may be useful to note, that the original moulds are still in existence, and that 'Portland Vases' from them are still produced by the Messrs. Wedgwood,

both with a black and with a deep blue ground, and are much and deservedly admired.

Once more, Josiah's flair for publicity was given full reign. In June 1790, he obtained from Sir Joshua Reynolds a signed certificate declaring that his vase was 'a correct and faithful imitation, both in regard to the general effect, and the most minute detail of the parts', and exhibited it to the public at Greek Street. Immediately afterwards, Wedgwood's son, also named Josiah, set off on a Continental sales tour, taking the vase with him to help create interest in his other goods.

*　　　*　　　*

IN the space available it is only possible to give a very brief outline of the life and achievements of Wedgwood. On his death in 1795, at the age of 65, a memorial to him was erected in St. Peter's Church, Stoke-on-Trent. Beneath a three-quarter head of the potter stand two of his most famous productions, basaltes and Portland vases, and a lengthy inscription. Of the latter, the most memorable line refers to the fact that he 'converted a rude and inconsiderable manufacture into an elegant art and an important part of national Commerce'.

His instinct as a potter enabled him to improve existing wares of red and white clay until they merited Royal and public approval, and his knowledge of earlier stoneware led eventually to the making of jasper. To the production of them both he added an unerring instinct for salesmanship that would do credit to a twentieth century tycoon, and at the same time he treated his workpeople with a consideration in advance of most employers of the period. He was content only with the highest attainable standards of workmanship, commissioned the best artists available, and led the market by continually producing better

Left, *Fig. 134: Black and white jasper-ware plaque depicting a chained negro slave, inscribed around the border 'Am I not a man and a brother?' Designed by William Hackwood in or about 1787 for the Society for the Suppression of the Slave Trade, of which Josiah Wedgwood was a member of the committee. Circa 1800. Height, 1¼ inches.* **Above,** *Fig. 135: The style of impressed mark found on vases and busts—see below.*

patterns, better types of ware and better ways of marketing them.

It has been argued, with some justice, that Wedgwood's success was the end of true ceramic artistry in England; that he was responsible for the death of native genius in pottery, and by industrialising the craft he took away forever its artistic content. In return for this he can be said to have given the county of his birth a world lead that has been maintained for two centuries.

Some Wedgwood Dates
Earthenwares

Creamware	..	..	from 1759
Pearlware	..	..	from 1780

'Dry Bodies'

Basaltes	..	..	from 1767
Jasper ..	..	..	from 1774
Jasper Dip	..	..	from 1777
'Rosso Antico' (red)	..	from 1776

Cane-colour	..	.. from 1786

These dates are only approximate, and in some instances the wares did not reach the market in quantity until a year or more later.

Wedgwood Marks

Domestic wares in cream-coloured pottery, termed by Wedgwood 'useful', were made at the Bell House, Burslem until 1772 and then at Etruria. They bore the impressed mark WEDGWOOD, although sometimes the initial only was in capitals.

Ornamental wares, in basaltes, jasper and other bodies, made at Etruria from 1769 by Wedgwood and Bentley in partnership, bore both of their names, until Bentley's death in 1780. The mark was impressed as Wedgwood & Bentley or WEDGWOOD & BENTLEY, or on vases and busts with the names in a relief between circles as Fig. 135.

10 Wedgwood's Contemporaries

IN Staffordshire and elsewhere secrecy has for long been synonymous with ceramics. In the late 17th century the Elers brothers had a reputation for being secretive over the processes they employed for making stoneware, which was new to the district. It was alleged that they had some type of speaking-tube between the house occupied by John Philip Elers at Bradwell Wood, and the pottery about a mile away. In about 1900 some alterations on the site of the latter, which had by then been transformed into a public-house, resulted in the excavation of some pottery pipes with flanged ends and a circular funnel-shaped object that could have been used as a mouthpiece or earpiece. Simeon Shaw repeated or invented in 1829 that the tubes had been used by Elers to give warning of approaching spies.

According to Shaw, Thomas Astbury went so far as to feign idiocy when employed by Elers, and duly set himself up in business on his own behalf to make use of what he had been able to learn. Again, it was Shaw who recorded that Thomas Whieldon was careful 'to prevent his productions being imitated in quality or shape, [and] he always buried the broken articles'. Why his competitors could not just as well, or better, copy the perfect pieces is not explained, but perhaps Shaw was only relaying some garbled legend that had reached him.

From the outset of his career, Josiah Wedgwood was fully aware of the possibility of prying eyes ranging in his direction. His early note-book, compiled when he was in partnership with Whieldon between 1749 and 1754, shows that he was on the alert. In an introductory paragraph he wrote:

In the following experiments I have expressed the materials by numbers, which in this instance are a species of

Fig. 136: **The Potteries.**

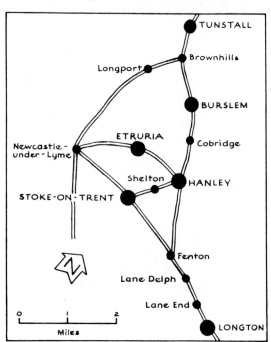

Fig. 137: Black stoneware vase, marked I. NEALE HANLY in a ring, with a replacement turned wood cover. Circa 1780. Height of vase, 6¾ inches.
(Sotheby's.)

shorthand, and saved much writing. They have also the advantage of not being intelligible, without the key, to any person who might happen to take up the book, which is often, in the course of making the experiments, unavoidably exposed to such an accident.

Wedgwood's fears were well-founded, and for most of his working life he was dogged by the 18th century equivalent of modern Industrial Espionage. In 1769, when he was planning what should be sent to Bentley in London, he wrote to his partner:

> The Encaustic will be imitated as soon as seen . . . there is nothing relating to business I so much wish for as being released from these degrading slavish chains, these mean, selfish fears of other people copying my works . . .

A few years later, when he was working to produce what was eventually named jasperware, Wedgwood was no less careful. As he is said to have made some ten thousand experimental samples before achieving success, it is perhaps remarkable that he remained for so long untroubled.

In the first biography of Wedgwood, written by Eliza Meteyard and published in 1865, there is a footnote which confirms the trouble taken by the potter to protect his formulas.

> At Etruria Hall, the places are still to be seen in which Wedgwood stored the cawk and other materials, and made his secret mixtures. They are a range of cellars shut off from the rest by thick partition walls, and heavy doors. Wedgwood's means of access was a trapdoor, and a flight of narrow brick steps leading from a room which was probably his study. . . The trap-door steps ended in a wide passage, and from this opened a door to the outer air, as also the cellar in which the mixtures were made, the bins or troughs still remaining. The outpost of this fortress is equally well guarded. It is approached from the rear of the Hall by a double wall screen, forming a sort of winding passage. At the end of this are wide steps, and the door before mentioned. Thus guarded and

masked, barrels and boxes could be brought in without the cognizance of anyone, except the immediate agents in the secret.

The foregoing remarks apply to Wedgwood's basaltes and jasperware, but the creamware caused him rather less concern. This is probably because it had a straightforward 'useful' purpose, was so much less novel, and certainly earned him fewer laurels in academic and aristocratic circles. Also, although in many ways he improved it, notably in shaping, decoration and marketing, it was largely developed by the time he established his first works, and was already being made by many other Staffordshire makers.

Nonetheless, in the early 1770's Josiah was still seeking to whiten his creamware and approximate it more closely to porcelain. He found that the addition of Cornish china-stone to the glaze would be a considerable help in achieving this, but the material was only allowed to be used in making porcelain. The patent granted to William Cookworthy of Plymouth in 1768 had established this, but when the patent still had several more years to run, an attempt was made to renew it. Wedgwood saw his chance, and rallying the potters of his county he opposed the renewal as being against the public interest. As a result, a bill was passed in Parliament in 1775 allowing the continuation of the patent, but permitting the Staffordshire potters to use both china-stone and china-clay for the making of pottery.

From then onwards, creamware was made in increasing quantity at a number of factories, some of which also manufactured all or most of the types of ware Wedgwood had pioneered. The following are the principal potteries active during the years 1770 to 1810. Not all of them engaged in deliberately pirating Josiah's original work, but they had it in common that they owed their prosperity to his energetic leadership of the industry.

Fig. 138: Jug with moulded and painted decoration; on the reverse the head of Captain Berry, who served under Nelson. Perhaps Staffordshire; circa 1800. Height, 6 inches. (County Museum, Truro.)

Hanley: Palmer and Neale.

Humphrey Palmer of the Church Works, Hanley, not only rivalled but blatantly copied Wedgwood's productions from about 1760. In 1766 the latter wrote to Bentley: 'I have only one objection to sending you a sortment of vases, which is that they would very probably some of them travel back again to Staffordshire'. Palmer's London agent, James Neale, as well as at least one other representative of a Staffordshire maker, constantly bought the very latest of Wedgwood's productions as they reached London. As quickly as they had been sent down to the London showroom, they returned northwards to be copied.

Two years later Josiah mentioned the matter again:

> You must try if you can recollect any particular Persons repeatedly buying a few pairs, or single articles of your new patterns as they arrive; very probably it may be some sham Gentn. or Lady equip'd for the purpose, with their footman or maid to carry them home to prevent a discovery.

Fig. 139: White ware (in imitation of Wedgwood's Pearlware) drug jar inscribed in blue S: DE. ALTHAEA within a rococo frame. Impressed mark TURNER. Circa 1790. Height, 7 inches. (E. N. Stretton, Esq.)

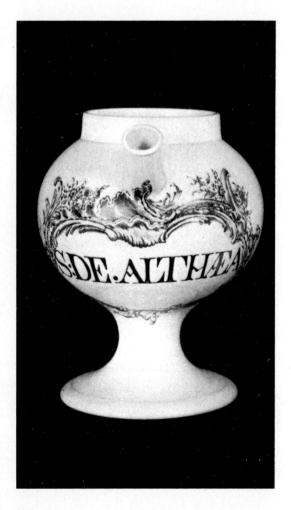

Within months, having been unable to prevent the abuse, he noted:

> I saw one of P's black vases yesterday. The body is very good, the shape & composition very well . . . upon the whole it is better than I expected.

Finally, in October 1770 it had been found that painted black-stoneware vases, similar to Wedgwood's, were being put on the market by Palmer and Neale. An injunction against their sale was obtained, and an action for infringement of Wedgwood's patent for encaustic painting was proposed. In the end, the matter was settled out of court, and Josiah never again resorted to litigation to determine such matters.

After John Voyez had served a sentence of imprisonment for his misdemeanours while with Wedgwood, he was employed by Palmer. There, he followed other former workers at Etruria in making copies of his late master's wares. He and Palmer did not hesitate to forge the Wedgwood mark on their imitations of seals, and were alleged to have disposed of them all over the country as being genuine. In 1776, after he had done Wedgwood considerable damage, Voyez left the district and exercised his talents in making seals of glass paste in the manner of James Tassie.

Humphrey Palmer's wife, who had played an important part in his business affairs, died, and in 1778 Wedgwood wrote to Bentley:

> Mr. P. married a young wife lately & settled pretty largely upon her, which threw his family affairs into disorder, & alarmed his creditors . . . it is imagined his affairs are irretrievable.

James Neale took over the factory, and while copies of Wedgwood wares continued to be made some original and prettily-coloured figures were also produced. Both Palmer and Neale marked their wares with their surname impressed, sometimes with the addition of the place-name HANLEY.

Lane End: Turner.

The first member of the Turner family to become a potter was John, the son of a

Fig. 140: (Left) *Cream-coloured and brown stoneware jug moulded with fighting cocks and spectators; height, 7 inches.* (Centre) *Caneware jug moulded with bacchanalian children; height, 6½ inches.* (Right) *Cream-coloured and brown stoneware jug moulded with toxophilites and a lady shooting; height, 7 inches. All with impressed mark* TURNER. *Circa 1800.* (*E. N. Stretton, Esq.*)

awyer who practised in Wolverhampton and lived outside the town not many miles from Stafford. John Turner began to make wares of current local types in about 1756, at a place named unpropitiously the Black Jump, at Shelton. Within a short time he removed to Lane End, near Stoke-on-Trent, where it was said he 'manufactured every kind of Pottery then in demand, and also introduced some other kinds not previously known'.

As the writer of those last words was Simeon Shaw and he penned them about seventy years after the event, they must be accepted with caution. It has been assumed that like many others in the area Turner manufactured salt-glazed stoneware, although there is no positive evidence of his early activities. Some specimens of salt-glaze recently in the possession of one of his descendants have been tentatively attributed to him, but they are unmarked and differ in no way from any others.

John Turner duly manufactured cream-coloured pottery, and in company with Josiah Wedgwood he visited Cornwall in 1775 to seek supplies of china clay and china stone. He was, however, soon able to make use of a material that lay near at hand. Again, the informant is Shaw, who wrote:

> About 1780 he discovered a vein of fine Clay, on the land at Green Dock, now the property of Mr. Ephraim Hobson, of Hanley. From this he obtained all his supplies for manufacturing his beautiful and excellent Stone Ware Pottery, of a cane colour. . .

In addition to this buff stoneware, which he mixed to varying shades from cream to ochre, Turner also made his own imitation of Wedgwood's basaltes, and duly found for himself a method of copying jasperware. For the latter he did not employ the same ingredients as in the original, and his colours were limited to blue and white.

While Turner was able to make tolerable versions of Josiah's most successful types of pottery, he was only occasionally able to

approach the standards of design and finish of the originals. Of his near-jasperware it has been pointed out that

> . . . its surface is more glossy than Wedgwood's jasper, while its texture is also notably different. . . . the colours obtained in it are also distinctly different from Wedgwood's colours; one shade of blue being more slatey and glossy than Wedgwood's light blue, while the darker blue is much greener, and indeed in many pieces is of distinctly green-blue tone.

Most of the Lane End output was neatly potted in comparison with that of many other makers, and while some pieces bore classical ornament copied from that of Wedgwood, a proportion of the designs was original. Turner did not, indeed, ally himself so closely to the neo-classical as Josiah, and made considerable use of subjects with a less sophisticated appeal.

These reliefs are to be found most often on the sides of stoneware jugs in large and small sizes. Judging by the quantity surviving they must have been made in large numbers. Examples usually have tall necks encircled by bands of fine reeding, and coloured brown in contrast to the cream

Above, Fig. 141: Caneware pie dish and cover simulating baked pastry. Impressed mark TURNER. Circa 1800. Length, 8⅞ inches. (City Museum and Art Gallery, Hanley.) **Right,** *Fig. 142: Creamware coffee pot and cover painted by David Rhodes. Leeds; circa 1765. Height, 9¾ inches. (Sotheby's.)*

or off-white body. Some were neatly mounted with a silver rim round the top.

The deeper buff-coloured ware was used also to make imitations of pie-crust at a time, around 1800, when flour was scarce throughout Britain. Turner and other manufacturers produced dishes with 'pastry ware' covers which, while they did nothing to fill the hungry stomach, undoubtedly must have provided subjects for conversation at dinner-parties and acted as good advertisements for the potters.

In 1781, or at about that date, Turner acquired a London-based partner, as had Wedgwood, and the firm was listed as 'Turner and Abbott, Staffordshire-potters china and glass men, 9 Old Fish Street in London'. In the following year they moved to 82 Fleet Street, and soon afterwards advertised themselves as 'Potters to his Royal Highness the Prince of Wales'. An

Fig. 143: Creamware table centrepiece with removable casters and dishes. Leeds; circa 1780. Height, 23½ inches. (Sotheby's.)

added inducement to the public were the words:

> N.B.—*Their Warehouse and Show-room are kept agreeably warm.*

John Turner died in 1786, and the business was continued by his sons, John and William. They built up a large trade with the Continent, and sent much undecorated creamware to Holland where it was painted locally. It can be recognised by a lavish use of orange-red, summary draughtsmanship and, when present, inscriptions written in Dutch. These and other productions of the pottery were marked with the name TURNER impressed. After 1800 the name of James Mist, who joined in partnership with Andrew Abbott, was sometimes stamped on wares, and is found with or without the name of Turner.

As a result of their extensive cross-Channel commitments the finances of the firm were affected seriously by the consequences of the French Revolution and the rise of Napoleon. In 1806 the factory at Lane End was sold, and the brothers were declared bankrupt. John Turner went to work for another pottery, Minton's, while William struggled on at Lane End until 1829.

Burslem: Adams.

There were a number of potters with the surname of Adams active in Staffordshire during the 18th and 19th centuries. William Adams of St. John's Square, Burslem was established in business by 1769 and quickly prospered. He is said to have owned two other manufactories in the Tunstall district, but in spite of the publication of books devoted solely to the history of the family there remains uncertainty about it. This is perhaps understandable in view of the fact that in addition to the William Adams mentioned above there were two others named William, whose life-spans were 1748 to 1831 and 1772 to 1829.

The St. John's Square Adams was born in 1746 and died in 1805. He made creamware, and from sometime in the 1780's began to produce jasper in close imitation of Wedgwood's. His blue was inclined to be deep in colour and tending to violet in comparison with that from Etruria, but unlike Turner he produced a range of colours. They included 'dark and light blue solid jasper, and pale green, dark green, lilac, pink and plum-coloured jasper dip'. He made also caneware and basaltes.

While a proportion of the designs used are traceable to Wedgwood, others were original and said to have been the work of the potter himself or a Swiss-born modeller Joseph Mongenot. A late Victorian collector and student of the ware stated 'that he could always recognise original Adams jasper from that of Wedgwood, Turner or Neale, by the elongated features

Plate 22 *Bowl inscribed* 'Success to the Trade and the Lads of Cornwall'; *probably a reference to the copper trade, in which the ore was sent to Swansea for smelting. Probably Swansea; circa 1800. Diameter, 6¼ inches. (Private collection.) Creamware teapot painted with a plough, and on the reverse with a wheatsheaf and* 'Success to the Grain return'd'. *Leeds; circa 1780. Height, 5 inches. (County Museum, Truro.)*

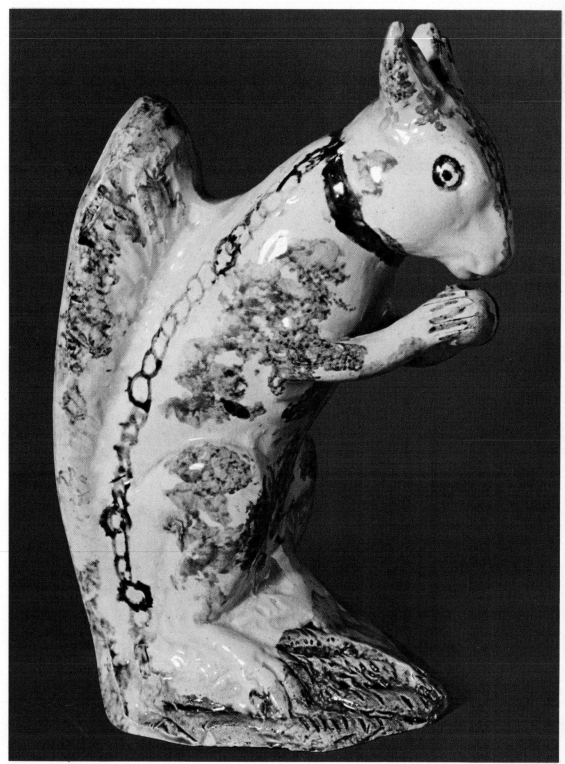

Plate 23 *Creamware figure of a squirrel decorated in underglaze colours. Staffordshire; circa 1790. Height, 6¾ inches.*

of the figure subjects'. This has been accounted for by the suggestion that most of the female heads were modelled on that of Mary Adams, daughter of William Adams, 'whose face was of the type stated'.

Impressed marks were used on all types of ware, and took the form of ADAMS & Co. or ADAMS.

Leeds.

A pottery was probably active in Leeds during the 1750's; it was enlarged in 1770 and one or more members of a family named Green were partners in the enterprise. Clay was brought from Poole, Dorset, and the flints to be pulverised and mixed with it came from Sussex. Coal was only a short distance away, and a primitive horse-drawn railroad ran through the property from the mine.

A windmill was used for grinding the flints and formed a part of the establishment, as is clear in a contemporary record:

> On Sunday, 31st July, 1774, the sails of the windmill belonging to the Leeds Pottery fell down with a tremendous crash; which being looked upon as a judgment for desecrating the Sabbath, the proprietors resolved that the mill should never be allowed to be worked afterwards on the Lord's Day.

While other types of ware were made, creamware was the principal production, and is normally recognisable by its good finish and even glaze. Table-wares formed the largest proportion of the output, some of them of daunting size and standing two feet in height (Fig. 143). A catalogue issued in 1817 lists and illustrates some three hundred items, ranging from plain meat-dishes to elaborate cockle-pots; the latter supported on figures of mermaids, and with a pierced cover topped by Neptune with trident and sea-horses.

Complicated pierced ornament, punched through the semi-hard clay, was used effectively, and is a characteristic feature of many articles. Handles were often made from two lengths of ribbed clay, inter-

Fig. 144: Creamware plate painted in Holland with portraits of Prince William of Orange and his wife, with an inscription in Dutch. Leeds; circa 1787. Diameter, 7 inches. (Sotheby's.)

twined, and with flowers and leaves where they joined the body of the piece. Such details, however, were not exclusive to any one factory, and are rarely acceptable without other evidence in determining the origin of a piece.

The Leeds firm enjoyed a good export trade with Russia and other countries, and in 1783 printed translations of its English catalogue in French, German and Spanish. As with Turner of Lane End, some of the plain creamware was decorated in Holland. The subjects popular there were either religious or political: the latter centring on the return from exile in 1787 of William V, Prince of Orange, and his wife, Sophia Wilhelmina of Prussia (Fig. 144).

In England, much of the decorated ware was painted at an independent establishment in Briggate, Leeds, where David

Rhodes and Jasper Robinson had premises. They advertised in the *Leeds Intelligencer* in 1760 and 1761 that they

> Enamel and Burn in Colours and Gold, Foreign and English China; and match broken Sets of enamell'd China Tea Wares . . . They also enamell Coats of Arms &c. . . .

Robinson went to London in 1768, where he worked for Josiah Wedgwood and it is thought that the factory then set up its own painting workshop. In about 1775 transfer-printing was used, but not on a large scale.

Black earthenware of basaltes type was made at Leeds, but only from about 1800. Its use was restricted to tea and coffee pots and other table pieces, and it would appear that purely decorative articles like vases were not made.

Towards the end of the 18th century figures were produced but they differ little from those of Staffordshire and elsewhere at the time. The most striking of them, and most original, is a large horse, which was executed in both creamware and pearlware (Fig. 147). Surviving examples vary from each other in detail, and a few of them are marked; one, in the Yorkshire Museum, York, with the initials L.P. (presumably for Leeds Pottery) painted on the saddle-cloth.

Eighteenth century Leeds pottery was only occasionally marked. When present, the mark comprises the words LEEDS POTTERY in capitals, sometimes separated by an asterisk. A variation is the addition of the name of the firm, Hartley, Greens & Co. A large proportion of surviving marked examples date from after 1888, when a

Left, *Fig. 145: Creamware vase and cover decorated with a print in black. Cockpit Hill, Derby;* circa *1770. Height, 10¾ inches. (E. N. Stretton, Esq.)* Below, *Fig. 146: Black stoneware sugar bowl and cover, impressed mark* HER-CULANEUM. *Liverpool;* circa *1795. Height, 5½ inches. (City Museum and Art Gallery, Hanley.)* Right, *Fig. 147: Pottery figure of a horse. Leeds;* circa *1790. Height, 16¼ inches. (Sotheby's.)*

Left, *Fig. 148: Creamware two-handled vase with moulded ornament. Cockpit Hill, Derby;* circa *1765. Height, 6¼ inches. (E. N. Stretton, Esq.)*

newly-formed company began to re-use the original moulds. To complete the deception they added marks, but although closely similar to the correct ones they have the letters set in a straighter line and are more carefully stamped than the genuine ones.

Derby.

In about 1750 a pottery was established at Cockpit Hill, Derby, and is thought to have made both stoneware and cream-coloured earthenware. Of the latter, some teapots with transfer-printed decoration include the words 'Derby Pot Works', 'Pot Works in Derby' or, simply, 'Derby'. The name of the engraver, Thomas Radford, is found on some examples.

Judging from characteristics of the marked pieces it has been possible to attribute others to the same source. All of them share a shiny yellow-green glaze which is frequently crazed: i.e. covered in a network of very fine cracks. The standard of craftsmanship was not high, and the undersides of teapots were sometimes left unglazed.

In 1779 the proprietors were bankrupt, and in the year following the contents of the pottery were advertised for sale. It comprised 'the whole stock in trade of that great and extensive factory commonly known by the name of Derby Pot Works . . . .', and included

> a large quantity of Enamelled Cream Ware, and plain Cream Tentable [? *a misprint for tea-table*] ware; a great quantity of White stone and Brown Ware. . .
> This Earthenware will be sold in different lots and is well worth the notice of Pot Carriers in and about the neighbourhood of Coleorton Moor.
> No less a quantity than two horse-loads will be sold to one person.

Distributed far and wide by the pottery-hawkers of the area, the Cockpit Hill wares have by now mostly vanished. Only a few printed pieces are marked, and the unmarked, which would have been the greater proportion, can only be attributed on the ground of a general resemblance. Research is continually bringing to light a little more information about the factory, and knowledge of its products is slowly widening.

Swansea.

In or about 1767 a pottery to make domestic wares for local sale was established at Swansea, in South Wales. The acquisition

Fig. 149: Creamware jug printed in black with the arms of the Cordwainers' Company and inscribed at the front 'Richd. and Elizth. Sampson, Penzance'. Liverpool; circa 1800. Height, 8¾ inches. (County Museum, Truro.)

of a new partner in the firm led to an enlargement of the existing premises in April 1790, and the whole was named the Cambrian Pottery. Creamware, basaltes and most of the other types popularised by Wedgwood were copied, and a whitened variety of the first-named, in competition with Pearlware, was duly developed. Transfer-printing was used for much of the decoration, and some of the designs used were engraved by a Staffordshire man, Thomas Rothwell.

A Derby-born painter, Thomas Pardoe, worked at Swansea from about 1790 until 1809. He is best known for his careful copies of flowers taken from illustrations in William Curtis's *Botanical Magazine*, which commenced publication in 1787. The artist inscribed the name of the subject in red or brown at the back of the plate or dish on which it appeared.

The wares made at the pottery prior to 1790 were unmarked, and are identifiable only from the few surviving inscribed examples. Of these, the earliest is a salt-glazed stoneware pocket-flask with wording in 'scratch blue' reading: 'Morgan John Swansea March ye 28 1768', which is in the possession of the Royal Institution of South Wales. At the time, the Portreeve (equivalent to a mayor) of Swansea was named Morgan John, and it is reasonable to suppose the flask was made for him.

From about the year 1791 the name SWANSEA in capital letters was used regularly as an impressed mark.

Liverpool.

Creamware was made in Liverpool and, as has been stated, Wedgwood sent some of his output there to be decorated by Sadler and Green at their printing establishment. Makers in the city appear to have been numerous, but there is little evidence of what they produced. A few pieces have been found bearing the name of Joseph Johnson, and an advertisement of 1773 stated that the pottery of Messrs. Okill & Co., was for sale, 'as also a large assortment of cream colour or Queen's ware, manufactured at the said work'.

At the end of the 18th century a pottery was opened at Toxteth Park and named 'Herculaneum'. Some of the productions were stamped with the factory name in capital letters. A marked Wedgwood-type basaltes sugar-bowl and cover is illustrated in Fig. 146.

11 19th Century Pottery: Part 1

Above, *Fig. 150: Interior of tankard shown in plate 24; probably made by Dixon & Co., Sunderland, circa 1815. Height, 4¾ inches. (Mrs. G. C. S. Coode.)*

ENGLISH pottery of the late 18th century and early 19th century is summarised broadly in the varied productions of the most prominent of the Staffordshire manufacturers, Enoch Wood of Burslem. He, himself, is an example of the continuity found in the trade, for he was one of a family descended from Ralph Wood, a miller of Cheddleton, near Leek. The miller's son and grandson, both named Ralph, were renowned potters in their day (see page 105), and Enoch was nephew of the one and cousin of the other.

The 'Father of the Potteries', as Enoch Wood was called by his contemporaries later in life, was born in 1759, is said to have worked for Josiah Wedgwood, and was apprenticed to the latter's imitator, Humphrey Palmer of Hanley. In about 1784, when he was 25, he joined in business with his cousin Ralph, and six years later was in partnership with James Caldwell. In 1818 he bought out Caldwell, and from being Wood and Caldwell the firm became Enoch Wood & Sons.

Wood, like many of his relatives, was not only a practical potter, but a modeller of some skill. His best-known work is a bust of the preacher, John Wesley, made in 1781, which was 'acknowledged to be the most faithful likeness of that eminent person ever produced, and has been the prototype of numerous copies subsequently promulgated' (Fig. 151). Among his other identified works is a large plaque in blue earthenware on a white background and resembling jasperware, depicting the *Descent from the Cross*. It is signed and dated 1777, and examples are at Hanley Museum and the Victoria and Albert Museum.

Some large-sized figures, standing up to 26 inches in height, including *Fortitude*, *St. Paul preaching at Athens* and *Bacchus and Ariadne*, were modelled by Wood. Also he made busts of such notabilities as Cleopatra, William IV and the Emperor Alexander I of Russia. They may be thought by many to merit the comment of a knowledgeable critic that they 'are in general without much artistic merit'. His *Night Watchman* (Fig. 152) and *Vicar and Moses*, the clerk leading home by lantern-light a befuddled parson, possibly have a greater appeal.

Enoch Wood has been credited with instigating a different manner of painting pottery from that hitherto employed in England. Up to about the mid-1780's earthenware had mostly been coloured by means of tinted glazes, usually flowing uncontrolled but occasionally manipulated to emphasise the details of the clay body. Exceptionally, Josiah Wedgwood had caused his painters at Chelsea to employ overglaze enamels, of the kind used on porcelain, to decorate the service he made for the Empress Catherine of Russia in 1774 (see Plate 19). Wood, or one of his contemporaries, used the same process for figures and groups. The result was a closer approximation to porcelain than had been attained before, but a complete loss of the quality that had given pottery its individuality.

The earlier process, in which the colour was part of the glaze, gave the finished work an unbroken glossy surface. The newer method, introduced on the Continent at Strasburg, with the colours painted on top of the glaze, resulted sometimes in a dull surface wherever the colours lay. The piece had to be glazed and fired, then re-fired after painting so as to fix the enamels. This second baking was carried out at a lower temperature than the first, and a special kiln, known as a 'muffle-kiln'

Left, Fig. 151: Portrait bust of the Reverend John Wesley (1703-91) modelled by Enoch Wood. Staffordshire; early 19th century. Height, 11½ inches. (County Museum, Truro.) **Below, *Fig. 152: 'Night Watchman' jug modelled by Enoch Wood. Staffordshire; circa 1800. Height, 9 inches.* Right, *Fig. 153: Figure of Cleopatra, modelled by Enoch Wood. Staffordshire; circa 1800. Length, 14 inches. (County Museum, Truro.)***

was employed for the purpose.

Whereas the colour-glazes tended to melt to some degree into the clay forming the article and do not easily come away, the overglaze enamels are often chipped. This occurs particularly with black, and can be seen on the shoes, breeches and hat of the Watchman jug illustrated in Fig. 152. Overglaze colours can be recognised, even when unchipped, by the fact that they are opaque and sometimes have a matt surface. The colours employed were more numerous than those obtained with glazes, and their effect is totally different from the muted shades of Whieldon and Ralph Wood, senior. This is apparent in a comparison between the food-warmer in Plate 17 and the figure of a stag in Plate 25.

Enoch Wood's expanding firm manu-factured most kinds of pottery. They included not only creamware and imitations of jasperware and basaltes, but also a variety that came into popular demand from the early years of the 19th century: blue-printed earthenware. For this, a whitened creamware was the basis, and the patterns were mainly, but not exclusively, based on Oriental originals.

Its introduction is often credited to Josiah Spode, who had been apprenticed to Whieldon in 1749 and eventually set up his own business. Whether he was the first to employ blue transfer on pottery is debatable, but certainly he made many improvements in the process employed. In the first decades of the 19th century, his son, also named Josiah, popularised some excellent patterns taken from contemporary book illustrations

and embellished with well-designed borders.

The best-known of the many transfer-printed blue designs is unquestionably the so-called 'Willow Pattern', which first appeared on English porcelain in about the year 1780. The story it allegedly illustrates concerns a girl named Koong-Shee, daughter of a wealthy and tyrannical mandarin, who fell in love with and wanted to marry her father's secretary. As ever, her choice was not approved, and the engraved scene shows the girl eloping with her lover and pursued by her angry parent. There were several variations of the pattern, some of which do not feature all three characters crossing the bridge and also vary in the number of ripe fruit shown on a tree overhanging the romantic scene. Opinions differ widely as to which is the 'authentic' one, and a modern parody of the subject, made for advertising purposes, has added a further variation for the consideration of students of the genre.

Blue-printed earthenware was made by almost every Staffordshire potter, and by others all over the country. A very extensive export trade was enjoyed, and patterns were designed especially to suit the tastes of buyers overseas. Several different views in and around Quebec were made for

Above left, *Fig. 154: Plate, transfer-printed in blue with a flower,* Hibiscus tiliæ folius. *Impressed mark* WEDGWOOD. *Circa 1810. (J. K. des Fontaines, Esq., F.R.S.A.)* Above, *Fig. 155: Plate, transfer-printed in blue with a view of the bridge at Solaro, copied from an engraving in a book published in 1797/98. Impressed mark* SPODE. *Circa 1810. Diameter, 10 inches.* Right, *Fig. 156: Dish, transfer-printed in dark blue with the arms of the State of Pennsylvania. Staffordshire; circa 1830. Width, 21 inches.*

Canada, and views of buildings and other subjects with a local interest went to the United States (Fig. 156). A writer in 1843 noted that Enoch Wood & Sons 'have of late years been reckoned the largest exporters of that article from Staffordshire to the United States of America'. A noticeable feature of the export wares is that they were printed in a very dark blue, whereas the home-market pieces were in a comparatively light shade.

Following the example of Wedgwood at Etruria, many of the early 19th century potters took pains to mark their wares. They used stamps for impressing them or, in the case of printed articles, a mark was applied in the same manner as the decoration. Many of the marks showed the name of the pattern or its reference number, and for some reason a majority of the firms coyly hid their identities by using initials. These can, however, usually be traced quite easily in an up-to-date book listing such marks. While a few makers, like Wedgwood and Spode, produced wares that were outstanding in design and finish, the greater number were of indifferent merit and varied little between one maker and another.

FOLLOWING the death of Josiah Wedgwood I in 1795, the firm was carried on by his son, also named Josiah, in partnership with his cousin, Tom Byerley. While continuing to manufacture the wares they had made in the past, several innovations were introduced during the years 1800-1820. Among them was the use of lustres, both pink (or copper) and silver, which were possibly the subject of experiments from 1790 but were not made in quantity until about 1800.

It was not long before other makers were producing similarly-decorated articles, although in many instances the glitter was applied carelessly. Wedgwood and a few of the better-class potters took more trouble, and their lustre wares were carefully finished. This was especially the case with the 'resist' pieces, which were made by covering the spaces where lustre was not wanted with a composition to *resist* it. In this manner it was applied to jugs and other articles, painted or patterned with transfer prints or, more rarely, on wares with a bright yellow ground (Plate 24).

The least rare is copper lustre found on

red clay jugs banded with blue, that have been made almost continuously for more than a century. Wedgwood and others used the copper to give a blotched effect that is unusual in appearance but not particularly endearing. Manufacture of all kinds of lustre ware was by no means confined to Staffordshire, and the potteries of Sunderland, Swansea and Bristol were among the several centres that added to the flood while it remained popular.

A further variety of decoration that grew up alongside lustre was 'Mocha'; so-called from its resemblance to the stone of that name, which is similarly but naturally

marked. The mocha-decorated pottery shows feathery tree-like shapes in dark brown or black, that were first made, it is said, by a tobacco-chewing potter expectorating on to the half-finished article. By carefully moving the ware about, and sometimes by the use of a blow-pipe, he was able to direct the shaping of the ornament into the horizontal or the vertical. Such wares are usually covered in bands of pale-coloured slips, and the majority of surviving examples are jugs and mugs (Fig. 161).

Wood of Burslem seem to have marked only a proportion of their output with their own name, and much left the premises unmarked. As was customary in the pottery trade, they also manufactured for other firms, and pieces have been recorded that were undoubtedly theirs but bear the

Fig. 157: Mug, printed in black with a steam engine and coaches. Perhaps Staffordshire; circa 1845. Height, $3\frac{5}{16}$ inches. (County Museum, Truro.)

impressed stamp of Wedgwood. Some of the other firms in Staffordshire, and elsewhere, similarly appear to have been capricious in their use of marks, and attributions have mostly to be made on grounds of design and colouring.

The name of 'Pratt Ware' is given to a large range of articles painted in colours that include a 'dirty orange', blue, green and brown, dating from the late 18th/early 19th centuries (Fig. 158). As Felix Pratt of Lane Delph, who is credited with their manufacture, was not born until 1780, it is to be wondered why his name has been associated with them for so long. Some of the earlier pieces are recorded with the name PRATT impressed, but the precise identity of the potter responsible for making these has not been discovered.

Ralph Salt of Hanley was responsible for small figures sometimes with shrub backgrounds (bocage), decorated over the glaze in a rough manner with a noticeably bright green and other colours. They were obviously made for selling cheaply, and the subjects are typified by one of a girl fondling a lamb which stands beside her on its hind legs, the base ornamented with leaves and stamped SHEPERDISS. Some of them bear the impressed mark SALT within a scroll, or the name on its own.

A contemporary of Salt, and making comparable wares, was John Walton, of Burslem, active between about 1810 and 1835. His figures were often given bocage backgrounds, and are likewise painted brightly. Walton sometimes used a mark showing his name in capital letters within a scroll, and unmarked pieces of the same type could be his or the work of an imitator.

Unlike the makers just mentioned, Obaliah Sherratt did not mark his productions, but a number have been attributed to him. He had a pottery in Burslem from about 1815, and it was continued after his death by his son, Hamlet, until sometime between 1851 and 1860. Most of the groups attributed to the Sherratts are of a larger size than

Fig. 158: Teapot of 'Pratt'-type pottery. Staffordshire; late 18th century. Height, 8½ inches. (Sotheby's.)

many others, and they often incorporate an element of rustic humour that distracts attention from their stiff modelling and crude colouring.

The example illustrated in Fig. 162 has a characteristic base in the shape of a low table, and the lettering has been done by impressing with printer's type and filling-in with black enamel. The modelling is wooden, to say the least, but the designer has succeeded well in conveying the appearance and atmosphere of the outside of a circus tent. Related groups depict a couple with a child at either side of a tea table, entitled 'TEE TOTAL', and a vivid representation of the favourite Staffordshire sport of bull-baiting. This shows the bull being attacked by a dog, while the latter's owner stands waving his arms and with his hat in his right hand. On the base are written his words of encouragement to the dog: 'NOW CAPTIN LAD'.

Left, *Fig. 159: Group of 'The Tithe Pig', decorated in brightly coloured overglaze enamels in the manner of Walton and Salt. Staffordshire; circa 1825. Height, 5½ inches. (County Museum, Truro.)*

Right, *Fig. 160: Lustre-decorated milk jug in the form of a cow. Glamorgan; circa 1820. Overall length, 6½ inches. (City Museum and Art Gallery, Hanley.)*

One variety of pottery that was particularly favoured for domestic use has endured in quantity until the present day: Mason's 'Ironstone China'. This was patented in 1813 by Charles James Mason, of Fenton, and was alleged to contain slag of iron as one of its ingredients. It was mostly decorated with transfer-printing in deep blue in combination with red and gold painting to give the effect of Japanese Imari ware, and was marked in blue transfer.

Ironstone is a thickly-potted and very strong product, so it is not surprising that much of it remains in an unbroken state. The garish designs with which it was decorated were in the taste of the time, and with its gay colouring and great durability it proved a welcome substitute for Chinese porcelain. The factory closed in 1854, and Mason himself died two years later.

Earlier, in 1805, Josiah Spode had introduced his 'Stone' china, which was a type of earthenware with china-stone added to give it a greater hardness and density. It was decorated in a manner similar to Mason's Ironstone, and was marked *Spode*

Stone-China in various forms with and without a simulated Chinese seal. In addition, many other makers produced pottery similar in appearance and composition to that of Mason and Spode (Fig. 163).

*   *   *

A RICH manganese brown glaze used at the Swinton pottery, Yorkshire, duly earned the name of 'Rockingham brown' after 1826. In that year the name of the manufactory was altered to that of the estate of its patron, Earl Fitzwilliam, later Marquis of Rockingham. All types of pottery were made there, and a distinctive product was a teapot copied from a Chinese wine-pot in the form of a peach. This article had no lid and was filled through a hole in the base, leading into a pipe projecting high inside so that the liquid did not spill when it was inverted. It was first made in about 1806, and named the Cadogan pot after a member of that family.

Some of the Swinton products were stamped with the surname of the owners,

Fig. 161: Tankard of 'Mocha' ware.
Staffordshire; circa 1830. Height
6 inches. (City Museum and Art Gallery,
Hanley.)

Plate 24 *Lustre-decorated wares: plaque, width 7 inches; goblet, height 4¼ inches; silver-resist jug, height 5¼ inches; cow milk-jug, length 7¼ inches; pink-resist vase, height 5 inches; tankard printed with a view of the Wear bridge, Sunderland, opened in 1796 (see Fig. 150), height 4¾ inches. All early 19th century. (Mrs. G. C. S. Coode.)*

Plate 25 *Figure of a stag painted in overglaze enamels. Staffordshire; early 19th century. Height, 7½ inches. (City Museum and Art Gallery, Plymouth.)*

Fig. 162: 'Polito's Menagerie', modelled by Obadiah Sherratt. Staffordshire; circa 1835. Height, 11½ inches. (City Museum and Art Gallery, Hanley.)

Brameld, and later with the word Rockingham. Much, however, was unmarked and
remains unidentified like so much else from
innumerable other sources.

One further type of pottery was being
made in the period under review: salt-
glazed stoneware. As in earlier times, its
manufacture continued at both Fulham and
Lambeth, and in the provinces in Derbyshire. Wedgwood's creamware had put
paid to its attempts to capture the market
for table-wares, so it was confined mainly
to tankards and jugs which would withstand hard usage and to small-sized ornaments.

Of the several stoneware manufacturers
active in Lambeth in the early 19th century
the most familiar name is that of Doulton,
whose descendants remained in business
there until 1956. John Doulton served his

*Below, Fig. 163: Junket bowl decorated
with a Japan pattern, and with a printed
mark* AMHERST JAPAN IRON
STONE. *Staffordshire; early 19th
century. Diameter, 7½ inches. (Mrs. G.
C. S. Coode.)*

Fig. 164: Salt-glazed stoneware spirit flask depicting Earl Grey, who was responsible for the passing by Parliament of the Reform Bill in 1832. Impressed mark BELPER & DERBY. BOURNE'S POTTERIES BELPER. *Circa 1835. Height, 7½ inches. (County Museum, Truro.)*

apprenticeship at the Fulham pottery, then owned by descendants of John Dwight, and when his time was up in 1812 went to work in a small stoneware pot-house in Vauxhall. Eventually, after various changes in title the firm of Doulton and Watts became established in Lambeth High Street.

They made the same types of brown and greyish stoneware as their competitors, and owed their living more to a steady output of commonplace bottles and jars for ink, jam, boot-blacking or beer, than to anything more artistic. The nearest any of the firms approached to the latter was in the quantities of pocket-flasks that were then popular. These took many forms, being modelled in the likeness of kings, queens and other personalities, and in the shape of objects such as pistols and powder-horns (Fig. 164).

At Mortlake, just outside London and by the river Thames, a small stoneware pottery was owned by Joseph Kishere between 1800 and 1811. He impressed his name and address, adding 'Surry' [*sic*], on brown-coloured jugs and other articles, which were ornamented with reliefs in the manner of earlier Fulham pieces (see Plate 11). A large amount of similar, but unmarked, ware has survived. As the same basic shapes and decoration continued to be used for at least one hundred and fifty years, each maker copying the other, attribution and dating can prove difficult.

12   19th Century Pottery: Part 2

Fig. 165: Child's plate with a printed central pattern, the border moulded and coloured. Circa 1860. Diameter, 4½ inches.

WHILE there was an ample supply of pottery of all kinds in the first half of the 19th century, both output and variety increased in the second half. Not only were more manufacturers producing a greater quantity of goods, but there remains a considerable amount of information about their activities. Written records were fuller and more accurate, and the comparatively short interval of time between then and now has ensured the preservation of much material.

Between the years 1842 and 1901 it was possible for potters and makers of other goods to register their designs with the Patent Office, and many took advantage of this facility. The drawn pattern and written details were deposited with the Office, and after the granting of the application the products were marked to indicate the fact. The mark took the form of a diamond enclosing the letters *Rd.* (for 'registered'), and at each of the corners a bracketed numeral or a letter of the alphabet. The latter were in two series, running

from 1842 to 1867 and from 1868 to 1901, and keys are to be found in books of china-marks.

While the Patent Registry marks on pottery are often illegible because of glaze obscuring their details, their very presence implies a date from 1842 onwards. However, it must be remembered that such marks only record the date when the design was registered. They do not necessarily announce the actual year of manufacture, which can be, and often is, some years later.

Research into the information given by the marks has revealed much about the succession of changes in design, and about the makers themselves. Of the latter, too, knowledge has been widened from studying printed lists of potters, in Staffordshire and elsewhere, given in contemporary Directories. From these it has been possible to trace the comings and goings of firms, and to relate the initials found on wares to those of makers.

Amongst the potters who showed their

Fig. 166: Child's plate with a printed central pattern, the border moulded and coloured.   Circa 1860.   Diameter, 5½ inches.

goods at the 1851 Great Exhibition were F. & R. Pratt, Fenton Potteries, Staffordshire, whose surname had been well-known in the Potteries since the late 18th century. In 1847 and 1848 the firm had patented methods of mass-producing circular lidded boxes, and also a way of decorating them in colour by superimposed transfer-prints. The surface was glazed after the prints had been applied, and the slightly-convex lids came from their final firing with a brilliant sheen.   The firm exhibited a number of pieces employing the process; amongst them picture-plaques, a bread plate and cheese dish and a pair of vases.

From Burslem, T. J. and J. Mayer showed
Various designs for meat pots, printed in colours, under the glaze.

In addition, the latter's exhibit was described as including
Bust of Wesley, from the original mould, belonging to the late Enoch Wood, Esq., the sculptor. (Wood had died in 1840, at the age of 81. See *Chapter* 11, Fig. 151.)

The decorated pots were used for fish and meat pastes or for hair dressings, and have for long been collected as assiduously as cigarette cards.   Many of the patterns

were designed and engraved by Jesse Austin, who worked for Pratts', and some of their lids bear his name or initials on them (Plate 27).

Single-colour printing in blue or another colour, introduced earlier, continued to be popular.   In many instances the printed pattern was given added attraction by hand-painted dashes of bright colour.   This was used for many kinds of ware, and often on small-sized plates between 3 and 6 inches in diameter, made for children.   The plates were ornamented with biblical texts, sayings of the great, nursery rhymes, views and many other subjects.   Their manufacture was principally in the north-east of England, but many Staffordshire firms made them, and among marked examples some from Swansea have been recorded.   Their popularity was long-lived and lasted from about 1830 for at least the next thirty years (Figs. 165 and 166).

Charles Mason, of Longton, was an exhibitor of 'patent ironstone china' in 1851, and his display included not only services and jars and covers, but also pieces of tableware 'made of the white patent ironstone china, used in the hotels of the United States of America'.   Among other unusual articles was a monumental tablet 'lettered under the glaze', and one may wonder if any were used and remain today in grave-yards or within doors.

Not unexpectedly Wedgwoods displayed a Portland Vase at the Exhibition, for this was still in the public eye following the smashing of the Roman original, while in the British Museum, in 1847. Their other goods included jasperware and creamware in 18th century forms, as well as a number of other types of pottery revived and re-designed. They included green-glazed wares (Fig. 167), black basaltes with painted Chinese flowers and pieces covered in a brown ('Rockingham') glaze. Most of them continued to be made for the remainder of the century, and some remain in daily production at Barlaston now; a continuity of output that gives collectors a headache.

It is helpful to remember that although the same impressed mark, the name WEDG-WOOD, has been used continuously since about 1771, there have been additions and variations from time to time. For instance, from 1860 a series of three letters was also stamped on a piece to indicate the month and year in which it was potted. Then, from 1891 onwards, Wedgwood and all other pottery was almost always marked with the word *England;* denoting the country of origin in order to comply with a newly-passed American law. Above all, the fineness of the finish and the softness of the ware are unmistakable clues to the experienced; once these have been recog-nised by a careful study of old examples there can be no possibility of confusing early, late and modern.

Much of the late 19th century Wedgwood took the form of painstaking copies of earlier jasperware, with emphasis on two- and three-colour specimens. Some of the creamware, however, showed more indi-viduality, due to the original painting of a Frenchman, Emile Lessore. He came to England in 1858 and shortly went to work at Etruria, where he stayed for five years before returning to his native land. His work is distinguished by competent drawing and his restricted palette of colours (Plate 27). While he decorated a considerable quantity of creamware during his stay in England, the firm continued to send plain pieces to him when he had gone back to France and he decorated for them until his death in 1876. His work is sometimes

Fig. 167: Plate moulded with vine leaves and covered in a green glaze. Impressed mark WEDGWOOD. Circa 1860. Diameter, 8¾ inches. (Victoria and Albert Museum.)

Left, *Fig. 168: Brown and buff stoneware jug with a central band of white figures in relief. Impressed mark of Doulton's, Lambeth, and Rd. No. 121031 (1899), Height, 8⅛ inches.*

Right, *Fig. 170: Grey stoneware jug decorated with blue glaze, the central panel in 'scratch blue' showing a potter at the wheel. Signed beneath the base by R. W. Martin, Southall, and dated 1878. Height, 15¼ inches. (City Museum and Art Gallery, Plymouth.)*

Below, *Fig. 169: Pair of figures of pet spaniels in white pottery with details in black and buff. Height, 10½ inches.*

signed with his initials, and sometimes *E. Lessore*.

A number of other French potters had come to England shortly before the arrival of Lessore, and they brought with them a practical understanding of their craft as well as a knowledge of its history. Chief among them was Joseph-Léon-François Arnoux, who had been appointed Art-Director of the Mintons factory, Stoke-on-Trent, soon after he reached England in 1848.

The first new type of ware introduced by Arnoux was in imitation of 16th century Italian majolica; employing an opaque white glaze over a pottery body, and using the surface for polychrome painting. Among the pieces Mintons displayed in 1851 were

> Wine coolers of porous ware: ornamented with views, and festoons of vine leaves and grapes, in buff; with a wreath of vine leaves, &c.; with festoons of vine leaves and grapes, and coloured in the majolica style; with wreath of vine leaves, &c., and coloured.

Also

> Variety of flowerpots and stands, coloured in the majolica style, &c.

Soon after, attention began to be paid to the long-forgotten work of the Frenchman, Bernard Palissy, who lived between *circa* 1510 and *circa* 1589. He became the subject of considerable interest, with his life-story becoming quoted as an exemplary one of genius rising above personal suffering. A Huguenot, he was attracted to potting, and during experiments was driven to burning his own furniture in order to fire his kiln. He eventually worked for Catherine de Médicis and other important patrons, but although spared in the massacre of St. Bartholomew was later imprisoned in the Bastille.

Palissy's wares were modelled with figure subjects in low relief or with life-like representations of reptiles, decorated all over with coloured glazes which he had

Above, left and right, *Figs. 174 and 175: Salt-glazed stoneware jugs exhibited in 1851 and produced continuously for many years afterwards. Meigh, Hanley, Staffordshire. (From woodcuts.)* **Right,** *Fig. 176: Jug with printed and hand-coloured decoration in the Chinese style: similar examples were made with Greek-style patterns. Staffordshire; circa 1860. Height, 6 inches.*

developed himself. The glazes became the subject of interest to Arnoux and his staff, and a range of them was evolved copying, more or less, those used three centuries earlier. Coatings of transparent greens, browns, yellows and blues were flooded thickly over tiles, plates and other objects, which had been moulded with patterns showing dimly through the semi-obscurity.

Llewellynn Jewitt wrote in 1878 that

In 1850 Majolica was added to the other art-productions of this manufactory, and in this it still stands pre-eminent. No firm has surpassed them in the sharpness of details; the purity of colours; the excellence of glaze, or the artistic character of these goods, which comprise every description of both useful and ornamental articles.

Then he added

In 1851 Della Robbia and Palissy ware were also here commenced.

Luca and Andrea Della Robbia were Italian Renaissance sculptors who modelled terra cotta (red clay fired hard) into reliefs and statues and finished it by covering it with white and coloured opaque glazes. These latter were in complete contradiction to the transparent glazes of Palissy, but were similar in type to those of the majolica artists.

During the present century there has been confusion between the Mintons majolica and their 'palissy-type' wares. For some reason it has been thought that the Victorians mis-named the clear-glazed variety as *Majolica*, which has been termed by more than one writer 'absurd'. In fact, it seems they did no such thing, and kept the two varieties separate as well as correctly designated.

Mintons were by no means the sole makers of any of the wares mentioned, and as soon as they had successfully made and marketed one of them it was speedily copied by one or more of their rivals. Many of the latter aided deception by not

Fig. 177: Match-container in the form of a fly, the inside of the top scored for striking, covered in transparent glazes. Impressed mark WEDGWOOD. *1872. Length, 5 inches. (Buten Museum of Wedgwood, Merion.)*

putting a mark on their products, whereas Mintons usually impressed their name on theirs.

A NUMBER of other Staffordshire makers were catering for a much less discriminating market than Mintons and their competitors. From sometime in the 1840's a type of white pottery figure, roughly and garishly finished, began to be made in large numbers for selling cheaply. The subjects were those with an instant appeal, and among the earliest of them to be modelled was the young Queen Victoria. In addition to politicians, there were figures of military men, boxers and cricketers, foreign notabilities, murderers and their victims, and, in fact, anyone who to-day would be called 'headline news'.

A large proportion of the surviving figures are to be recognised only by their appearance and some remain unidentified, but many were finished with their name in raised letters or written in gilt script on the front of the base (Plate 26). In recent years named examples have been eagerly collected and their variations carefully recorded. Needless to say, this has caused a steep rise in their value, and the appearance on the market of fakes of a few of the rarer examples.

Manufacture of the ornaments lasted throughout the remainder of the 19th century. While rough dating is possible according to the history of the person or

event portrayed, it is probable that each model remained in production over a period of years. The distinctive colouring relies largely on a brilliant deep blue and an orange-red, and the modelling is mostly confined to the front of the piece. Backs will usually be found devoid of shaping or decoration, neither of which would be required on pieces intended for display on a mantelpiece.

One of the known makers of these figures, sometimes termed 'flat backs', was Sampson Smith, of Longton, who began manufacture in 1859. He died in 1888, but the business was continued by successive owners and managements to the present day. The figures were made continuously until 1918, but their making was re-commenced, with the aid of the original moulds, in 1948. Sampson Smith also made the familiar figures of dogs (Fig. 169), some of which are marked in relief with his name and the date 1851.

O NE of the objects of the Great Exhibition was to act as a stimulus to better design, and as a result a number of Schools of Art were started in different parts of the country. One of them was at Lambeth in south London, where in 1864 the owner of the nearby Doulton pottery, Henry Doulton, began to take an interest in the project and commissioned some work from the students.

From a humble start as makers of stoneware bottles, the Doulton pottery had prospered following the publication of Edwin Chadwick's 1842 report on sanitary conditions in Great Britain. When the Government took steps to alleviate the prevailing state of affairs, in which a lack of drainage went hand-in-hand with dirt and disease, it was decided that stoneware pipes would provide the best answer. Doulton quickly adapted his pottery to providing quantities of them, and by so doing reaped a deserved fortune.

Within two years of his having encouraged the students in the School of Art, Doulton took into his employ one of the more promising of them, and set him to work designing and making ornamental ware. Similar clays and processes to those for producing drain-pipes were employed, and a study of old stoneware, English and foreign, led to the conclusion that past methods of decoration could hardly be bettered. The simple technique of 'scratch blue' was revived for the purpose (page 88

and Plate 14), and was well received by the limited number of members of the public who saw specimens of it.

In 1873 Doulton's little department had six working in it, and by 1890 the staff had increased to 345. The best-known of the modellers was the man who had been the first employee, George Tinworth, whose range of productions extended from large- and small-scale religious groups to ornaments depicting frogs and mice in human attitudes. A typical example of the latter shows a rowing-boat containing half-a-dozen mice, one playing an accordion and singing while a third leans unhappily over the side, entitled 'The Cockneys at Brighton'.

Fig. 178: Game dish and cover decorated with moulded ornament and coloured glazes. Staffordshire; circa 1870. Length, 10¼ inches. (Mrs. G. C. S. Coode.)

Another Doulton artist who is remembered is Hannah Barlow, whose sister and brother also worked at Lambeth. Hannah was proficient at incised patterns of animals, in which her sure touch is readily distinguished. She and most of the other employees signed or initialled their work, and the firm rarely sold anything that had not been stamped with its name.

In addition to the use of 'scratch blue', much of the stoneware was stained brown, or decorated with stamped reliefs (Fig. 168). Pieces were ornamented also by using coloured slips, and in the early 1880's some shaped and delicately carved vases were made in the prevailing Oriental style. Certainly there was no lack of variety and about a dozen differently-named wares came and went between 1873 and the end of the century.

Also making use of saltglazed stoneware were the three Martin brothers: Robert Wallace, Walter and Edwin Martin. The first-named had been trained at Doulton's, and the trio set up a pottery in Southall,

Middlesex. Between about 1873 and 1900 (the pottery continued in operation until 1915) they made large quantities of ware, much of it in the form of rather odd-looking birds and animals with a facial resemblance to human-beings. The clever use of the material, in making the most of its texture, and the employment of sombre browns and blues to colour it, add to the somewhat disturbing appearance of many of the Martin's productions. They incised their name and other details beneath the base of each piece.

Roughly contemporary with the foregoing was William de Morgan. He was both a writer and a craftsman, and his work shows strongly the influence of William Morris; a man who similarly combined literature with practical handiwork. From his study of 16th and 17th century Syrian pottery, de Morgan was able to reproduce its lustre decoration (Fig. 171). This he was able to achieve by throwing sawdust or wood-chippings into the kiln at the vital moment, and the carbon in the ensuing

Plate 26 *Figures and groups: 'Napoleon & Albert', height 11¼ inches; castle, height 7⅝ inches; 'The Death of Nelson', height 8 inches; 'K. of Sardinia', height 11½ inches; Napoleon, height 2¾ inches; dog, height 3 inches; lady and gentleman (? Jenny Lind), height 4 inches; Queen Victoria on horseback, height 4¼ inches. Staffordshire, second half of 19th century. (Mrs. G. C. S. Coode.)*

Plate 27 (Top) *Plate painted by Emile Lessore, inscribed on the back 'Latest from Paris'. Impressed mark* WEDGWOOD. *Circa 1860. Diameter 8 inches. (Private collection.) Colour-printed pot-lids:* (top left) *'Pegwell Bay', with four shrimpers, diameter 4⅜ inches;* (top right) *'Wellington', diameter 4⅜ inches;* (centre) *'The Listner* (sic), *diameter 4 inches;* (bottom left) *'Shooting Bears', diameter 3⅜ inches;* (bottom right) *Queen Victoria, Windsor Castle in background, diameter 5¼ inches. Staffordshire; mid-19th century. (County Museum Truro.)*

thick smoke caused the effect he sought.

Between 1882 and 1888 de Morgan had a pottery at Merton Abbey, Surrey, where Morris was endeavouring to revive tapestry-making. Then, in the following year, in partnership with an architect, Halsey Ricardo, he established the Sands End Pottery, Fulham. After further business changes he retired from potting in 1907. He, Ricardo and Dr. Reginald Thompson made the designs, and fifteen painters were employed at one time or another. While some pottery was made on the premises, some was supplied in biscuit form (baked, undecorated and unglazed) from Staffordshire.

As in earlier times, many of the Staffordshire makers continued to manufacture stoneware alongside other types of pottery. Charles Meigh, of Hanley, was amongst them and the jugs in Figs. 174 and 175 are typical productions of the last half of the century. Specimens of them, one with Gothic motifs and the other with ivy leaves on geometrically arranged stalks, were displayed at the Great Exhibition in 1851 and were still in demand many years later.

Fig. 180: Group of pottery exhibited in 1862 by Clews, Cobridge, Staffordshire. (From a woodcut.)

13   Chelsea

THE history of pottery-making in England has been described and illustrated in the preceding *Chapters,* and attention will now be paid to the rival material: porcelain. This first began to reach the country from China during the 16th century, and imports increased until the first few specimens rose to a great flood numbering millions of pieces a year. The trade was general throughout Europe, where each nation was eventually engaged in trying to perfect a similar material. Scientists, philosophers, geologists and others spent their years in efforts to gain for their countrymen a share of the commerce flowing so heavily between East and West.

The Chinese manufactured their porcelain from two natural products that were abundant in a part of their country: chinaclay and china-stone. Suitably treated and mixed, they fused in the heat of a kiln and became the translucent, resonant and attractive substance that, to quote Macaulay, a lady valued 'quite as much as she valued her monkey, and much more than she valued her husband'.

In Italy there had been a short-lived, but locally successful, manufactory at Florence in the late 16th century. Under the patronage of the Medici family an imitation porcelain had been invented and made, but not on a large scale. It was composed basically of glass and white clay, and was the first of many successors of a comparable nature: the so-called 'soft-paste' as opposed to the Oriental compound of 'hard-paste'. A century later the French were making a comparable ware, and then in 1745 the same began to be made near London, at Chelsea.

A number of small jugs have survived, each modelled in the form of two seated goats supporting a vase-shaped body with a realistic bee and a twig handle. A few of them have a triangle cut into the unglazed base, and of these a proportion also bear the name Chelsea and the date 1745.

It should be noted that the marks were all cut into the clay when it was in a semi-hard state prior to firing, so the edges of the lines are slightly burred. Forged markings are not by any means unknown, but these will have been added to the finished article by means of a lapidary's-wheel, and the different result is obvious under a magnifying-glass.

The origin of the Chelsea factory has been suggested to have lain in the visit to London in 1743 of a 'Mr. Bryand'. Described at the time as 'a Stranger' (the word used to denote a foreigner) he showed to members of the Royal Society 'several

Specimens of a sort of fine white Ware made here by himself from native materials of our own Country . . .'. No further mention has been found of this Bryand (or Briand) but his name is probably a French one. The first man who had a positive connection with the new manufactory was certainly a Frenchman, named Charles Gouyn, who had been established in London as a jeweller since 1737. His partner, also from across the Channel but in this instance from Liège, was a silversmith, Nicholas Sprimont.

The earliest discovered printed reference to the manufactory appeared in the *Daily Advertiser* on 24th February 1749, and announced that 'Tea and Coffee Pots, Cups and Saucers of Various Forms, besides several other Things as well for Use as Ornament' would be offered for sale at Chelsea on the following Tuesday, the 28th. A week or so later Sprimont, using his own

Fig. 182: Teapot and cover modelled as a seated Chinaman grasping a snake. Triangle period, 1745-49.   Height, 7 inches. (Sotheby's.)

name instead of calling himself 'The Undertaker of the Manufactory' as previously, stated that the sale had been so successful that it would now be suspended to give time for further stock to be accumulated. At the end he added:

He also gives Notice, that he has no sort of Connexion with, nor for a considerable Time past has put any of his Ware into that Shop in St. James's Street, which was the Chelsea China Warehouse.

A reply to this took the form of a further notice, this time in the *General Advertiser*, which ran:

CHELSEA CHINA WAREHOUSE

SEEING it frequently advertised, that the Proprietor of *Chelsea Porcelaine* is not concerned in any shape whatsoever in the Goods exposed to Sale in St. James's-street, called *The Chelsea China Warehouse*, in common Justice to N. Sprimont, (who signed the Advertisement) as well as myself, I think it incumbent, publicly to declare to the Nobility, Gentry, &c. that my China Warehouse is not supply'd by any other Person than Mr. *Charles Gouyn*, late Proprietor and Chief Manager of the Chelsea-House, who continues to supply me with the most curious Goods of the Manufacture, as well useful as ornamental, and which I dispose of at very reasonable Rates.

S. Stables.

Chelsea China Warehouse,
St. James's Street, Jan.
17th, 1750.

It would appear clearly from the foregoing that Charles Gouyn had ceased to be a partner, and at the same time the west-end showroom, in St. James's Street, was

Fig. 183: Teapot and cover moulded and painted with leaves of the Hart's Tongue fern (Scolopendrium vulgare). Raised anchor period, 1749-52. Height, 5 inches. (Sotheby's.)

Left, *Fig. 184: An example of the raised anchor mark.* **Right,** *Fig. 185: A man and a woman dancing, the former wearing a mask. Marked with an anchor in red.* Circa 1755. *Height, 7 inches.* (*Sotheby's.*)

given up and selling was conducted on the factory premises. Within a few years, however, a showroom was opened in Pall Mall, and annual sales by auction began to be held.

The first of the public sales was announced for April 1754 and lasted 15 days. No copies of the catalogue have survived, but press announcements specified 'Epargnes and Services for Deserts, beautiful Groupes of Figures, &c. complete Table Sets of round and Oval Dishes, Tureens and Plates'.

Further auctions held in 1755 and 1756 were advertised, and catalogues of each of them have been preserved and reprinted. They enable an idea to be obtained of the various wares that were introduced in each year, and many have been identified from the descriptions given. There were no sales in 1757 and 1758, and it was stated that this was because the manufactory 'has been very much retarded by the Sickness of Mr. Sprimont'.

Rumour at the time, and since, has persistently connected the names of George II's son, the Duke of Cumberland, and his secretary, Sir Everard Fawkener, with patronage of the factory. Either or both of them may have come into the picture following the split with Gouyn, and the death of Sir Everard in 1758, together with Sprimont's illness, may have been responsible for a slowing of activity in that year. Certainly the Duke owned some of the ware, and a visitor to his home in 1766, a year after he had died, recorded seeing 'a chandelier of Chelsea china, the first of that manufacture, and cost £500'. Whether these men had a financial interest in the china-works is unknown, and their rôle, if any, in its conduct remains undiscovered.

In 1759, 1760 and 1761 there were further annual auctions. Then, after an interval of a year the usual advertisement was concluded with a statement that Sprimont would shortly be disposing of the contents of the manufactory: '. . . all the unfinished Porcelain and Materials; his valuable and great Variety of Models; all the Moulds, mills, Kilns, Presses, &c. . .'.

In January 1764 the final auction at Chelsea was announced to take place in the following year, but apparently this did not occur. Time passed, and five years later, in 1769, Sprimont offered more of his finished stock and again announced the disposal of moulds and other items in the factory. Finally, in August of that year he sold the concern, and soon afterwards it passed into the hands of the proprietor of the Derby porcelain works, William Duesbury, and the twenty-four-year-long story came to an end.

IN considering the productions of the Chelsea factory during its lifetime it has been found convenient to divide it into four periods. While the output within one sometimes overlaps into another, it is usual to classify the wares according to the mark most commonly used at the particular time, viz: Triangle, Raised Anchor, Red Anchor and Gold Anchor.

Triangle Period, circa 1745-49. The 'goat and bee' jugs, mentioned earlier, are the key pieces of early Chelsea, but they pose at least two queries that have never

been answered satisfactorily and perhaps never will be. The fact that they are well-finished articles suggests that they may not be the first experimental productions of a newly established industry; and there is no clue as to why these particular items should bear on them the word Chelsea, when nothing else has been found similarly marked. The design, too, has been discussed, and the possibility mooted that it was the handiwork of the silversmith Sprimont.

In view of Nicholas Sprimont's connection with the craft, and as porcelain was being made to replace silver articles at the table, it is to be expected that their forms had much in common. It was doubtless encouraged, also, because the better kinds of chinaware were for sale in the shops of

Fig. 186: Dish, modelled after an original in silver and painted in colours by Jeffryes Hamett O'Neale with The Tiger and the Fox *from Aesop's fables. Raised anchor period, 1749-52. Width, 13 inches. (Sotheby's.)*

Plate 28 *Drunken Fisherman, and* (right) *Fisherman, after Meissen models of* circa *1745. The last-named marked with a small anchor in red. Circa 1755. Height, 7¼ inches. (Saltram House, Devon: The National Trust.)*

Plate 29 *Boxes and covers; (left) in the form of a melon with a floral knob; and (right) as an apple with a caterpillar for handle; the latter marked with an anchor in red. Circa 1755. Widths, 3¼ and 3½ inches. (City Museum and Art Gallery, Plymouth.)*

Plate 30 *Bonbonnière modelled with a boy playing a flute to two sheep, height 2⅞ inches; scent-bottle formed as fish and an eel in a net, height 3¾ inches; seals: (left to right) dovecot inscribed* Amoureux et Heureux, *height 1 inch; a woman holding flowers, height 1¼ inches; the Marquis of Granby, inscribed* Genereux et Brave, *height 1¼ inches; a parrot, height 1½ inches.*

silversmiths. The establishment dealing exclusively in pottery and porcelain did not appear until sometime after the mid-century, and eventually directories listed an increasing number of traders who earned their living as 'chinamen'.

The early pieces of Chelsea frequently came from the kiln warped, with jagged fire-cracks and exhibiting pin-pricks in the glaze. The latter also shows an opacity due to the presence in it of tin oxide, which had earlier been an important ingredient of the white coating on delftware. A like employment of tin oxide on porcelain occurred in France, at the Chantilly factory founded in 1725, and this feature as well as some Chelsea shapes have been traced to the same source. Whether they were brought across the Channel by an emigrant potter, or were copied by chance is unknown.

Marking was not general, but many pieces with the characteristics enumerated are attributable on those grounds. A few examples of similar type bear a crown and trident superimposed, in underglaze blue. The best-known example with this latter mark is a group of lovers in the British Museum, of which there is an unmarked version, having the modelling slightly and facetiously varied, in an American collection. Some cups and saucers, the former moulded with overlapping strawberry leaves and the latter with a garland of oak leaves, are known in both marked and unmarked versions; the marked ones variously with the triangle, blue crown and trident and the later raised anchor.

Sparse painting ornaments some triangle pieces, but the larger proportion of surviving examples is plain. The absence of decoration allows the glossy surface, which varies in tint from cream to white to be admired, but some or all may have been coloured at the time with 'cold' oil-paints that have long-since worn or been scraped away.

Raised Anchor Period, circa 1749-52.
The consistent use of a mark, in the form of a small anchor in relief on an oval pad (Fig. 184), dates from about 1749. Why an anchor should have been chosen, and adhered to for the remainder of the factory's life, has not been explained.

It was during this period that the much-described 'moons' began to appear. They are vari-sized circular areas of translucency, visible when the piece is held up against the light, but they are neither invariably found in Chelsea ware nor is their presence a guarantee that an article was made there. As far as Chelsea is concerned, they are to be seen in pieces made

Fig. 187: Figure of a Chinaman. Red anchor period, 1752-58. Height, 7 inches. (Sotheby's.)

between about 1750 and 1755, and along with other characteristics can assist in attribution.

A notice in the *Daily Advertiser* of 9th January 1750 lists pieces then being manufactured ready to be sold in the March of that year. It specifies different kinds of ware for the table, but tantalisingly groups ornaments in a brief phrase:

> . . . a Variety of Services for Tea, Coffee, Chocolate, Porringers, Sauce-Boats, Basons and Ewers, Ice-Pails, Terreens, Dishes and Plates, of different Forms and Patterns, and. . . a great Variety of Pieces for Ornament in a Taste entirely new.

Surviving pieces for the table include some painted with illustrations to Aesop's Fables; a popular subject for decorative inspiration throughout the century, and one that was not confined to porcelain. The decoration, which was based on engravings by other artists, is attributed to Jeffryes Hamett O'Neale, an Irishman who

worked in London. He did similar work on porcelain from other factories, and it occurs on Chelsea of both the Raised Anchor and succeeding Red Anchor periods (Fig. 186).

Figures bearing the raised anchor mark would not seem to have been made in large numbers. While some are close copies of Meissen, others were modelled especially from contemporary and earlier engravings. The latter were mainly the work of a fellow-countryman of Sprimont, Joseph Willems, later anglicised to 'Williams', who is surmised to have worked for the factory from about 1750 until 1766.

Some marked figures of birds are known to have been modelled from the engraved illustrations to a book published between 1743 and 1747. The author was a prominent naturalist of the time, George Edwards, and the work *A Natural History of Uncommon Birds*. In contrast with the output of the preceding period, much of the raised anchor ware was decorated, either at the factory or by men working independently outside. They purchased their requirements 'in the white' and used either oil-colours, or china-enamels which they fired in a kiln.

Red Anchor Period, circa 1752-58. A document in the British Museum, most probably composed by Nicholas Sprimont and datable to between 1752 and 1759, requests the Government to use the law to the full in prohibiting illegal imports of Meissen ware. These, it alleges, were taking place either under the cloak of being the private possessions of diplomats or for the personal use of the importer. In the accommodating 'diplomatic bag' no duty was payable, otherwise it was levied at no more than a low charge. For straightfor-

ward commercial sale its import was prohibited, so that any in the shops must have been brought in by 'collectors' or 'ambassadors'. To mitigate the evil, it was suggested that Meissen on sale should be seized by the Customs, otherwise the Chelsea concern would shortly be faced with ruin.

Newspapers of the early 'fifties record instances of such seizures by the authorities, but it would seem that Sprimont himself found the answer to the competition. As though responding to the current advice 'If you can't beat it, join it', he produced increasing numbers of accurate copies of Meissen figures, groups and dishes. On many of them the anchor mark was drawn very small and concealed among flowers and

Left, Fig. 190: Jar and cover painted with flowers in colours. Marked with an anchor in red. Circa 1755. Height, 11 inches. (Stourhead, Wiltshire: The National Trust.) **Below,** *Fig. 191: Tureen and cover in the form of an eel, painted in natural colours. Marked with an anchor in red. Circa 1755. Width, 7½ inches. (Christie's.)*

foliage. It could be overlooked, and it is possible that much of the output was purchased by the public as genuine Meissen; a mistake easily made today by anyone not familiar with the differences between hard-paste and soft-paste.

Much of the ware made was for the table, and included tea and coffee services, ice pails, sauce boats, porringers and dishes of many shapes and sizes. Also for the table, were tureens modelled as birds, fishes, flowers, fruit and vegetables (Plate 29), of which the largest and most spectacular is that catalogued in 1755 as

A large and curious TUREEN, in the shape of a SWAN.

Two of these life-size pieces were disposed of in 1755 and two more in the following year. At the present day there are examples of them at the Victoria and Albert Museum, London, and the Cecil Higgins Art Gallery, Bedford.

Figures took many fanciful forms, among the most popular being characters from the Italian Comedy. The *Commedia dell'arte* appeared on the stages of all countries in the West during the 18th century, and the participants were universally known. Even today, although their origins are largely forgotten, the names and appearance of Harlequin, Columbine and Pierrot remain familiar, while the other dozen or so one-time favourites have faded almost into oblivion. All of them live on in engravings, and in the porcelain made at Chelsea and many other factories.

During the course of the red anchor period tin oxide ceased to be included in the ingredients for the glaze, and it became transparent. The standard of painting was high, colours were applied with taste as well as skill, and many of the models were exceedingly well designed. In their praise the late W. B. Honey wrote: 'The Chelsea porcelain figures of this period are by general consent among the finest ever made'.

Gold Anchor Period, circa 1758-69. The

longest-lasting period in the factory's history saw a number of important changes. The rococo fashion, beginning to wane rapidly in architecture, furniture and silver, reached its height in porcelain design. Figures and groups were raised upon bases moulded into scrolled shapes and bedecked

Fig. 192: Vase and cover painted with Les Amants Surpris *after François Boucher within gilt borders on a ground of 'mazarine-blue'. Marked with an anchor in brown, used occasionally during the Gold Anchor period. Circa 1760. Height, 23½ inches. (Sotheby's.)*

with flowers and leaves, and masses of shrubbery formed backgrounds for them. Bright gilding was much to the fore, and the ware itself was hidden beneath painted ornament.

Table wares were equally brightly painted, and the influence of the French royal factory, at Sevres, is to be seen in mazarine blue, claret and other coloured grounds. These were used also, and with considerable effect, on sets of vases which showed panels

Left, *Fig. 193: Figures of a shepherd and a shepherdess, each marked with an anchor in gold. Circa 1760. Height, 11¾ and 11¼ inches. (Fenton House, London: The National Trust.)* **Below,** *Fig. 194: Figure of a girl seated in a swing. 'Girl-in-a-swing' factory. Circa 1749-54. Height, 6¼ inches.*

Fig. 195: Europa and the Bull. 'Girl-in-a-swing' factory. Circa 1749-54. Height, 6¼ inches. (City Museum and Art Gallery, Plymouth.)

of carefully-painted subjects within areas of rich colour and burnished gold (Fig. 192).

The glaze continued to be clear and free from tin, but collected thickly round bases and is often found to be crazed. As had been done earlier at Bow, a new ingredient, bone-ash, was added to the clay mixture to improve its qualities.

The 'Girl-in-a-Swing' Factory, circa 1749-54.

Some decades ago the Victoria and Albert Museum acquired a white porcelain figure of a girl seated on a swing suspended between two leafy tree-trunks; the trunks had originally been topped with candle-holders and they have short hollow branches intended for holding metal mounts with porcelain flowers (Fig. 194). The figure can be dated by its style to about 1750, and an analysis of the porcelain body showed that it was similar in composition to that of Chelsea. Although it had this feature in common with triangle-marked pieces, the resemblance ended there; the modelling had several distinctive features not seen in other wares.

Subsequently other figures and groups have come to light and within the past few years a suggestion as to their origin has gained ground. It is based in a statement penned by Simeon Shaw, who wrote in 1829 that he had been told about half-a-dozen Staffordshire potters who came to work at Chelsea and then left in disgust. They were said to have given up their employment because they found that 'they were the principal workmen, on whose exertions all the excellence of the porcelain must depend'. Thereupon they set up for themselves in opposition to Sprimont. The advertisements published in 1749 and 1750 (see page 197) have been quoted as evidence of what took place when, apparently, Charles Gouyn seceded from the original firm and took charge of the new one.

It seems not improbable that the Staffordshire men were the makers of the eighty or so surviving examples of 'girl-in-a-swing' type, of which about one-third are painted. Their number has been swelled further by a theory that they initiated the manufacture of 'toys': small objects such as seals, patch-boxes and so forth (Plate 30). These had hitherto been accepted as the work of Sprimont's factory, but it is now suggested that when the second establishment failed, in about 1754, Sprimont bought their remaining stock of the trifles and then began to manufacture them himself. It may be mentioned that so far no tablewares with 'girl-in-a-swing' characteristics have been identified, and it is assumed at present that only ornaments and toys were made.

Bow

Plate 31 (Top) *Mug painted with the 'partridge' pattern after a Japanese original, height 4¾ inches;* (bottom) *octagonal plate and cup and saucer decorated in the Chinese 'famille rose' style. Circa 1755. Diameter of plate, 7⅜ inches.* (F. T. W. Collection.)

THE founder of the Bow porcelain factory was a versatile Irish artist, Thomas Frye, who was an accomplished painter, miniaturist and engraver. In partnership with a merchant from Bristol, Edward Heylyn, Frye took out a patent in December 1744. It was for

> A new method of Manufacturing a certain material whereby a ware might be made of the same nature or kind, and equal to, if not exceeding in goodness and beauty, China or Porcelain ware imported from abroad.

Frye and Heylyn proposed using for the purpose 'an earth, the produce of the Chirokee nation in America, called by the natives unaker'. It would seem that one or other of the men had arranged importation of the earth with a man named Andrew Duché, who visited England from Georgia in May 1743 and did not re-cross the Atlantic until about two years later. He is known to have attempted porcelain-making when in America, and is assumed to be the unnamed man referred to in a letter of May 1745. In it, the writer stated:

> He [*presumably Duché*] is gone for a cargo of it [*the clay: unaker*], having

bought the whole country of the Indians where it rises. They can import it for £13 per ton, and by that means afford their china as cheap as common stone ware.

The factory was established at Bow, but regrettably many of the vital documents which might help to locate the precise site are missing. The earliest relevant ones show that in 1744 Heylyn, together with a London linen-draper, George Arnold, bought some land which was on the west side of Bow bridge and in the county of Middlesex. There follows an unrecorded interval until 1749, when it is known that 'Alderman Arnold & Comp' were occupying premises across the bridge and in Essex. Strictly speaking, therefore, the factory was not in Bow at all, but in Stratford.

George Arnold, an Alderman of Cheap Ward in the City of London and President of St. Thomas's Hospital, died in June 1751, but prior to that date Frye had taken out another patent. This one specified the inclusion of bone-ash: burned animal bones which produced a white powder giving improved stability in the kiln. Heylyn almost vanished from record until he was

adjudged bankrupt in 1757, but it has been suggested that he established a rival concern, across the river and actually in Bow, which lasted from 1752 to 1756.

In 1753 a warehouse was opened in the City, in Cornhill, and one of the staff there, possibly manager, was John Bowcock. Some details of his life are known because of the fortunate preservation for a while of some of his note-books and some of the firm's account-books. Like the papers of John Dwight, mentioned earlier (page 84) they were in the possession of Lady Charlotte Schreiber, but most of them have since disappeared. Extracts from the missing books were printed in 1869, and one complete volume has subsequently come to light.

Left, *Fig. 197: Kitty Clive in the character of the 'Fine Lady' in David Garrick's farce* Lethe, *modelled after an engraving by Charles Mosley. Circa 1750. Height, 10 inches. (Royal Scottish Museum, Edinburgh.)* **Below,** *Fig. 198: Plate painted in underglaze blue with a Chinese pattern, and marked at the back with a painter's numerals 15. Circa 1755. Diameter, 9¼ inches.*

Bowcock began his career in the Navy, and while with the Bow concern made notes of daily affairs that give clues as to what was being ordered and supplied. His jottings include many references to John Weatherby and John Crowther, china dealers of St. Katherine's, in the City, who were associated with the Cornhill premises.

Early contemporary printed reports state that manufacture at Bow comprised 'large Quantities of Tea-Cups, Saucers &c. which by some skilful persons are said to be little inferior to those which are brought from China'. Just what they were like is difficult to judge because, unlike Chelsea, the factory did not use a mark. However, it is known that the building was named 'New Canton', perhaps because it set out from the start to emulate the goods sent westwards from that port, and some surviving articles are inscribed '*MADE AT NEW CANTON*' and dated 1750 and 1751.

The latter are small circular inkwells, probably presented to demonstrate the standard of workmanship that had been attained (Fig. 196). Some of them are painted in colours in an Oriental style which, perhaps oddly in view of the name given to the factory, is Japanese and not Chinese. Similar inkwells are painted in underglaze blue, but in the Chinese style.

Also of the same period are some uncoloured figures modelled from engravings, and a salt-cellar in the form of a shell with

Below, *Fig. 199: Cups painted with Chinese patterns in underglaze blue. Circa 1755. Height of tallest, 3 inches.* **Right,** *Fig. 200: Mug painted in underglaze blue. Circa 1755. Height, 5⅛ inches.*

a shell-encrusted base. All of them have 1750 incised beneath, and these, too, were doubtless prestige pieces. A small group of painted wares has been attributed to the years immediately prior to 1750. They have in common a greyish body, and the neatly-painted decoration is in imitation of contemporary Oriental work.

A series of newspaper advertisements tells a little of the progress of the manufactory, and indicates the types of ware in demand at various dates. In 1753 decorators were being sought eagerly, and the Midlands enamel-painters were appealed to through a notice in *Aris's Birmingham Gazette*, which ran:

> This is to give Notice to all Painters in the Blue and White Potting Way, and Enamellers on China-Ware, that by applying at the Counting House at the China-Works near Bow, they may meet with Employment, and proper Encouragement, according to their Merit;

likewise Painters brought up in the Snuff-Box Way, Japanning, Fan-painting, &c. may have Opportunities of Trial; wherein, if they succeed, they shall have due Encouragement.

Two years later, the Cornhill premises advertised

> The finest painted Blue in the Manner of that called the Nankeen, enamelled and burnt in to the finest old Japan and Chinese Patterns, so as not to be distinguished from the Manufactures of those Countries: Also Branches [*candelabra*] fitted up in the compleatest Manner with a large Variety of Figures. Knives and Forks of all Sorts, fitted up by the best Workmen, &c.

In April 1757 an auction sale, on the Chelsea model, took place, and included

Below, Fig. 201: Sauceboat with moulded and gilt decoration. Circa 1755. Height, 5½ inches. **Right,** *Fig. 202: Bowl inscribed and dated beneath the base:* JOHN & ANN, BOWCOCK, 1759. *Diameter, 8 inches. (British Museum.)*

blue and white as well as coloured wares. In the following year there were two such sales, of which the second specifies a greatly increased variety of goods.

To be Sold by Auction
By MR. LAMBE

At his House in Pall-Mall, St. James's on Monday the 10th of April 1758 and the five following Days (by order of the Proprietors of the Bow Manufactory of Porcelain). All the intire Stock of their Warehouse, on the Terrass in St. James's Street, they having intirely quitted the same; consisting of fine Epergnes, Chandeliers, Branches decorated with Flowers and Figures, fine Essence Pots, beautiful Groups and other figures of Birds, Beasts, Jars, Beakers, Bottles, &c. Service of Dishes and Plates, Sauceboats, Bowls, Compleat Tea and Coffee Equipages, a large Assortment of fine Enamel and fine Partridge Sets, which are most beautifully painted by several of the finest Masters from Dresden, made up in Lots proper for the Nobility and private Families. There is a large quantity of the Chelsea Manufactory among the Stock.

The final paragraph should be taken as a caution in accepting the articles described as all having had a Bow origin. A mixed stock held at the manufactory's own showroom may seem a little surprising, but it was normal practice throughout the 18th century. Wedgwood, who dealt exclusively in his own productions, was a notable exception, but even he supplied goods made by others. The difference was that he usually had them stamped with his name and they were disposed of as having been made by him.

A small number of inscribed and dated pieces of Bow have been recorded, the majority having been exhibited in a special display at the British Museum in 1959. Amongst them was the bowl, which belongs to the Museum, illustrated in Fig. 202. The outside is painted with shaped panels of Chinese scenes in blue and with a powdered-blue ground, while beneath the base is written *JOHN & ANN, BOWCOCK,* 1759. The significance of the date is undiscovered, nor is it known why the interior depicts Bowcock 'landing and sailors with staffs in their hands'.

In the same year Thomas Frye retired, his health requiring a year's recuperation in Wales prior to a return to London. He then re-commenced engraving and, so far as is known, severed all connection with china-making. Apart from his name having appeared as patentee at the start of activities, there is no knowledge of what role he played in the factory: whether he was responsible for shapes and patterns, and whether he actually did any of the modelling and ornamenting. After his death in 1762 it was said that he was 'the Inventor and first Manufacturer of Porcelain in England', and as the man who introduced the use of bone-ash he has earned an enduring fame.

In 1762 the death occurred of John Weatherby, and in the following year John Crowther was declared bankrupt. The former's widow instituted proceedings against Crowther for dishonesty during the partnership, but the upshot is unknown. He apparently carried on the factory himself after 1762, and there followed an auction of the contents of the Cornhill stock together with 'some of the finest of the said Porcelain, removed from the Manufactory at Bow near Stratford'. From about 1770 Crowther had a warehouse in St. Paul's Churchyard, and in 1775 or 1776 he disposed of the manufactory and its equipment to William Duesbury, owner of the Derby porcelain works.

John Crowther had been a member of the Skinners' Company since 1747 (he received

Below, *Fig. 203: Woman cook carrying a leg of mutton on a dish, and the companion man cook carrying a dish holding two trussed chickens. Circa 1755. Height, 6¾ inches.* **Right,** *Fig. 204: Pair of figures sometimes called 'dismal hounds'. Circa 1755. Height, 3½ inches. (Both Sotheby's.)*

his Freedom in 1748), and was Master in 1759. In 1774 he was awarded a pension of £10 a quarter, and at a later date went to live at Morden College, Blackheath, an almshouse for pensioned merchants, where he died sometime in 1790.

*　　*　　*

THE Bow manufactory would seem to have had a very large output. Sources for this statement are figures from the account-books, and the written statement of one of their painters, Thomas Craft. The books show that in the year 1755 a total quantity was sold amounting in value to over £10,000, which must represent a very large number of individual pieces at 18th century prices. In Bowcock's 1756 note-book there are records of typical charges:

    1 cook, 7s. (Fig. 203)
    1 pint printed mug (Fig. 208)
    1 sprig'd teapot, 4s. (Fig. 209)
    1 sprig'd upright teapot, 3s.
    1 enamelled pero [*pierrot*], 6s.
    1 pair sprig'd [*sauce-*] boats, 6s.

Craft's statement is with a bowl he decorated, now in the British Museum, and gives some details of the piece of china. He also noted that the Bow manufactory 'employed 300 persons; about 90 painters (of whom I was one), and about 200 turners; throwers, &c., were employed under one roof'.

Of surviving Bow porcelain the largest proportion is decorated in underglaze blue with Oriental patterns, many of which can be exactly matched with contemporary Chinese specimens. Much of it lacks careful finishing, and many of the plates show warping received when in the kiln. Additionally, plates show three marks round the rim where they rested on pegs in the sagger. Usually such marks are on the underside, but Bow laid their ware face-downwards and the scars are usually clearly visible amid the decoration.

The white porcelain made at Fukien (*blanc de chine*) was also copied, as was done at Chelsea and at more than one French factory (Fig. 209). Like the original Chinese ware, this was unpainted, and relied on reliefs of prunus blossom for ornament. Bowcock referred to it as 'sprig'd ware', in reference to the process by which the reliefs were applied (see **page 112**).

The earlier figures, dating from 1750, have been attributed to a single unnamed modeller who, because he executed a

series of distinctive figures of the Muses, is known as the 'Muses Modeller'. Some of his work is copied directly from Meissen examples, but much is original and based on engravings. The figure of Kitty Clive, the actress, was taken from a print published in 1750, and the companion, of Henry Woodward, from one of the same year (Fig. 197). All the 'Muses' series have their draperies boldly shaped to overcome the thick glaze, and their faces often show a decidedly vacant expression with protruding eye-balls and an open mouth. Most of the figures and groups were left unpainted, although many may once have been finished with unfired oil-colours.

Flat bases, sometimes square or oblong were usual up to about 1755, when they began to be ornamented with rococo scrollwork. This was gradually augmented until the model was raised on scrolled feet, often centred on a pierced shell-like motif. Colouring also increased in intensity as well as in complexity of pattern, and by 1760 an opaque light blue, a reddish-mauve and a strong yellow were liberally used. The popular bocage backgrounds are found less often than at Chelsea, but the exuberance of the Gold Anchor period was occasionally equalled. The brilliantly coloured figures in Fig. 207 vie with those made at the Thames-side factory, although a lack of 'movement' in the modelling is not disguised by the elaborate painting.

Printed decoration was used from as early as 1755, and it has been suggested that it was executed at the Battersea enamel works. As this establishment closed in 1756 and much of the surviving Bow ware has on it blue printing of about 1760, it would appear that by then they certainly did their own work. The tankard in Fig. 208, which is printed in dark lilac and has a painted brown rim, exhibits a heart-shaped terminal at the base of the handle. It is a noticeable feature on many Bow tankards or mugs, but was not exclusive to that factory and its appearance cannot be taken on its own as grounds for attribution.

Fire-cracks developed in the kiln are sometimes to be seen on Bow figures and groups. Their presence did not apparently affect the saleability of a piece, for such blemishes were disguised by painting over them a leaf or some other suitably-shaped ornament. A further feature, seen mostly on blue and white tablewares is brown staining at edges where glazing ends.

Fig. 206: Scaramouche and Isabella from the Italian Comedy.   Circa 1755. Height, 7¾ inches.   (Christie's.)

THE site of the Bow factory has twice been the subject of excavations, from which much has been learned about the different wares. In 1867 sewerage operations were being carried out on the premises of a match factory then standing there, and a large quantity of Bow material was revealed. Finds included broken saggers, lumps of clay and animal bones; perhaps the latter were for making bone-ash, but more probably this arrived ready made and the find was only a coincidence. Most of the many fragments of porcelain were unglazed but some were decorated and had not received a final firing. Moulds for sprigging were found, and a report printed two years later mentioned:

> Among other relics are pieces which have been injured in the kiln by falling into ugly and distorted shapes, plates and saucers that have inadvertently gone in contact with each other and could not be separated. . . . There are a large number of china biscuit knife-

handles, some plain, others with rococo scrolls in relief, heightened with blue. . . . There are two pug dogs nearly perfect, with collars, on which are roses. . . . The Bow paste is exceedingly hard, and the fracture very close and compact; consequently the pieces, as a rule, are very heavy for their size, but many of the cups and saucers are almost of egg-shell thickness. The colour is a milky white.

The second excavation took place in 1922, and unlike the first was not an accidental occurrence. Mr. A. J. Toppin, who conducted it, a keen collector and student of English porcelain, was unrivalled in his knowledge of many aspects of the subject. He found more of the types of ware that had been discovered earlier, including portions of figures identifiable with known specimens. There were also numbers of moulds made of lead and of fired pottery or porcelain; some for sprigging and others for parts of figures and dishes.

Early examples of Bow decorated in underglaze blue sometimes bear numerals put on them by the painter, but no proper works mark was used. Imitation Chinese characters occasionally appear on plates, and a blue crescent or a red anchor beside a dagger were used on figures after about 1760. The last-named is thought to be the mark of a painter working outside the factory who bought the pieces uncoloured.

Fig. 209: Teapot and cover with 'sprigged' prunus ornament copying Chinese Fukien porcelain. Circa 1755. Height, 4½ inches. (F. T. W. Collection.)

15 Derby

Below, Fig. 210: Sauceboat in the shape
of a shell, the base of rock and shells and
the handle with a crayfish and pieces of
coral. Circa 1750. Length, 6¾ inches.
(Saltram, Devon: The National Trust.)

IT is thought probable that the Derby
porcelain factory owes its origin to a
French refugee named Andrew Planché,
who is known to have been living there in
1751 and probably earlier. A statement
made in the 19th century related that

About 1745 a man, said to be a foreigner
in very poor circumstances, living in
Lodge Lane, made small articles in
china, such as birds, cats, dogs, sheep,
and other small ornamental toys, which
he fired at a kiln in the neighbourhood
belonging to a pipe-maker named Woodward.

According to the same informant, the foreigner was approached by William Duesbury, a man who was at that time working in London as an enameller of ware bought undecorated from various factories. There is, however, a record of a document having been drawn up some years later, in 1756, but apparently never signed, in which Planché and Duesbury were allied with a local banker, John Heath, who was already a partner in the earthenware manufactory at Cockpit Hill, Derby (see page 168). It has been assumed that Planché quickly faded from the scene, and Duesbury took charge of the manufactory with financial assistance from Heath.

The earliest known Derby pieces are three small jugs incised variously *D*, *D1750* and *Derby*. Opinion about these specimens is non-committal, but is agreed that they show little or no resemblance to anything else made there. However, proof of activity is to be seen in the surviving note-book of Duesbury, in which he listed the work he carried out between 1751 and 1753. Among the numerous entries are

1 pair of Dansars, Darbey Figars
3 pr. of Darbishire sesons
1 pr. of Larg Darbey figars.

Although the spelling is a trifle unorthodox, the meaning is plain.

A number of obviously early wares have been grouped together because of features they share, and are attributed to Derby. All are well modelled, and they include a

Below, *Fig. 211: Basket painted in underglaze blue.* Circa 1760. *Width, 9½ inches. (F. T. W. Collection.)* **Right, Plate 33:** *Man playing a flute.* Circa 1755. *Height, 5½ inches. (F. T. W. Collection.)*

Plate 34 *Bagpiper with a dog.* Circa *1760. Height, 11¾ inches.* (*County Museum, Truro.*)

Fig. 212: Mug painted in underglaze blue. Circa 1765. Height, 4 inches.

set of five groups representing the Senses: sight, hearing, smell, taste and touch, depicted by quasi-Chinese men, women and children. A version of the figure of Kitty Clive was probably moulded from the Bow model (see Fig. 197), as it is smaller in size than the original; a result of shrinkage while in the kiln. Others of the pieces were copies of Meissen, and a pair of life-like boars have become sufficiently well-known and valuable to have received the attention of a maker of fakes within the present decade.

The wares survive undecorated, and with simple but attractive painting in which a strong iron-red is contrasted effectively with other colours in pale shades. The glaze is thick and glass-like with a tendency to gather in places at the base of a piece and make it stand unsteadily. Where this has occurred it has been necessary to grind the surplus away, but the defect was

Above left, *Fig. 213: Vase painted in colours with birds. Circa 1760. Height, 5 inches. (County Museum, Truro.)* **Above,** *Fig. 214: Candelabrum modelled with children and a dog beside a tree on which sits a bird. Circa 1755. Height, 10 inches. (Museum and Art Gallery, Derby.)* **Right,** *Fig. 215: Figures of a boy and girl holding flowers; models made also at Longton Hall. Circa 1760. Height, 11½ inches. (Stourhead House, Wiltshire: The National Trust.)*

usually avoided by wiping round the lower edge. This resulted in a glaze-free area, the so-called 'dry edge', which is one of the hall-marks of the pieces. The other characteristic is a funnel-shaped hole beneath the base; a hole that looks as if it had been made by a large-sized screw. It is not, however, confined to any one factory and some of the earlier Bow figures have a similarly shaped orifice.

A later series of Senses shows men and women in contemporary costume, and two sets of Seasons have been recorded. There are also figures of classical gods and goddesses, and some Paris street-traders copied from Meissen originals. Most of these are on scrolled bases in contrast to the earlier plain ones, but colouring, when present, is not dissimilar (Plate 33).

The first effect of Duesbury's management would seem to be an advertisement which appeared in mid-1756:

Richmond Wells in Surrey.
On Monday next there will be a Ball at the large Assembly-Rooms. It being the full of the Moon, there are expected many Persons of Quality and Distinction: and as it is thought this Assembly will be very numerous and brilliant, the Doors will be open'd at Five O'clock. To be sold by Hand at the said Rooms a large Quantity of China . . . the greatest variety of the Derby Porcelain, in Figures, Jars, Candlesticks; Sauce-Boats, Fruit-Baskets, Lettices, Leaves, Roses, and several curious Pieces for Desserts, finely enamelled in Dresden Flowers, reckoned by Judges who have

been Purchasers, to excel, if not exceed, any Thing of the kind in England.

Later in the same year came an announcement in the *Public Advertiser* of an auction-sale 'By order of the Proprietors of the Derby Porcelain Manufactory', which included

A Curious Collection of fine Figures, Jars, Sauceboats, Services for Deserts, and great Variety of other useful and ornamental Porcelain, after the finest Dresden models, all exquisitely painted in Enamel, with Flowers, Insects, India Plants, &c.

A year later the same newspaper printed a paragraph regarding an auction then being held near Whitehall, where

There were Numbers of Quality and the Gentry, who expressed great satisfaction at seeing . . . the great Variety of the English China Manufactories; and admired at the great Perfection the Derby Figures in particular, are arrived to, that many good Judges could not distinguish them from the real Dresden.

Advertisements of the auction stressed the likeness to Meissen with references to 'Derby or Second Dresden', which underlines the hold on the market of the foreign porcelain. Although in some instances examples of Chelsea come so close to Meissen as to cause confusion, the same cannot be said for Derby. Presumably the publicity was aimed at the less discerning members of the buying-public, who could not afford to purchase the better quality, but more costly, imported product.

Some further evidence of what was being made in the early 1760's was given by Llewellynn Jewitt, who stated that

> in 1763, in an account of 'goods sent to London', not less than forty-two large boxes appear at one time to have been despatched to the metropolis, and the proceeds, I presume, of the sale of a part of them, on the 2nd of May, in that year, amounted to no less a sum than £666 17 6d.

The wares included several patterns of sauce-boats, plates, vases, figures of Shakespeare and Milton, cats, coffee pots, 'blue guglets [*small jugs*] and basins to ditto', butter tubs, teapots, figures of Mars and Minerva, sets of the Elements, Neptune, the Muses, and what are described as 'Chelsea jars' and 'Chelsea-pattern candlesticks'.

None of these pieces bear a factory mark, but all have in common the well-known 'patch' marks under the base. They resulted from their having stood upon circular pads of clay when in the kiln, and the finished articles, almost without exception, show three roughly circular patches (Fig. 216). While these marks are obvious beneath the bases of figures, other wares do not exhibit them so noticeably. However, although they occur with such frequency on Derby, similar markings are occasionally seen on the products of other factories so attributions must be verified by further indications.

On figures it will be found that cheeks are usually painted to give a 'rouged' look, and there is frequent use of an opaque turquoise-blue with a tendency to acquire a brown stain. The modelling is usually stiff, and in conjunction with the colouring gives many of the figures the appearance of dolls. This is not always unattractive in its own right, but is far from confirming the claim of the makers 'to excel, if not exceed, any Thing of the kind in England'.

The foregoing pieces, in particular the figures, were at one time attributed unhesitatingly to Chelsea, and it was not until the late twenties of the present century that their correct origin was determined. Having accepted them as Chelsea for so long, collectors were reluctant to down-grade their possessions and it was many years before they were described universally as Derby.

Duesbury completed his purchase of the Chelsea establishment in February 1770. Some of the Chelsea workers were then sent up to Derby, while production on a small scale continued at Chelsea. A little information about the latter can be gleaned

Below, Fig. 218: Candlesticks modelled with a man playing bagpipes and a woman playing a mandoline. Circa 1765. Height, 9 inches. (Saltram, Devon: The National Trust.)

Below, *Fig. 219: John Wilkes (1717-97), a cupid at his feet holding the Cap of Liberty. Circa 1780. Height, 11½ inches.*

Right, *Fig. 220: Biscuit group of two cupids. Incised numerals 48, listed as 'Elements in two Groups'. Late 18th century. Height, 9 inches. (Museum and Art Gallery, Derby.)*

from the reports sent to Duesbury each week, of which the following extract is typical:

> Work done this Week (May 12 to 19, 1770) at Chelsea.
> Reparing 4 figures in Clay to go to Darby. Making 1 Ornament Beaker. Dry rubbing the 2 Large Jarrs, helping at the Kiln, &cc. Making Jarr for Perfumes on 4 feet. Mending the 2 Large Quarters of the World, and helping at the Kiln, &cc. Roberts at Case making, and working in the Kiln, &cc. Piggot working in the Mill and helping at the Kiln, &cc. Inglefield Cutting Wood, Case [*sagger*] making, and helping at the Kiln.

Other lists refer to decorating, and include:

Seals, 3 dozen Bull finches ..	3. 6d.
2 dozen of parrots	2. 4d.
3 Hart Shape Perfume Potts, with handles	3. 9d.
1 dozen and 6 Chinease Men a smoking	1. 9d.
Seals, 3 dozen Arliquens	2. 4d.
30 Seals painted in Mottowes, by Boarman and Wollams ..	3. 1½d.
34 Figure Seals, painted by Jinks, at 2d. each	5. 8d.
Modling of a Pedestol .. ..14. 0d.
21 Snuff boxes of Cupid and Lamp	1 4. 6d.
Seals made overtime, 6 Cocks	7d.

There is also a record of 'fine Clay' and bone-ash being sent to Derby, but at about the same time 100 loads of wood for the kiln were bought for £38. 15s.

Finally, on December 11th, 12th and 13th, 1783, James Christie held a sale of the stock and fixture 'on the premises', the sum realised being £686. Two months later Robert Boyer, one of the painters wrote to Duesbury at Derby, and began his letter with the words:

Left, *Fig. 221: Vase and cover and two cups and saucers painted with panels in colour reserved on coloured and gilt grounds. The marine scenes probably painted by George Robertson, and the butterflies by William Dexter. Late 18th century. Height of vase, 9 inches.*

Below, *Fig. 222: Set of four figures representing The Continents, the bases inscribed* (left to right): AFRICA, EUROPE, AMARICA (sic), *and* ASIA. *Late 18th century. Height, 8½ and 8¾ inches. (Sotheby's.)*

Sir, -I Wright to Inform yow how we are pretty forward in the pulling Down of the buildings at Chelsea. I think a little better than a fortnight they will be all down to the ground and Cleared of the premises, wich I shall be glad to my hart, for I am tired of it.

Earlier, in 1771, James Christie held 'the First Public Sale of the Chelsea and Derby Manufactories', and the catalogue marks the first appearance of a type of ware new in England. This was the so-called 'biscuit': porcelain without glaze or painting, which had been made at Sèvres twenty years earlier.

As the articles were completely unadorned by anything to conceal blemishes they had to be modelled and finished with great care. Biscuit figures were sold at slightly higher prices then their coloured and glazed duplicates, and as an example the well-known Shakespeare, from Scheemakers' statue in Westminster Abbey, cost 25s. enamelled and gilt, and 31s. 6d. in biscuit (Fig. 217).

With increasing output it became essential to have a London retail outlet, and in 1773 premises were acquired in Bedford Street, off the Strand. From there was issued a

> List of the principal additions made this year to the new invented Groups, Jars, Vases, Urns, Beakers, Cups, Chalices, &., of Mr. Duesbury's Derby and Chelsea Manufactory of Porcelaines, Biscuits, and China Ware, both Ornamental and Useful.

This did not conflict with the holding of periodic auctions, and these lengthy dispersals continued to take place under the direction of 'The Specious Orator', James Christie.

THE names of three modellers of the period are known: John James Spängler, Pierre Stephan and William Coffee. The first-named was son of the director of the Zurich porcelain factory in Switzerland, and worked at Derby from at the latest 1790. Stephan was at Derby from 1770, and Coffee was there in 1794. All three men, like many others connected with ceramics, were somewhat restless and moved from place to place usually with only short stays at each. There has been argument as to which particular figures and groups they designed, and some attributed to them are no more than adaptations from Continental models. One of Coffee's best-known figures, a shepherd, is stated to have been copied from an antique bronze of Adonis which was made to look the part by the addition of some clothing.

The painters working at Derby in the last quarter of the 18th century are known by name, although much of the work attributed to them is based on tradition: rarely a reliable guide. Information is given in some surviving fragments of pattern-books, which record details of shape and colour and often name the artist responsible. These men, however, came and went and very rarely had a recognisable individual style, so that even this apparently-authoritative source has to be treated with reserve. Many of the painters were versatile artists, and while specialising in, say, human figures, could equally well take a turn at landscapes, flowers or birds.

The pattern-books depict cups, saucers and plates, which were frequently the subject of elaborate and carefully-painted decoration of high quality. Gilding was used effectively, applied thickly and burnished. In the majority of instances such articles were not intended for use, but for display in a cabinet. Although entire services were made, most of the output of this nature took the form of specimen cups and saucers and plates, singly or in pairs or, occasionally, tea-sets for one or two persons. These were complete with a matching tray and have become known as carbarets; a name that was not applied to them until some time in the 19th century.

It was with some of these wares in mind

that Samuel Johnson wrote to Mrs. Thrale
on 20th September 1777:

> I took Boswel yesterday to see Keddle-
> ston, and the silk mils, and china work
> at Derby, he was pleased with all.
> The Derby China is very pretty, but I
> think the gilding is all superficial, and
> the finer pieces are so dear, that perhaps
> silver vessels of the same capacity may
> be sometimes bought at the same price...

Of the many painters employed, the most
renowned is William Billingsley, who was
born in Derby and served his apprenticeship
at the works from 1774. He remained there
until 1796, and developed a style of flower-
painting that has become almost legendary.
When he left the factory his work had
become sufficiently esteemed for Duesbury's
London agent to write:

*Fig. 223: (Left) cup and saucer painted
with powder-blue and gilt designs, the cup
with naval and other trophies in colours,
and the dates* August 1st. 2d. 3d. 1798
*in commemoration of the Battle of the
Nile; (right) cup and saucer painted in
green and gilt, the cup with a marine
scene probably painted by George
Robertson. (Christie's.)*

... his going into another factory will put them into the way of doing flowers in the same way, which they are at present ignorant of.

The range of productions was very wide and can be judged from the summary printed on the cover of the catalogue of the 1783 auction-sale. It took place during six days in May, and comprised:

An Elegant and Extensive Assortment of Derby and Chelsea Porcelane, consisting of a great Variety of Table and Desert Services, Tea, Coffee and Chocolate Equipages, Caudle and Cabinet Cups and Stands; Dejeunes, &c. of the most beautiful Séve and other Patterns, richly finished with the fine Mazarine and Ultramarine Blue and Gold; also a beautiful Assortment of superb Ornaments for Chimney Pieces, Toilets, &c. in Vases, Urns, and Tripods, elegantly painted with Figures, and embellished with chased and burnished Gold; Groups, and single Figures in Biscuit, &c. accurately model'd.

Fig. 224: Vase painted with an illustration to James Thomson's poem The Seasons *on a ground of gilt stripes. Marked with a D below a crown in gold on top of the plinth. Circa 1785. Height, 10 inches. (Victoria and Albert Museum.)*

John Heath became bankrupt in 1779, and William Duesbury was then sole owner of the concern until he died in 1786. His son, of the same name, carried it on until 1795, when he took as partner an Irish miniaturist, Michael Kean. The partnership did not endure for long, because a year or so later the younger William Duesbury died, but Kean married his widow and the firm continued in existence under the style of Duesbury and Kean.

A variety of marks was used by the Duesburys. The Chelsea anchor in red, brown and gold is found on some pieces dating from after the purchase of that factory in 1770 and perhaps up to as late as 1780. A crown over a script 'D' in blue, green, puce or gold was used from about 1770 to 1782. The more familiar crown, crossed batons with dots and a script 'D' occurs painted in puce, blue and black between 1782 and 1800, and is often accompanied by a pattern number. Figures made after 1770 usually have an incised script 'N' or 'No' followed by numerals denoting the model, some of which can be checked in a list first printed in John Haslem's *The Old Derby China Factory*, published in 1876.

The men who assembled figures from the moulded pieces, known as 'repairers', sometimes incised their symbols under the bases. The most prolific in this respect were Isaac Farnsworth who used a roughly-drawn star, and Joseph Hill who cut a small triangle. This latter must not be confused with the mark of the same form appearing on early Chelsea.

16 Lund's Bristol & Worcester

As he proceeded on one of his tours of England, Dr. Richard Pococke noted while in Bristol in 1750:

> I went to see a manufacture lately established here, by one of the principal of the manufacture at Limehouse which failed. It is at a glass house, and is called Lowris (?) china house. They have two sorts of ware, one called stone china, which has a yellow cast, both in the ware and the glazing, that I suppose is made of pipe clay and calcined flint. The other they call old china; this is whiter, and I suppose this is made of calcined flint and the soapy rock

Fig. 225: A West Prospect of the Worcester Porcelain Manufactory, *after an engraving by Robert Hancock, 1757.*

Left, *Fig. 226: Advertisement from the* London General Evening Post, *August, 1755.* **Foot of page,** *Fig. 227: Pair of sauceboats painted in colours. Circa 1750-55. Length of each, 6½ inches. (Stourhead, Wiltshire: The National Trust.)*

at Lizard Point, which 'tis known they use. This is painted blue, and some is white, like the china of a yellowish cast; another kind is white with a blueish cast, and both are called fine ornamental white china. They make very beautiful white sauce boats, adorned with reliefs of festoons, which sell for sixteen shillings a pair.

The foregoing lengthy extract from the observations of a reliable witness calls for comment, as much has come to light at later dates to prove its accuracy. In the first place, advertisements have been reprinted, the first dated 1st January 1747, announcing that

The Proprietors of the Limehouse Ware give Notice, that they now have a large Assortment at their Manufactory, near Dick Shore in Limehouse.

Further announcements mention 'The new-invented blue-and-white Limehouse Ware', and 'Limehouse Ware Tea-Pots, sauceboats and Potting-Pots' of various sizes. The venture did not last long, for in June 1748, 18 months after its brave start, a meeting of creditors was held and the establishment closed. Records of the stay at Limehouse of several potters have been located, and the most probable of them to have been concerned in this establishment

252

Right, *Fig. 228: Mug with coloured decoration.* Circa 1750-55. *Height, 2⅝ inches. (F. T. W. Collection.)*

would seem to be William Ball, who paid rates for premises very close to Dick (or Duke) Shore at the relevant date. It is possible that he is the man of the same name who was later concerned in a porcelain factory in Liverpool. In spite of the finding of these tantalising details, it is unfortunate that to date not a single piece of chinaware can be attributed to Limehouse.

The editor of the Pococke papers, which are in the British Museum, was himself unsure of his reading of the words 'Lowris china house' and appended a question mark to them. It is now known that what was written was 'Lowdn's china house': a reference to premises in Redcliff Street formerly occupied by William Lowdin, a glass-maker, the word 'china' having been substituted by a later hand over the original writer's 'glass'. The premises were put up for sale in 1745, and later became the property of a local copper and brass merchant, Benjamin Lund, and a banker, William Miller. Lund also acquired, in 1748 (1749 by the modern calendar), a licence to take soapstone, named by Dr. Pococke 'soapy rock', from near the Lizard, Cornwall.

Soapstone or steatite is aptly named because of its 'soapy' feel and softness. It had perhaps been employed at an earlier date for porcelain-making by the Chinese,

and it has been suggested that William Cookworthy, who later founded the Plymouth manufactory, was responsible for its discovery and use in this country. By 1749, following the acquisition of a regular supply of soapstone, the Bristol proprietors would seem to have started operations, and in the year following they inserted in a Bristol newspaper an advertisement for apprentices. They would, it stated:

> learn the Art of Pottery, as practised in Staffordshire, and . . . may be learned to draw and paint by Persons appointed for that purpose, that they may be qualified to paint the said Ware, either in the India or Roman taste, whereby they may acquire a genteel Subsistance.

By 1751 the china was being sold either at the factory or from a warehouse on Castle Green, but during the year an announcement was made that it was obtainable solely at the latter address:

> For the future no Ware will be Sold at the Place where it is Manufactured; nor will any Person be admitted there without Leave from the Proprietors.

It is now known that the reason for this sudden secrecy was that negotiations were in progress to dispose of the concern to a company in Worcester.

A number of sauce and cream boats are known with the words *BRISTOL* or

BRISTOLL in raised letters beneath the base, and these certainly came from Lund's factory. In addition, a few examples of the figure of a Chinese god, probably moulded direct from an Oriental one, bear similar marks plus the date 1750 at the backs of their bases and came from the same source.

The dozen or so marked boats that have been recorded are mostly of long and shallow shape with prominent lips, shaped rims, and handles with forward-curving thumb-pieces. The majority of them are painted with Chinese scenes in underglaze blue varying in tint from dark to greyish, while others have polychrome decoration of similar design. Related to the marked examples are a quantity of unmarked ones, which show similar characteristics of shape and colouring as well as of body and glaze. All of them are notable for neat potting, a bluish or greyish glaze and careful painting with a fine brush.

In years past all ware of this type was named 'Lowdin's Bristol', to distinguish it from the Cookworthy hard-paste Bristol of 1770-81. Nowadays it is usually referred to as Lund's Bristol; admittedly a trifling point, but mentioned here because readers of older books on the subject may be confused on finding only the now out-dated name and may not realise that Lowdin and Lund mean one and the same.

* * *

FROM surviving documents it appears that sixteen men, all from Worcester except Edward Cave who printed the London *Gentleman's Magazine*, became proprietors of the licence to quarry soapstone at the Lizard by purchasing it from Benjamin Lund. The business was conducted on their behalf by a Worcester glover,

Plate 35 *Two cups and a jug painted with Chinese subjects. Circa 1750-55. Heights, 2 $\frac{1}{16}$ and 3$\frac{1}{2}$ inches. (F. T. W. Collection.)*

Plate 36 *Two butter- or sauce-boats. Circa 1750-55. Lengths, 6 and 4$\frac{1}{4}$ inches. (County Museum, Truro.)*

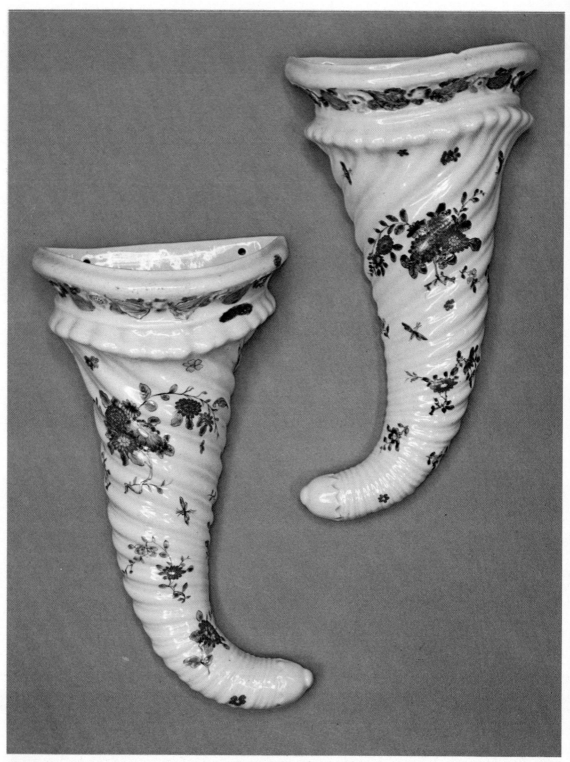

Plate 37 *Pair of wall vases in the form of cornucopias. Circa 1750-55. Length, 10 inches. (City Museum and Art Gallery, Plymouth.)*

Richard Holdship junior, who was, like Lund, a Quaker. The deal was concluded by the two men on 6th February 1752, and on the 21st of the same month the Bristol concern was bought as it stood; 'the stock, utensils and effects and the process of manufacture of the said Bristol Manufactory' and Lund and Miller were restrained from continuing it. Then, on 25th March 1752, Holdship transferred his purchases to his brother, Josiah, who was acting for his fellow-partners in the Worcester venture.

The original partnership had been formed in the previous year, had acquired premises at Warmstry House, on the Severn, and was named the 'Worcester Tonquin Manufacture': perhaps for the same reason as Bow called itself 'New Canton', i.e. because it set out to emulate the Chinese. In both instances the pseudo-Oriental names soon fell into disuse, although rivalry with the Far East was continued.

As the moulds had been included in the purchase, it is not unexpected to find that many of the Bristol articles continued to be made in the Midlands. In addition, Benjamin Lund went to live in Worcester, and it is probable that he did so in connection with the factory, where he would have exerted an influence on production. Thus it cannot be a surprise that Bristol and early Worcester wares are so similar that it is often difficult to decide their origin. Usually they are claimed for Bristol, and much more is labelled with the name of that factory than could possibly have been produced during its short life.

A smokiness often seen on what are probably Bristol pieces would seem to have been rectified following the transfer to Worcester, and the wares were, from then onwards, of a consistently good quality. A feature that appeared with increasing regularity as the years continued was the so-called 'glaze-shrinkage': an apparent pulling away of the glaze from the foot-rims of cups, saucers, dishes and other

Fig. 230: Front view of a tankard printed in black with birds in trees and in flight. Circa 1760. Height, 4 inches. (Bearne's, Torquay.)

pieces. In fact, it has been pointed out that no shrinkage is involved, and that in order to prevent the glaze collecting in the angle between foot and base it was carefully scraped away by a workman before firing. As the glaze melted it tended to flow a little, and this results in an appearance akin to shrinking.

As before, much of the decoration was in underglaze blue, but a proportion was coloured. The same neatness of workmanship is to be seen, and the 'cleanness' of finish is outstanding against most other English porcelain of the time. According to one of the partners its price was competitive, for in August 1752 the *Gentleman's Magazine* printed a woodcut view of the manufactory and against it were appended the words:

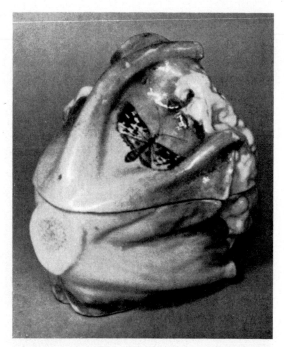

A sale of this manufacture will begin at the Worcester music meeting, on Sept. 20, with great variety of ware, and, 'tis said, at a moderate price.

Three years later it is known that teapots 'round, fluted, panelled and octagonal' cost 15s. to 30s.; chamber pots 4s.; tart and potting pans, in three sizes, 24s. to 28s.; scallop shells, four sizes, 14s. to 27s.; and high-footed sauce-boats, three sizes, 14s. to 27s. All prices were 'per dozen', wholesale, and subject to 15% for prompt payment; the latter reflecting on the tardy business habits of china-dealers at the time.

The first recorded auction of Worcester china took place in 1755, when the advertisement reproduced in Fig. 226 appeared in the London *General Evening Post* during August and September. The wording of the later announcements was varied somewhat: the date of sale was to be 8-10 October, and a footnote explained

> N.B. The above was the Sale advertised for the 17th, 18th and 19th of September, but was postponed on account of the large Quantity of Goods which could not be got ready so soon.

Above left, Fig. 231: Tureen and cover in the form of a cauliflower, coloured naturally and with butterflies printed in black. Circa 1760. Length, 4⅛ inches. (City Museum and Art Gallery, Plymouth.) **Above,** *Fig. 232: Tankard printed in black with the King of Prussia and a group of military trophies, the engraving dated 1757. Height, 4⅝ inches.* **Right,** *Fig. 233: Tankard printed in black with three masons and emblems of Freemasonry, engraved by James Ross who became assistant to Robert Hancock in 1765. Height, 5⅞ inches. (F. T. W. Collection.)*

Further, the sale was to be of 'about 300 Lots of Worcester China-Ware, lotted for Traders'. The result of the auction is unrecorded.

From the year 1757 are dated the first successful appearances of a new decorating process: transfer-printing. As with so many other innovations there is argument as to where and when it was introduced. After having for long been thought to have originated at the Battersea enamel works, just outside London, it is now known to have been employed by the Birmingham enamellers in or about 1750. Battersea certainly did make use of it on enamel, and the fact that the auction-sale of the stock-

in-trade, following the bankruptcy there in 1756, included 'stone plates' (salt-glazed stoneware) is significant. If pottery was stocked for transfer-printing then it is not improbable that porcelain may have been decorated in the same manner.

The first application of the process was claimed by two Liverpool men, John Sadler and Guy Green, who stated that on 17th July 1756 they had printed 1,200 pottery tiles in the space of six hours, and that they had spent seven years in developing the method. In spite of a sworn declaration to the effect the claim is not now accepted as valid, but Sadler and Green set up a factory where printing was carried out principally on pottery.

Transfer-printing is so simple that one might imagine it scarcely needed inventing. All it requires is that an engraved copper-plate should be printed with special ink onto a thin paper, the latter is then placed on the article to be decorated and by gentle rubbing the printed impression is transferred. The specially-compounded ink fixes in the heat of the kiln in the same manner as enamel, and being applied over the glaze does not need a very great heat. The thin paper is necessary so that a curved object can be decorated as easily as a flat one. An advance in the process was achieved within a few years, in about 1760, when the Worcester decorators were able to print in blue under the glaze. It required the plates to be engraved more deeply, so that the lines held more ink and

Right, *Fig. 238: Pseudo-Chinese mark on the back of a plate painted in underglaze blue. (J. W. Jenkins Collection.)*

showed satisfactorily through the coating of glaze.

At one time it was thought that some rather blurred small prints of squirrels, men o' war and other subjects, often found on the sides of sauce boats, were the first experimental uses of the process at Worcester. Now it is concluded that the fuzziness of line is not due to inexperience but to the use of worn plates, and the results are later in date than their appearance suggests. The first positively datable print is one of the King of Prussia, which usually adorns tankards and is dated 1757 (Fig. 232).

The King of Prussia and two variations of the design were engraved by Robert Hancock, who was born in the Midlands in about 1731 and apprenticed to a Birmingham engraver in 1746. He is supposed to have worked at the York House, Battersea, enamel works, and to have gone to work and reside in Worcester in about 1756. Certainly he was established there by the year following, and from then until 1775, when he had a disagreement and sold the share in the concern he had only recently acquired, he produced a large number of engravings. These not only proved his mastery of the process and the effects that could be achieved by its application, but have evinced considerable interest among modern collectors.

A study of Hancock's work has resulted in the publication of two books listing between them 180 different designs which he engraved, and the catalogue is probably by no means complete. Most of them were copied or adapted from the work of French and English artists of the time, and many of his engravings were printed in illustrated books, compiled for potential artists to copy, published between 1760 and 1798. Thus, artistic originality cannot be claimed for his output, but he did master the particular problems of transfer work with conspicuous success, and his prints on 18th century Worcester have a charm that elevates them far above the dully mechanical into which the process later sank.

The King of Prussia tankards were apparently ready for sale in December 1757, for some verses by a pseudonymous contributor to the *Gentleman's Magazine* were printed in that month's issue. As the print was signed with the initials *R. H.* the writer had credited it to Richard Holdship, and two lines from his poem were:

What praise, ingenious Holdship! is
    thy due,
Who first on porcelain the fair
    portrait drew!

This was countered soon by an equally anonymous correspondent to *Berrow's Worcester Journal*, who wrote:

Hancock, my friend, don't grieve, tho
    Holdship has the praise
'Tis yours to execute, 'tis his to wear the
    bays.

After leaving Worcester, Hancock lived successively in the Midlands, London and Bristol. He drew portraits, engraved trade cards, book illustrations and maps; of the latter, Worcester in 1764, Birmingham in 1785 and Bath in 1793 are known, but more

may be undiscovered. He died in Bristol in 1817 at the age of 87.

In addition to printed work, which was executed in black, lilac, brick-red or blue, and underglaze blue painting in the Oriental style, a proportion of the output was decorated in a full range of colours. Some of this followed Chinese and Japanese models, but much of it imitated Meissen where European shapes and subjects largely originated at the time. Flowers were painted profusely and skilfully, and native as well as exotic birds reflected a current taste for woodlands and aviaries. The recent discovery of a small-sized mug painted with a bird and inscribed '*I. Rogers Pinxit* 1757' has led to the attribution to this man of much else with more or less similar decoration.

The company had by 1755 already acquired an outlet in London, at London House, Aldersgate, a large mansion, which was a former home of the Bishops of London. Three years later the china-trade was informed in *Aris's Birmingham Gazette*

Above, *Fig. 239: Cups and saucers and a teapot and cover with printed decoration in underglaze blue. Circa 1770. (J. W. Jenkins Collection.)*

Fig. 240: Jug with moulded ornament, the decoration painted in colours. Circa 1760. Height, 8 inches.

That all Dealers may be supplied with Worcester Porcelain, in Variety of assortments, at the Warehouse, in Aldersgate-Street, London; and at the Manufactory in the city of Worcester. On the whole, however, the factory appears to have flourished without recourse to advertising, and was probably able to rely on sales promoted by the dependable standard of quality of the output. Compared with that of other English factories it was remarkably consistent, and its strength in use was an important point in its favour.

Although, as has been mentioned, underglaze blue printing would seem to have been introduced in about 1760, painting by hand continued to be done. The London *General Evening Post* on 12th December 1761 printed an advertisement reading:

> Worcester Porcelain Manufacture.
> Wanted,
> Painters in Blue and White: Good Workmen, who are sober and diligent, will meet with proper encouragement, by applying to the Manufactory in Worcester.

As competent painters were always scarce, there was possibly a purpose behind the notice and it was aimed at a particular target. This may have been the Bow factory, which had a large production of blue and white, and was at about that date quite possibly running into difficulties. The manager, John Crowther, was adjudged bankrupt in 1763, and in the previous year a news paragraph referred to the fact that 'the china-works at Bow overflowed' through the river Lea being in flood. The latter event has been suggested as a contributory cause to the bankruptcy, which it may well have been, but the main reason for it was perhaps of longer standing.

17 Worcester

IN 1763 an anonymous contributor to the *Gentleman's Magazine* wrote at some length on the various types of pottery and porcelain then available. He enumerated their advantages and disadvantages, and stated:

> We have, indeed, here, many other manufactories of porcelain which are sold at a cheaper rate than any that is imported; but, except the Worcester, they all wear brown, and are subject to crack, especially the glazing, by boiling water: The Worcester has a good body, scarce inferior to that of Eastern China, it is equally tough, and its glazing never cracks or scales off.

Below, *Fig. 241: Cup and saucer painted in colours with 'Watteau' figures within pink scale borders.* Circa 1765.
(Sotheby's.)

The writer pointed out that although the Worcester makers supplied all that was needed for the tea table, little or no provision was made for the dinner table except by way of small 'toys for pickles, and *hors d'ouvres*' (*sic*) and sauce boats. It was not for a further quarter century or so that dinner services began to be made, but by early in the 1760's the existing range of wares began to be made much more brilliant in appearance.

As with the figures produced at Chelsea,

Bow and elsewhere, Meissen was the dominant influence. The use of bouquets of naturally-coloured flowers painted on porcelain spread from there to both East and West, and it was the coloured grounds on vases and other pieces that inspired the Worcester firm.

The best-known of all, the 'scale' grounds were used at Worcester by 1761, for there is a pink-scale cream jug dated that year in the Works museum. In addition to pink, a yellow scale was occasionally employed and, the most popular of all, a blue scale. All were used to frame shaped panels in which were painted a variety of subjects including flowers, butterflies, figures and exotic birds.

Similar use of plain colours, as opposed to the scale effect, in emulation of Sèvres, was developed by 1769. In that year a

seven-day sale held in an auction room in Berkeley Square announced the inclusion of:

Complete Table and Desert Services, Leaves, Compotiers, Tea and Coffee Equipages, Baskets, Vases, Perfume Pots, Jars, Beakers, Cisterns, Tureens, Porringers, Bowls, &c. in the beautiful Colours of Mazarine Blue and Gold, Sky blue, Pea-green, French-green, Sea-green, Purple, Scarlet, and other Variety of Colours, richly decorated with chased and burnished Gold. . .

In the previous year a press announcement had mentioned that the Worcester proprietors had acquired the services of 'the best Painters from Chelsea', and it is assumed that these men brought with them information about the colours used so successfully at the London manufactory. Certain styles of painting have allegedly

been recognised as common on wares from both factories, but as in most instances each of them copied from a common source one might expect only slight evidence of distinctive features. Nonetheless, it has been possible to assign certain work to particular artists, mostly as yet un-named, but who can be recognised under such a title as 'the Painter of the Dishevelled Birds'.

Fig. 243: (Left to right) *Vase and cover with ground of pink scale; height 14⅛ inches. Dish with ground of dark blue (Mazarine blue) painted by Jeffryes Hamett O'Neale with an illustration to Aesop's fable 'Of Two Friends and the Bear'; diameter 9¾ inches. Vase and cover with blue scale ground; height 13¼ inches. All circa 1770. (Fenton House, London: The National Trust.)*

Below, *Fig. 244: Figure of a Turk. Circa 1770. Height, 5¼ inches.*

(Christie's.)

The work of this last man has been found to occur on porcelain from Bow, Plymouth and Longton Hall, as well as Worcester. It is assumed, therefore, that he was not actually employed at any of these factories, but was an 'outside decorator': he painted ware bought in a plain state from the various sources. As has been noted earlier, William Duesbury, of Derby, began his career in this manner (see page 228), and his surviving notes record the different makes of pottery and porcelain on which he worked.

The most prominent of such men in London during the third quarter of the eighteenth century was James Giles. He had a decorating establishment in Berwick Street from at least 1749, and by about 1760 also had a kiln in Kentish Town. In the columns of the *Public Advertiser* of 28th January 1768, he stated that he decorated all kinds of china to order and had 'a great Variety of white Goods by him'. His advertisement opened thus:

> J. Giles, China and Enamel Painter, proprietor of the Worcester Porcelaine Warehouse, up one Pair of Stairs in Cockspur Street, facing the Lower End of the Haymarket, begs Leave to acquaint the Nobility, Gentry, &c., that the said Warehouse is daily opened with a great Variety of Articles of the said Manufactory, useful and ornamental, curiously painted in the Dresden, Chelsea, and Chinese Tastes, superior to any thing before exhibited to the Public on that Porcelaine.

A few months later the notice was repeated, but significantly without the words 'Proprietor of the Worcester Porcelaine Warehouse'.

Considerable light was thrown on the output of Giles's workshop following the acquisition by the Victoria and Albert Museum of some Worcester plates, which had descended in his family. Their last owner having been Mrs. Dora Edgell Grubbe, they are usually referred to as the 'Grubbe' plates. Each of them is differently painted, and from a study of them it has been possible to link much other Worcester china with the workshop. It has been shown that a good proportion of the more sumptuously decorated pieces, hitherto unquestioningly accepted as factory painted, were executed in London.

Much more awaits clarification on this aspect of decorating. Additional names have been recorded from time to time as 'outside decorators', but no work has yet been found which they may have executed. One of them had a sufficient reputation in his day to have had a brief obituary notice in the London *General Evening Post* of 4th May 1758:

On Sunday died Mr. Hughes, a China Painter.

It is known also that Hughes took two apprentices in 1749 when he was living in Clerkenwell, and that he was buried in St. Pancras. There are two similarly tantalizing references in the *Universal British Directory* of 1790:

Shaw, Joseph China gilder.
Fletcher, Samuel China painter.

No doubt there were others whose names did not appear in print and who are completely unremembered.

Signed painting on English porcelain is rare, but a few pieces of Worcester manufacture bear the name or initials of Jeffryes

Fig. 245: *Teapot, cover and stand painted in green and black with figures, buildings and ruins; probably decorated in the workshop of James Giles. Circa 1770. Width of stand, 5¾ inches. (Saltram, Devon: The National Trust.)*

Hamett O'Neale, who also decorated
Chelsea (see Fig. 186), and John Donaldson,
a Scottish-born miniaturist. While O'Neale
is known to have been living in Worcester
between 1768 and 1770 and may, therefore
have worked at the factory, there is no
evidence of Donaldson being there. It is
probable that he worked in London,
perhaps for James Giles.

An announcement in the *Public Advertiser* in December 1769 referred to an
auction by James Christie of

A large and elegant Assortment of the
Worcester Porcelaine; consisting of . . .
Services, rich sets of Jars and Beakers,
Figures, Bowls, Basons, and other
Articles . . .

The catalogue of the six-day dispersal
reveals, however, that no figures were
included, and it was assumed that someone
had made an error in mentioning them.
Confirmation that none apparently existed
in 1766 is found in a letter written in that
year, which stated that 'They have not
yet debased it [*Worcester china*] by making
vile attempts at human figures, but stick
to the useful'.

On the other hand, five years later (two
years after the auction) they were seen
being made by visitors to the factory, but
it is only since 1933 that Worcester figures
have been positively identified. Earlier,
attempts made to allocate them had been
based largely on marks, and a few figures
bearing an underglaze blue crescent, similar in appearance to that found on some
Worcester tablewares, were accepted tentatively. Many collectors remained un-
convinced by this attribution, and it is now
known that no mark was used on Worcester
figures, and the crescent-marked ones were
made at Bow: a confirmation of the advice
that marks alone are not to be relied on.

The identified Worcester figures are only
few in number, and include a pair of a Turk
and companion, a hunter and companion
(Plate 37), and a gardener and companion.
All are decorated with colours and gilding
that are typical of the factory, and some
bear beneath the base the incised mark *To*.
The same mark appears on wares from
other factories, Bow and Plymouth, and it
is thought it denotes the work of a Frenchman, Thibaud. He is perhaps the same man

Plate 38 *Figure of a sportswoman, a bird in her left hand and a powder-flask in her right.* Circa *1770. Height, 7¼ inches.* (County Museum, Truro.)

Above, *Fig. 247:* (Left and right) *Tea caddy and sugar bowl and cover with pea-green borders; heights,* 5¼ *and* 4⅝ *inches.* (Centre) *dish painted with the coat of arms of the Plumbers' Company; diameter 7 inches.* **Left above, Plate 39:** *Basket, the interior painted with flowers and the exterior coloured yellow.* Circa *1770. Diameter,* 8¾ *inches.* **Left below, Plate 40:** *Claret, turquoise, and pea-green (sometimes called apple-green) grounds.* Circa *1775. Width of spoon tray in centre,* 6⅛ *inches.* (County Museum, Truro.)

referred to by Josiah Wedgwood in a letter in 1774 as 'Mr. Tebo', who had 'made a shocking ugly Thing of the Lamp'. If he did indeed also model the figures, it is not surprising that Wedgwood was dissatisfied with his work, for they have a noticeable stiffness and lack of originality. Perhaps it explains why they ceased to be produced only about two years after their first appearance.

THE proprietors of the company changed in name and number over the years, and in 1776 died the most renowned of them, Dr. John Wall. At one time it was considered that he was the most important of the partners and that he had been responsible for inventing the successful formula, but now it is accepted that this

was a Bristol innovation. A local medical practitioner of eminence and a skilful amateur artist, he may well have initiated the original project, but the precise rôle he played is uncertain.

Many years ago his name had become a household word among collectors, and the term 'Dr. Wall period' was used to describe all Worcester wares made between the years 1751 and 1783. The latter including the seven years after the doctor's death until the original manager, William Davis, died. During the past decade, use of the term 'Dr. Wall period' has gradually faded from use, and is now replaced by the impersonal, but more accurate, 'First Period Worcester'.

Following the demise of Davis, in 1783, the remaining partners sold the entire concern to their London agent, Thomas Flight, who purchased it for his two sons, Joseph and John. With the change of ownership came a change of style in the china: the shapes and patterns that had altered little in the preceding years were abandoned, and the rococo vanished almost overnight in favour of the more up-to-date neo-classical.

John Flight's diary reveals some details of the day-to-day running of the warehouse in London and the works which lay just over a hundred miles to the north-west.

His description of a visit from George III and Queen Charlotte, who were attending the Music Meeting in the town, is interesting because it gives a first-hand picture of an event of great importance to the firm. The Royal party arrived on the 5th August 1788:

> the same day my Brother had moved [*from 33 to 45 High Street, Worcester*] and opened his new Shop. The next, in the afternoon, the Sovereign and his family honoured us with a visit, totally unexpectedly, and came in without any form as a Common person woud ... They behaved exceedingly familiar and affable, orderd a good deal of China. I took the Liberty to ask the Queen to honour us with a visit at the Manufactory, which She condescended, after mentioning it to the King, to accept and fixed Saturday morning.

Fig. 248: Pair of vases painted with hunting scenes by Jeffryes Hamett O'Neale (see Fig. 243), one signed O'Neale pinxt, *the ground of dark blue with gilding. Circa 1770. Height, 13¾ inches. (Sotheby's.)*

On the following day John Flight showed the Queen some patterns

> and had the honour of taking further orders . . . and the King told me to bring the Bill which he woud pay as I did not know much of him.

As a result of this patronage, the firm was granted the privilege of styling themselves 'Manufacturers to Their Majesties', and the ensuing publicity was of great benefit.

In October 1788 John Flight recorded that he went to Paris, and spent £300 on china. Early in the next year premises were taken in the West End of London, at No. 1 Coventry Street, and John returned to Paris. While there he negotiated an agreement with the Angoulême factory in the rue de Bondy, which involved the

Fig. 249: Knife and fork, the handles painted with butterflies and insects within borders of scale-blue. Circa 1770. Lengths 8½ and 6¾ inches. (F.T.W. Collection.)

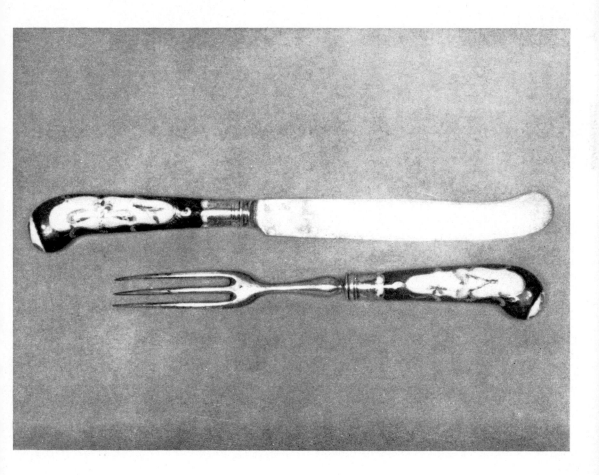

Left, *Fig. 250: Jug moulded with a pattern of overlapping cabbage leaves, the spout with a bearded mask, painted with the 'Queen Charlotte' pattern in red, blue and gold. Marked* Flights *in script.* Circa *1790. Height, 8¾ inches. (F.T.W. Collection.)*

Below, *Fig. 251: Plate of a service made in 1789 for the Duke of Clarence, fourth son of George III. From a woodcut.*

purchase of china annually to the amount of 50,000 livres (about £2,000). The French hard-paste ware was doubtless for sale in the new shop, for Joseph had been told earlier by a member of the Royal entourage that 'there are a great many French shapes in China that woud take well here'. Back in England, he noted that his father and his brother

> approved what I had done, but I was sorry to learn Chamberlain and his Son had taken our old House [33 *High Street, Worcester*] and intended setting up a Retail Shop.

Robert Chamberlain and his son, Humphrey, had been employed at the factory as painters. In their new establishment they decorated wares bought from Caughley in the white, but within a few years they set

up a manufactory of their own. The earlier products had a 'lumpy' greyish body, but towards the end of the century this was improved.

Both the Worcester factories were in rivalry with one another and with Derby in producing painting of miniature-like quality. Of Humphrey Chamberlain's work 'it was proudly said that the brushstrokes could not be discerned, even with a glass'. Other artists showing similar characteristics were employed at both establishments, and were able to exercise their powers on some of the many large services made to the order of royalty and the nobility.

Less costly, and many may consider less vulgar, tablewares were produced by Flight and by Chamberlain. Cups and saucers and other tea-table china were made with spiral fluting, painted naïvely with blue or some other colour set off with good-quality gilding (Fig. 252). The effect is cold, and it is interesting to notice an equal demand at the time for both the very sumptuous and the very sober.

*   *   *

Above, *Fig. 252: Cup and saucer moulded with spiral ribbing and decorated in mauve and gold. Marked* Flight *in script. Circa 1785.*

A VARIETY of marks was used at Worcester between 1751 and 1800. The most familiar of them is the so-called Square Mark (Fig. 253); a neat version of a Chinese fret and possibly used as an indication of origin at the 'Worcester Tonquin Manufacture'. Others which are more realistically Chinese in appearance include one with the initial letter *W* semi-disguised with cross strokes (Fig. 238). The Meissen crossed swords was used, mostly with the numeral *9* between the blades, and not always on the types of wares that would have come from that factory. On blue-painted pieces it is not uncommon to find small cyphers which are probably the private marks of individual painters. One

Below, *Fig, 253: Fretted square or 'Seal' mark found painted in underglaze blue and used between about 1755 and 1775.*

Left, *Figs. 254 and 255: Base, showing mark, and side view of a cup with the initials of Thomas Flight and his wife, Christian. Circa 1785. Height, 4 inches.*

of them, which resembles a *T* and an *F* in monogram was once taken to be the personal sign of Thomas Frye of Bow, but this is now recognised as incorrect. Finally, there is the script *W* and the crescent; the latter probably most frequently seen of all, but easily confused with similarly marked Caughley.

From 1783 Flights wrote their name in script, and added a crown above it after the royal visit of 1788. On John Flight's death in 1791, when he was only 25, Martin Barr became the partner of Joseph Flight and both names were used. Chamberlains wrote their name in red on their productions, but a varying proportion of the output from 1751 onwards bore no mark whatsoever, and must be attributed on other grounds.

Nineteenth and twentieth century imitations of Worcester are not difficult to find, but few of them will deceive anyone who is aware of their existence. French and German hard-paste copies and those in modern Staffordshire pottery are so different in appearance and weight from genuine examples that they should be quickly recognised by those who have handled old pieces. More dangerous are specimens to which decoration has been added, principally in the form of coloured grounds, so yellow and apple-green, particularly, should be examined with due caution.

18 Longton Hall

THE Longton Hall porcelain factory had become almost forgotten by the middle of the 19th century when, in 1862, Mr. A. W. Franks (later, Sir Augustus Wollaston Franks, a departmental keeper and a generous benefactor of the British Museum) wrote:

> I feel certain that if the newspapers of the period [*the 18th century*], both local and metropolitan, were carefully examined, much curious matter might be brought together, which would throw light on many debated points in the history of porcelain.

The hint was taken by J. E. Nightingale, whose book *Contributions towards the History of Early English Porcelain* was published in 1881 in Salisbury for private circulation. It contained a considerable quantity of material culled from old news-

Below, *Fig. 256: Interior of the sauceboat in Plate 42, showing the work of 'The Castle Painter' who was possibly John Hayfield. Circa 1755. Length, 8½ inches. (City Museum and Art Gallery Plymouth.)*

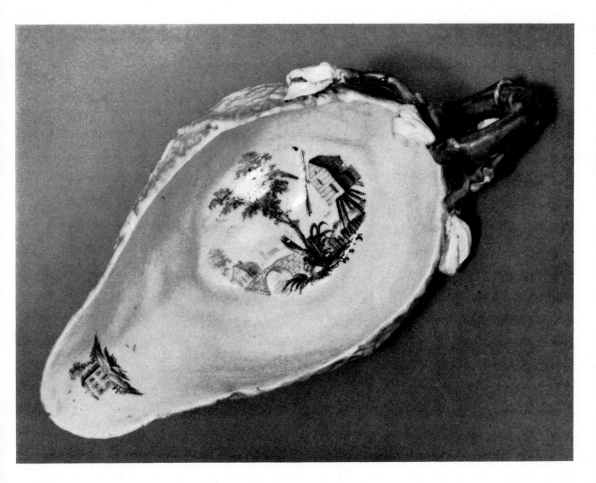

papers, and amongst the more interesting discoveries were some announcements concerning the long-lost establishment at Longton Hall.

Previously, in 1829, the indefatigable Simeon Shaw had written of specimens of the porcelain, and in so doing had added some inaccuracies to the words of an earlier author. Somewhat later in date Enoch Wood, the prosperous potter and keen collector, had authenticated in writing a tea-caddy which he had presented to the museum at Hanley. Wood stated that it had been given to him in 1809 by a man who remembered it being made 'by Mr. William Littler, at Longton near Stoke, about fifty-five years ago, say in 1754'. Notwithstanding, this well-attested piece is now ascribed to one of the Liverpool factories.

On the occasion when Mr. Franks printed the words quoted above, he drew attention to 'three specimens of a rare English manufacture of porcelain', which were then attributed to an unknown source. They are now in the British Museum, and are catalogued as Longton Hall. All three pieces are partly decorated in a peculiarly brilliant blue; one in the form of a leaf-shaped dish, and the others 'a large plate, and a bowl and cover formed of overlapping leaves'.

One of the advertisements re-printed by Nightingale appeared in the *Public Advertiser* in April 1757, and announced an auction sale of:

A New and curious Porcelain of China of the Longton-Hall Manufactory, which has had the Approbation of the best Judges, and recommended by several of

the Nobility to this public Method of Sale. Consisting of Tureens, Covers and Dishes , large Cups and Covers, Jars and Beakers, with beautiful Sprigs of Flowers, open-work'd Fruit Baskets and Plates, Variety of Services for Deserts, Tea and Coffee Equipages, Sauce Boats, leaf Basons and Plates, Melons, Colliflowers, elegant Epargnes, and other ornamental and useful Porcelain, both white and enamell'd.

The reference to 'leaf Basons and Plates' and various other scraps of evidence led a later writer, William Bemrose, to publish a book on the subject in 1906. Although he included in it many pieces that are now known to have come from factories other than Longton Hall, he was able to add to the growing number and variety of specimens that had originated there. Increases in knowledge were slight for some years to come, but with the formation of the English Porcelain Circle, later the English Ceramic Circle, in 1927 interest in the subject widened.

More recently, in 1957, Dr. Bernard Watney published his book, *Longton Hall Porcelain*, in which he was able to unfold dramatically almost the whole history of the factory and the men concerned in it. Not only did he discover some of the original documents, but much of the speculation which had surrounded the subject for so long was terminated by a series of fruitful excavations carried out on the site of the kilns.

*   *   *

THE mansion of Longton Hall, near Stoke-on-Trent, was leased in about

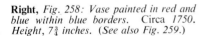

Left, *Fig. 257: 'Wasters', portions of knife-handles and a figure, excavated on the site of the factory. (City Museum and Art Gallery, Hanley.)*

Right, *Fig. 258: Vase painted in red and blue within blue borders. Circa 1750. Height, 7¾ inches. (See also Fig. 259.)*

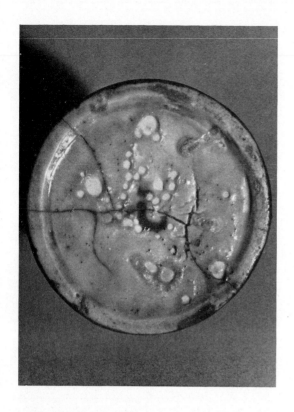

the year 1749 to William Jenkinson, described in documents as 'a gentleman'. He had 'obtained the art secret or mystery of making a certain porcelain ware in imitation of china ware', but we do not yet know how he acquired the knowledge. A clue may lie in the words written by Dr. Pococke, who was in the Newcastle-under-Lyme area in mid-1750, and wrote:

> ... there are some few potters here, and one I saw at Limehouse, who seem'd to promise to make the best china ware, but disagreed with his employers, and has a great quantity made here for the oven.

Jenkinson might have learned the 'secret' from the ubiquitous Limehouse potter, who was in Bristol later in the same year (see *Chapter* 16, page 251). Equally he may have been in contact with one or more of the Staffordshire potters who are thought to have worked at Chelsea. Such guesswork, however, is hardly profitable and it is to be hoped that one day the facts will be known.

One of the advertisements found by Nightingale concluded with the words:

> ... all Gentlemen and Ladies who please to honour him with their Commands, may depend upon having the Favour greatly acknowledg'd and all Tradesmen who favour him with Orders, may depend upon having them faithfully executed by their most obedient humble Servant William Littler.

Littler, the son of a Staffordshire potter of the same names, had been known as a maker of stoneware in partnership with Aaron Wedgwood, a member of the famous

family. Their pottery was at Brownhills, near Burslem, and they have been credited with inventing a brilliant blue colour known as 'Littler's blue' (see *Chapter* 6, page 96 and Fig. 90).

Dr. Watney revealed that one of the documents he found (which is now in the Victoria and Albert Museum) disclosed the fact that William Jenkinson signed an agreement in October 1751 with William Nicklin and William Littler to make use of the secret the first-named had acquired

> . . . and Agree to Enter into Co-partner-ship together and to become Co-partners and Joint Dealers in Making Burning and Selling the said porcelain Ware and All Other Sorts of Wares which the said partners should Agree to make or Deal in and in the painting Japanning Gilding and Enamelling thereof . . . during the said Term of Fourteen Years. . . .

Jenkinson is known to have had interests in mining, and it has been suggested that he was particularly concerned in the venture because, unlike any other manufactory at the time, this one was dependent on the use of coal, not wood, to feed the kilns. Nicklin was in the legal profession and in the present circumstances was no more than a sleeping partner. It has been suggested that Littler had worked for Jenkinson from the start and that the agreement quoted signified approval of his work and his promotion to the position of manager. It may be added that the partners held between them twelve shares, of which Littler held two and the others had five apiece.

A few months after the signing of the agreement, in July 1752, an advertisement was printed in *Aris's Birmingham Gazette*, and repeated in successive issues. It ran:

> This is to acquaint the public that there is now made by William Littler and Co. at Longton Hall near Newcastle, Staffordshire, A Large Quantity, and great Variety, of very good and fine ornamental PORCELAIN or CHINA WARE, in the most fashionable and genteel

Taste. Where all Persons may be fitted with the same at reasonable Rates, either Wholesale or Retale.

Thirteen months later a further agreement was drawn up and signed. In this, Jenkinson sold his five shares: Littler and Nicklin acquiring one each, and the remaining three were bought by a London maker of metal buttons, Nathaniel Firmin, who held a Royal warrant to supply buttons

Fig. 261: Vase painted in colours with flowers. Circa 1755. Height, 3⅛ inches. (County Museum, Truro.)

to George II. It may be added that his successors continued to hold such warrants, down to the present day.

Nathaniel Firmin died only a few months after he had purchased his quarter-share in the business, and in his will this was left to his son, Samuel. However, just over a year later a third agreement was concluded. Dated 1st September 1755, it brought in a fresh partner, some much needed capital, and in its particulars gives some important information about the manufactory and those concerned with it.

The new partner was a wealthy man, the Reverend Robert Charlesworth, of Bakewell, Derbyshire, and by adjustments of the various holdings he became owner of a one-third share in the concern. For this he advanced the sum of £1,200, and it was agreed that 'the said William Littler shall make and keep a true plain and perfect account of all Goods wares and merchandize made at and bought for the Use of the said Work'. Littler's wife, Jane, and a painter named John Hayfield, were each to be paid one guinea (21s.) a week.

By supplemental agreement Charlesworth advanced more money; £300 at thirty per cent interest, which is indicative of the state of affairs at the time, October 1756. In the following year, in April 1757, the auction mentioned on page 276 took

Fig. 262: Pair of figures of a man and a woman reading. Circa 1755. Height, 4 inches. (County Museum, Truro.)

place, but it would seem to have been unsuccessful in staving off difficulties. On 1st October of that year a further supplemental agreement stated that Charlesworth would accept the more realistic rate of interest of 5% for his money, and would advance a further sum.

A London warehouse in St. Paul's Churchyard opened in 1758 endured for under a year; in 1760 it was announced that Charlesworth had used his powers, embodied in the third agreement, and was

dissolving the partnership: all debts, etc., to be paid 'into the Hands of Mr. Samuel Boyer, Attorney at Law, in Newcastle under Lyme, for the use of the said Robert Charlesworth . . .'.

Within a few days the announcement was countered by one from Littler stating that production was being continued, but it was in vain. The stock was seized on behalf of Charlesworth, sold by auction at Salisbury, Wiltshire, in September 1760, and the first attempt to make porcelain in Staffordshire came to a close.

* * *

I⊤ is thought very probable that the first wares made at the factory were of the type now called 'snowman' figures: so-named because they are invariably found to be covered in a heavy and shiny coating

Fig. 263: Dish, the border moulded with strawberries and leaves and the centre painted with exotic birds. Circa 1755. Width 12¼ inches. (Christie's.)

Left, *Fig. 264: Negro with a prancing horse, copied from a Meissen group by J. J. Kändler. Circa 1755. Height, 8 inches. (Victoria and Albert Museum.)*

Above, *Fig. 265: Advertisement from the London General Evening Post, 14th July, 1759.*

Right, above, Plate 41: *Figures in typical Longton Hall colours: mauvish-pink, rich yellow-green, and warm yellow. The centre boy may be compared with the Derby version. Circa 1755. Heights, (left to right) 4¾, 4½ and 6 inches. (County Museum, Truro.)* **Right, below, Plate 42:** *Sauce-boat modelled with overlapping cabbage leaves coloured naturally (see Fig. 256). Circa 1755. Length, 8½ inches. (City Museum and Art Gallery, Plymouth.)*

of glaze. All of them owe their inspiration to outside sources, and are either direct copies of Meissen itself, of Chelsea versions of the same, or are taken from the Chinese. Some of the figures exist also in Staffordshire pottery and salt-glazed stoneware of the same date, so it is not unreasonable to suppose that all of them emanated, if not from the same hand, at least from the same county.

Among the thirty or forty different models known are the pair of horses illustrated in Fig. 269. Not only have they the thick glaze that covers all but the boldest modelling, but their bases are decorated with applied leaves and flowers in a noticeably unrealistic manner. Further, a pair of salt-glazed stoneware horses, posed in the same attitudes as these specimens, dating also from about 1750, is now exhibited at Colonial Williamsburg, Virginia. The unearthing of two porcelain 'snowman' figures on the Longton factory site points to the possibility that they may have been the wares seen and remarked on in 1750 by Dr. Pococke.

At the same date, useful wares were also made. Some pieces were decorated with Littler's vivid and distinctive blue with reserved panels painted in colours, and much of this at one time bore gilding. As the gold leaf was held only with some kind of size or varnish, most of it has now been worn away completely and it is difficult to imagine what it must once have looked like. Gilding no doubt masked the edges round panels, and would have made their raw look more acceptable.

Many pieces bear raised scroll and floral patterns, of the types found on silverware of the time. More significantly, there is a use of leaves, carefully shaped and veined, that became one of the characteristics at a later date. The clay mixture in use was not

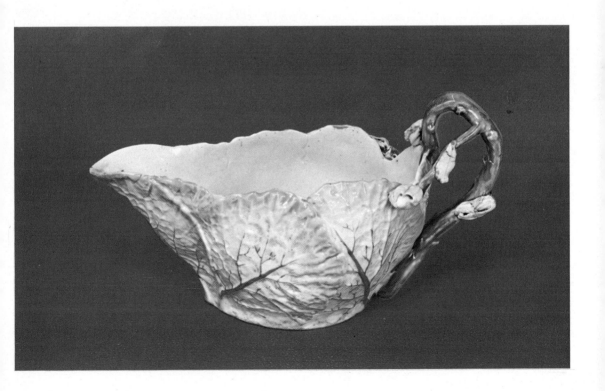

Plate 43 *Group of Hercules and the Nemean Lion, complete with a separate stand.* Circa *1755. Height,* $7\frac{1}{2}$ *inches.* (*County Museum, Truro.*)

Fig. 266: Jug moulded with strawberry leaves and an auricula plant, and painted with buildings in underglaze blue. Circa 1755. Height, 8 inches. (City Museum and Art Gallery, Plymouth.)

conducive to delicate workmanship, and
most of the pieces are thickly potted.

The middle period of production covered
the years 1754 to 1757, with an increase in
the range of goods made and advances in
their design. Figures were more numerous,
and in some instances were well-designed;
the spiralling rococo base blending with
the subject in a manner seen occasionally
in early Derby (Fig. 260, and see Plate 41),
and to perfection in Bustelli's work at
Nymphenberg. Meissen was again a
fruitful source of inspiration, although it
can be argued whether, as has been suggested, the Staffordshire versions were
ever an improvement on the originals.

A few types of vases were made, some of
them very colourful. A well-known example,
standing 16 inches high, is of assymetrical
form (as the plain small-sized example in
Fig. 261), and topped by a cover smothered
in modelled flowers. Amongst the latter,
and startlingly out of proportion with one
another and with the flowers themselves,
are a cock and hen, wild birds of various
breeds, and a girl dancing.

Table wares of the period include dishes

*Above, Fig. 267: Sauceboat painted in
underglaze blue with an Oriental subject.
Circa 1755. Length, 5½ inches. (Stephen
Simpson Collection: City Museum and
Art Gallery, Plymouth.) **Right**, Fig. 268:
Mug painted in colours with flowers by
William and Jane Littler at West Pans,
Scotland. Porcelain, circa 1755; decora-
tion, circa 1765. Height, 4½ inches.
(F. T. W. Collection.)*

and other pieces moulded with realistic oak
and strawberry leaves. Basins, teapots and
sauce-boats (Plate 42 were similarly treated, and with their naturalistic colouring
are among the more memorable of the
factory's products.

The quality of painted work could be
high, and many pieces bear small scenes
executed with great care. They often depict
architectural fantasies with a group of bent
grasses in the foreground, as on the interior
of the sauce-boat in Fig. 256. Long known
as the work of a single hand, named con-
veniently 'The Castle Painter', it is thought
that he may have been the John Hayfield,
mentioned as working as a painter at the
factory in 1755. It is known, also, that
William Duesbury, early in his life an
enameller working in London, was living

in Longton from 1754 to 1756 and he may well have been employed by Littler.

The final period of Longton production included much that had been made in preceding years, as well as additions to the ranges of figures and tablewares. An indication of what was in production at the end of the factory's life is given in the advertisement of the final auction-sale at Salisbury. It comprised:

> The Genuine large and valuable stock of the Longton Porcelaine China Factory, which, as the partnership is dissolved, will be sold without reserve or the least addition; containing upwards of ninety thousand Pieces of the greatest variety of Dresden Patterns in rich enamell'd, pencil'd, Blues and Gold; as Figures and Flowers, mounted in Chandeliers, Essence Jars, Beakers, Vases and Perfume Pots, magnificent Dessert Services, sets of Bowls, Mugs, Dishes and Plates, ornamented with Columbines and Central Groups, Tea Coffee and Toilet Equipages, of elegant patterns superbly furnished, equal to a national Factory, so eminently distinguish'd, with a profusion of useful and ornamental articles.

Why Salisbury, in Wiltshire and 150 miles away, was chosen for the disposal of the stock has never been explained. Nor is it known exactly what was sold, as no catalogue, if one ever existed, has been preserved.

Some of the ware may have been retained by Littler, or have been purchased by him

Above, *Fig. 269: Pair of seated horses of 'snowman' type. Circa 1755. Length about 8 inches. (Victoria and Albert Museum.)*

at the sale, because a quantity was decorated by him at a later date in Scotland. By 1764 he was at West Pans, near Musselburgh, where he and his wife painted tablewares with sprays of flowers and coats of arms and crests. The latter were those of Scottish nobles and gentlemen, and an example is on the front of the jug in Fig. 270. The coat of arms and motto (*Nescit abolere vetustas*) are those of Sir James Adolphus Dickenson Oughton, Commander-in-Chief of the Forces in North Britain. When he travelled in Scotland with James

Fig. 270: Jug painted with bouquets of flowers, on the front the coat of arms and motto of Sir James Adolphus Dickenson Oughton (1720-80). Porcelain, circa 1750; decoration, circa 1765. Height, 8⅝ inches. (F. T. W. Collection.)

improved and the resulting wares are better finished. The glaze has been compared in appearance to 'paraffin-wax or candle-grease' (Fig. 259).

The history of the Longton Hall porcelain factory is such a romantic one that it has tended to lift many of the products into a prominence unjustified by their appearance. Much of the output was damaged in one way or another during manufacture, but this did not prevent the makers decorating it and hiding the blemishes, as well as they could, before selling the ware. On the other hand, the very crudity of many of the pieces is no small part of their attraction, and epitomises the struggles of the makers. Not only had they to combat a deficiency of scientific knowledge, but also shortage of money and, sometimes, a lack of skill on the part of employees. With such disadvantages, it is remarkable that so many successes were achieved.

No mark was used regularly on Longton productions, but some examples are recorded with an underglaze blue pair of initials placed facing one another as was done at Sèvres from about 1745. In the case of Longton, the blurred letters, sometimes with one or more added dots, may stand for Littler or Longton, or may be 'J's' for Jenkinson.

It should be noted that some of the figures and groups originating at Longton were copied closely at both Plymouth and Derby. Derby versions of a pair of the figures (Plate 41, centre) are shown in Fig. 215.

Boswell in 1773, Samuel Johnson told an officer at Fort George: 'Sir, you will find few men, of any profession, who know more. Sir Adolphus is a very extraordinary man; a man of boundless curiosity and unwearied diligence'. Such a testimony to its former owner gives an added interest to the piece of china.

Some pieces with transfer-printed decoration by Sadler and Green of Liverpool are known. Many of the designs commemorate personages connected with the Seven Years' War of 1756-63, but others bear the arms of private individuals and of societies. While a proportion of them may have been executed during the end of the factory's career, others date from after the closure.

The earlier productions were, as have been mentioned, thickly-walled, and when held to the light show a bluish-green translucency. Often there are 'moons'; areas of lighter colour probably caused by air-bubbles trapped in the clay during manufacture. From about 1754, the mixture was

19 Liverpool

IT has long been known that there were several manufactories of porcelain in 18th century Liverpool, but because they were mostly sited close to one another and made goods destined for the same market it is difficult to differentiate between their products. In recent years a serious attempt has been made to attribute specimens to each of them, although a lack of marks and other positive evidence has involved a considerable use of detective work. There remain, however, many outstanding problems offering a rewarding field for research, and much guesswork that awaits confirmation.

Fig. 271: Sauceboat with coloured floral decoration. Circa 1770. Length, 4¾ inches.

The first known porcelain works to be established in the city was that of Richard Chaffers, who served an apprenticeship from about 1735 in the delftware pottery of Alderman Thomas Shaw (see page 66). Chaffers established a pottery of his own in the mid-1740's on Shaw's Brow (now William Brown Street), and progressed from tin-glazed earthenware to the making of creamware. In December 1756 he announced in *Williamson's Liverpool Advertiser:*

Chaffers and Co., China Manufactory. The porcelain, or china ware, made by Messrs. Richard Chaffers and Co., is sold nowhere in the town, but at their manufactory on Shaw's Brow. Considerable abatement for exportation, and to all wholesale dealers.
N.B. All the ware is proved with boiling water before it is exposed for sale.

In the preceding year Chaffers and his partner, Philip Christian, signed an agreement with Robert Podmore. The latter had been one of the original workmen at Worcester, when operations commenced there in 1751. He knew the secrets of their formula, and had been paid extra money as a reward for his work and 'the better to

Left, *Fig. 272: Vase and cover painted in colours with exotic birds. Chaffers' factory. Circa 1765. Height, 15½ inches. (City Museum and Art Gallery, Plymouth.)* **Below,** *Fig. 273: Mug painted in colours with a Chinese subject. Circa 1770. Height, 2⅝ inches. (County Museum, Truro.)*

Fig. 274: Bowl decorated with flowers in underglaze blue. Circa 1760. Diameter, 8¼ inches. (F. T. W. Collection.)

engage his fidelity'. It was said that he had worked for a short time with Wedgwood, and then had the idea of going to America to start a pottery there. En route, at the port of embarkation, he called on Chaffers, who finding that he had 'so much intelligence and practical knowledge, induced him, by a most liberal offer, to forego his American project, and enter into his service'.

It is assumed that Chaffers had been experimenting until then with a porcelain incorporating bone ash in the body, but Podmore told him of the Worcester success in using soapstone: the basis of that factory's claim that their products did not crack in boiling water. Chaffers, probably accompanied by Podmore, set out for Cornwall, to locate a supply of the stone. A story related by his grandson, tells how Chaffers went on horseback, with a supply of clean linen, one thousand guineas and a brace of pistols. Arriving in the West-country, he employed a party of local miners to assist him in his quest, and just as he was on the very point of disconsolately giving up the search, one of the party shouted and signalled that he had struck a vein of the stone.

In fact, the soapstone was found close to the source of that used at Worcester, so there was possibly less romance to the story than was supposed. In any case, the stone was obtained, and it would seem that Chaffers personally returned home with it. The story concluded by describing how he

> Obtained an ample supply of the long-sought-for clay, which was conveyed to the nearest port, and thence shipped to Liverpool; on his arrival, the vessel entered with its precious freight into the Old Dock, dressed in colours, amidst the cheers of the spectators.

While most of the output was decorated with Oriental patterns in underglaze blue, some was painted with similar designs in colours. They resemble painting in the same style on Longton Hall, and there are examples of mugs with grooves at the base that are like some of those made at the latter factory. However, such similarities are common not only with regard to Longton;

there are few English factories with which the products of one or other of the Liverpool establishments have not been confused.

Employing the same distinctive ingredient, soapstone, it is no surprise to find that Chaffers' wares with blue decoration are very like those from the Worcester and Caughley factories. A similarity in designs is due to a common emulation of Oriental imports, but they resemble one another also in the dry appearance of the inside of the foot-rim of cups, saucers and plates. As at Lowestoft, the use of numerals, written inside the foot-rim or on the base of wares, is not uncommon, and one specimen that has been illustrated and described as Chelsea is now re-allocated to Chaffers.

Against the light, the porcelain shows a translucency varying from brown-yellow to greenish for the early bone ash type, and greenish for the phosphatic variety.

Inscribed and dated specimens are rare, and only four have so far been noted. They are: a bowl with a verse concluding

This bowle is round, it is for you
If you'l be constanet I'll be true.

a mug commemorating the successful election to Parliament of Sir William Meredith in 1761; a jug inscribed 'A free gift to John Fell, China house joiner, 1762'; and an inkwell initialled *I.H.* and dated 1765. Of these, the first two are in the British Museum, the Fell jug is in the museum at Bootle, Lancashire, and the last-mentioned is in private ownership.

On the death of Chaffers in 1765, Philip

Christian and his son carried on the manufactory. Their output would seem to have been little different from that of preceding years, although it is said that the underglaze blue painting was greyer in tint than that of Chaffers'. On the other hand, Christian did make use of a rich, dark blue for borders, and this was occasionally marbled with gold.

Jewitt printed a receipt for 'Christian's china body (January 1769)', which consisted of the following:

> To 100 parts rock: flint, 24 parts; best flint glass, 6 parts; small glass, 6 parts; crown glass, 6 parts; To every 20 lbs. of the above put 1 lb. of salts. Glaze—4 china body (foreign); 16 flint glass; 3 white lead; 12 oz. of pearl ashes.

It is interesting to notice the inclusion of broken glass, which is specified in three different qualities, and the fact that the glaze contained 'china body (foreign)'. This was doubtless broken Oriental hard-paste porcelain, of which a writer in 1758 had made a mention in a similar connection. He reported: 'I have seen, at one of those [*china factories*] carried on near London, eleven mills at work grinding pieces of the Eastern china'. If this was being performed in the capital, or just outside it, there is no reason why the same process should not have been employed in the provinces.

In 1776 the remainder of the soaprock lease was sold to the Worcester partners, and the making of porcelain by Philip Christian and Son ceased.

A variety of pieces made from a bone ash porcelain, and often imitating shapes introduced by Christian were possibly made

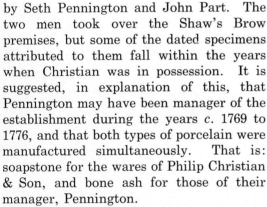

Opposite, below, *Fig. 277: Plate painted in underglaze blue with a Chinese subject. Circa 1765. Diameter, $8\frac{1}{8}$ inches.*

Right, *Fig. 278: Mug painted in underglaze blue. Circa 1765. Height, $2\frac{1}{2}$ inches. (City Museum and Art Gallery, Plymouth.)*

by Seth Pennington and John Part. The two men took over the Shaw's Brow premises, but some of the dated specimens attributed to them fall within the years when Christian was in possession. It is suggested, in explanation of this, that Pennington may have been manager of the establishment during the years *c.* 1769 to 1776, and that both types of porcelain were manufactured simultaneously. That is: soapstone for the wares of Philip Christian & Son, and bone ash for those of their manager, Pennington.

Alternatively, the Pennington & Part pieces may have been made by the former's brothers James and John. James was listed in the Directory of 1769 as having a 'china works' in Park Lane, and five years later in a similar capacity at Copperas Hill. He is said to have left Liverpool at a later date and to have gone to Worcester, where 'one of his children painted a dinner service for the Duke of York'.

The Shaw's Brow property was mortgaged by Pennington & Part in 1788, and they dissolved their partnership a few years after 1800. No other particulars of the two men are recorded, and if any remain they have so far eluded discovery.

The wares attributed to the factory are decorated with either painting or printing, and are mainly poor-quality versions of the Christians' productions. Shapes include sauce-boats with the handles terminating in a snake's head (Fig. 283), and tall teapots moulded round the base with leaves and about the body with palm-trees (Fig. 279). Dated pieces range from 1772, and include a well-known jug in the British Museum, which is inscribed *Frederick Heinzelman Liverpool* and dated 1779. The piece bears decoration printed in blue which includes two birds with sprigs of liverwort in their beaks, creatures featured in the arms of the City of Liverpool, and a border of hexagonal diaper pattern. This last is commonly found on Chinese work, and although sometimes known as the 'Heinzelman' border is by no means exclusive to the Pennington or any other Liverpool factory (see Fig. 281).

Next door to the above-mentioned premises, occupied successively by Chaffers, Christian and Pennington, was the short-

306

Left, *Fig. 279: Teapot moulded with leaves and palm trees and painted in colours.* Circa *1770. Height, 7 inches.* (County Museum, Truro.) **Above,** *Fig. 280: Two jugs painted in colours with Chinese figures.* Circa *1770. Heights, 3 and 3½ inches.* (County Museum, Truro.)

lived pottery of Samuel Gilbody. His father, who bore the same names, appears in a local baptismal register on the occasion of the birth of a daughter, the entry reading:

25 September 1736.
Hannah, daughter of Samuel Gillbody [*sic*], Lord Street, potter.

Earlier, he had been described in a document as a brick-maker, and on a further occasion was a 'dealer in white earthenware'.

To further confuse the story, both father and son took wives named Hannah, and the younger man's birth in 1733 followed the elder's second marriage. The latter died in 1752 and it is probable that Samuel Gilbody jnr. took over the management of the pottery, which had been left to his mother, when he came of age in 1754. He did not, however, live for long afterwards, and in a document dealing with his estate

is a mention of a windmill 'usually occupied with the pothouse'.

There seems to be no absolute proof that Gilbody actually manufactured porcelain. A mug in Liverpool Museum had for long been accepted as evidence of the fact, because the printed decoration on it was signed 'Gilbody maker. Evans Sct.'. Presumably the engraving must have been made for use on some of Gilbody's productions, but this oft-quoted example is now stated to be of Worcester manufacture. The presence of the print on it has been explained as a mistake on the part of Sadler and Green, who are known to have decorated Worcester occasionally.

A small number of pieces have been attributed to Gilbody. Some are painted in colours and others in blue, and many show similarities in their decoration to Chaffers' wares. The appearance of the ware is compared to some of the output of Longton Hall, in that the earlier examples are heavily made and thickly glazed. Later pieces show more expert technique, but it may be thought a somewhat speculative exercise to divide the production of a mere seven years into early and late.

Above, left, *Fig. 281: Tankard decorated with underglaze blue printing, the border of 'Heinzelman' pattern.* Circa *1775. Height, 6⅝ inches. (Stephen Simpson Collection: City Museum and Art Gallery, Plymouth.)* **Above,** *Fig. 282: Jug printed in underglaze blue.* Circa *1775. Height, 3¾ inches. (County Museum, Truro.)* **Right, Plate 44:** *Jug painted with birds. Chaffers' factory.* Circa *1765. Height, 8⅝ inches. (F. T. W. Collection.)*

Near the centre of Liverpool, on Brownlow Hill and with its own colour-mill nearby, stood the manufactory of William Reid. The first public mention of its existence appeared in *Williamson's Liverpool Advertiser* on 24th September 1756, when the undermentioned advertisement was printed:

Wanted, several apprentices at Messrs. Reid and Co. China Manufactory, at Brownley Hill, near this town, Any young persons with capacities for drawing and painting may meet with suitable encouragement by applying to the Proprietors.

N.B.—Any persons that can supply the work with cord wood [*cut into lengths suitable for burning*] are desired to apply to the managers; a large quantity being wanted.

Two months later, in the same newspaper, a further advertisement announced the opening of a showroom situated near the docks. It read:

Liverpool China Manufactory—Messrs. Reid & Co., Proprietors of the China Manufactory, have opened their warehouse in Castle Street, and sell all kinds of blue and white china ware, not inferior to any make in England, both wholesale and retail. Samples sent to any gentleman or ladies in the country that will pay carriage, good allowance for shopkeepers or exporters.

The showroom was later transferred to larger premises at Castle Hey, which was duly renamed Harrington Street. Finally, the same journal which had served for earlier notices carried a third, printed in the issue of 4th December 1761, reading:

309

Plate 45 *Coffee pot with moulded and blue-painted decoration. Circa 1765. Height, 10½ inches. (City Museum and Art Gallery, Plymouth.)*

To be sold by public auction on the 5th of January next at 6 o'clock, all those new erected buildings now used as a china manufactory with the colour mill and premises appurtenant thereto, situated on Brownlow Hill near Liverpool and lately occupied by Reid and Company, held by lease under the corporation of Liverpool. Any person desirous to view the premises may apply to Mr. Wedgwood at Burslem or to Mr. John Dobson in Liverpool. There is now on sale at Mr. Reid's shop, the upper end of Harrington Street, best blue and white cups and saucers at 3s. per set, second best do. at 2s. per set. Enamelled coffee cups from 6s. to 2s. a dozen. And all sorts of china cheap in proportion.

It is not known how or why Josiah Wedgwood became involved in the firm and its bankruptcy, but Wedgwood's *Experiment Book* records the ingredients used 'for the Liverpool china being made by Messrs. Reid and Baddeley'. It included bone ash, along with Dorset clay and sand from the Isle of Wight. It is also known that a licence to quarry soaprock on Viscount Falmouth's land was signed on 1st January 1760. It was granted to 'John Baddeley of Shelton in the County of Staffordshire, Gentleman, and William Yates of Newcastle under line in the same county, Gentleman'. Baddeley is recorded as having been connected with some of William Littler's porcelain-making activities in 1751, and was himself bankrupt within a few days of the same fate overtaking William Reid.

A few pieces, hitherto unallocated, have been attributed within recent years to the Reid factory. Those apparently of early date reveal traces of bone ash through the presence of phosphoric acid, while later examples have been found to contain soaprock. Both types differ little to the eye, and are finished with a glaze to which a small quantity of tin-oxide has been added to whiten it and make it opaque. The name

Fig. 283: Sauceboat, printed in underglaze blue, the handle moulded with a snake's head. Circa 1775. Length, 7½ inches.

of one of the artists employed is recorded: that of Ralph Wilcox, who worked for Reid's after an apprenticeship with a maker of Liverpool delftware. He later married the daughter of Thomas Frye of Bow, and the two of them took employment with Wedgwood. None of the work executed by Wilcox while at Liverpool has been identified, but it has been suggested he may have been responsible for some country landscapes seen on a few of the wares attributed to Reid.

At about the same date as Chaffers, Gilbody and Reid were starting their manufactories, another was begun by William Ball, who appears in Gore's *Liverpool Directory* of 1766 as a china maker, of Ranelagh Street. He has been described appropriately by a recent writer as 'elusive', as his name does not figure in any other records of the place. It is thought that he is quite possibly the man of the same name noted in the baptismal register of St. Anne's, Limehouse:

Below, *Fig. 284: Cup and saucer printed in puce with a shepherd and shepherdess, the border hand painted. Circa 1785. Diameter, 4⅞ inches. (County Museum, Truro.)*

Fig. 285: Saucer printed in dark blue with rural lovers copied from an engraving after Thomas Gainsborough published in 1760. Circa *1785. Diameter, 4⅞ inches.*

8 March 1747/8. Elizabeth, daughter of William Ball, potter, Fore Street, and Mary.

Ball was a ratepayer in Limehouse at that date, but by August 1748 he had gone (see *Chapter* 16, page 245).

There was an Isaac Ball making pottery in Burslem between about 1670 and 1700, and the surname was not uncommon in both Staffordshire and in the Liverpool area. However, it is tentatively thought that the William Ball in question may have left Limehouse for Staffordshire, and after a few years stay there moved on to start a concern in Liverpool.

Wares attributed to the manufactory are likened to both Bow and Longton Hall, and with a preponderance of Oriental patterns in underglaze blue of a bright tint. Sauce-boats attributed to Ball include some raised on an oval pedestal foot, which are of a type made at Bow (see Fig. 201, page 226). Coloured decoration was also used, and printing in colours, by means of several differently-coloured transfers app-

lied on top of each other, is thought to have been employed occasionally. The polychrome prints were usually additionally painted by hand to increase the range of colours.

Finally, the factory of Thomas Wolfe and Company, in Folly Lane, was in operation for about ten years between 1790 and 1800. The firm is supposed to have made porcelain with a greyish-looking body frequently decorated with transfer prints in various colours.

The foregoing owes a great debt to the energetic researches of Dr. Knowles Boney and Dr. Bernard Watney, who have bravely allocated wares that were once considered to be of Bow, Worcester or Longton Hall manufacture to the different recorded Liverpool makers. It is a start to what promises to be a lengthy and interesting exercise, during which there will doubtless continue to be many further changes of label.

313

20 Lowestoft and Caughley

THE soft paste porcelain made at Lowestoft, Suffolk, has acquired a disproportionately high status among English wares because of an error made by William Chaffers, the antiquary, in 1863. In that year he published the first edition of his *Marks and Monograms on Pottery and Porcelain*, and in it he allocated to Lowestoft all the 18th century Chinese porcelain made to English order of which he had knowledge. As a large quantity of the latter porcelain existed, the factory sprang suddenly from its rustic semi-obscurity to an unwarranted position of importance. Writing in 1878, A. W. Franks dealt firmly with the theory, which he termed a 'singular hallucination' and gave his opinion that 'the evidence of hard paste having been made there [*at Lowestoft*] is of the most unsatisfactory kind; chiefly the indistinct recollection of persons not acquainted with the difference between hard and soft paste.'

The controversy dragged on for some further years, and although a Chinese origin was accepted eventually for the hard paste porcelain it defiantly retained the name 'Lowestoft'. It is only during recent decades that it has been dropped, and on both sides of the Atlantic it is now usually known as 'Chinese Export Ware'.

The east coast manufactory was founded in 1757 by a group of local fishing-boat-owners, who appointed a chemist, Robert Browne, to manage the concern. By 1770 the style of the firm had become Robert Browne & Co., and in the same year a

London newspaper printed the announcement:

> Clark Durnford, Lowestoft China Warehouse, No 4, Great St Thomas the Apostle, Cheapside, London. Where Merchants and Shopkeepers may be supplied with any quantity of the said Ware at the usual Prices.
> N.B. Allowance of Twenty per cent for Ready Money.

It has been said that Browne used information he obtained after he had contrived to obtain employment at Bow. The story relates that

> Here, after a short time, he bribed the warehouseman to assist him in his design, and soon accomplished his purpose. The warehouseman locked him up secretly in that part of the factory where the principal was in the habit of mixing the ingredients after the workmen had left the premises. Browne was placed under an empty hogshead, close to the counter or table on which the principal operated, and could thus see through an opening all that was going on. From his hiding-place he watched all the processes, saw the proportions of the different ingredients used, and gained the secret he had so long coveted.

Fig. 287: Two inkwells decorated with painting in underglaze blue, and inscribed and dated 1782 and 1779. Diameters, (left) 2⅝ inches, (right) 2⅞ inches. The left hand piece was once in the Rix Seago collection.

The cloak-and-dagger episode apparently took him only a matter of two or three weeks, after which Browne returned to Lowestoft to put his newly-acquired knowledge into practice. The possibility that there was some kind of link between the factories, although not necessarily forged in the manner described, is borne out by a recognisable resemblance between the two wares. Not only did both of them contain bone ash as an ingredient, but each decorated a high proportion of its output in underglaze blue. Other factories also copied the popular Chinese blue-painted ware, and Lowestoft products have been confounded at one time and another with the similar wares of Worcester, Caughley and the Liverpool area. As such a high proportion of the output of all these establishments bore no marks of origin there has always been ample ground for errors, and even today confusion is not uncommon.

Fortunately for modern collectors, the Lowestoft management did some of their trade with people who liked to have their names or initials painted on their purchases. Together with inscribed dates,

Fig. 288: Bases of the inkwells in Fig. 287. The initials S.A on the left hand piece are probably those of Samuel Aldred, who was one of the partners in the Lowestoft manufactory.

Fig. 289: Mug painted with an Oriental scene in underglaze blue. Circa 1770. Height, 4⅝ inches. (City Museum and Art Gallery, Plymouth.)

Captain Osborne from COLCHESTER. Success to the Frances.

Another shows a fishing-boat, together with a ribbon on which is its name: *THE JUDAS*. A different trade is recorded on a coffee pot with the wording:

JOHN LEARNER
Sadler Cap and Harnefs-maker,
Upper Market St. Peter's,
NORWICH.

Further interest attaches to many of these pieces because they have been recorded in print by successive writers during the past hundred years. Thus, the cup and saucer in the foreground of Plate 45 is from a service made at the factory for the wedding of Robert Browne, son of the factory's first manager of the same name. The grandson of the latter (confusingly with the same name once more) swore an affidavit in 1895 regarding some china then in the collection of William Rex Seago, a former Town Clerk of Lowestoft. The document opened with the following words:

> The first things in Mr. Seago's collection, identified by me, was my Father's Wedding Tea Service, consisting of 6 Tea Cups and Saucers, Tea Pot, Sugar Basin, slop Basin, Cream Jug, all Pink Flower, and White with Gold Edging.

Much of the very extensive Seago collection was bought by F. A. Crisp, a noted antiquary and collector. When his collection was dispersed in 1935 the teaset formed lot 88 and was one of about sixty Lowestoft items. Following the sale, most of the teaset was bought by Edgar A. Rees, of Penzance, and on his death in 1959 it formed part of his bequest of pottery and porcelain to the County Museum, Truro. The set has an almost continuous history of two centuries, and the same is true of quite a sizable proportion of the output of the little factory.

Almost all the named specimens had a connection with someone living in the Lowestoft area or in the county of Suffolk. A notable exception is a small sauceboat in the Castle Museum and Art Gallery,

these provide a valuable key to the shapes and styles of decoration employed during the forty-five years between the opening in 1757 and closure in 1802.

In July 1968 a list of the known inscribed specimens was compiled, and the total reached 271. They are divisible into pieces on which are names, initials, arms and crests, mottoes, and those with legend 'A Trifle from . . .'. In the first category are the circular tablets, 2¼ to 3 inches in diameter, on which are written the name and date of birth of a child, usually with a pattern of some kind on the reverse side. They exist in coloured and in underglaze blue painting, and range in date between 1761 and the end of the century. Thirty of them have been recorded, of which one commemorates the birth of a girl and also poignantly, the death of her five-year-old sister.

Other pieces were made for the masters or owners of boats using the port. One of them is a punch-bowl bearing the words

Norwich, inscribed in blue with the words:
    Made at Lowestoft, Sepr 6
    in the preseence of J S Browne.
    Wardrobe Court Doctors Commons
    London 1770
That visitors were shown round the concern is made clear in the diary entry of one, Silas Neville, who was in Lowestoft in 1772. On Wednesday 26th August of that year he wrote:

Lowestoft stands upon the cliff very near the beach, consists of one pretty long street, & is a very poor disagreeable place. We all thought so, & therefore changed our resolution of spending the night there.   Dined at the Crown. After dinner [*then eaten at between 3 and 5 in the afternoon*] visited the China Manufactory carried on here. Most of it is rather ordinary.   The painting branch is done by women.

Neville's opinion that the ware is 'ordinary' is broadly true, for only rarely did the quality of it rise above that requisite for sale in country districts. Much of the decoration was painted in underglaze blue,

and Oriental subjects were the most popular (Fig. 289). Worcester was frequently and closely copied, and the similarity to Bow was probably also deliberate. Blue printing was employed, sometimes on its own and on other occasions in combination with hand painting. Only a few of the patterns showed much originality, and the painters and engravers devised their own versions of current favourites.

Shapes were equally unadventurous, but a few moulded designs on sauce-boats, teapots and other pieces have been recorded as being exclusive to Lowestoft. One of them centres on the initials *I H* and date 1761, which is thought to have been designed to commemorate the birth of James Hughes, grandson of Robert Browne.

Fig. 290: Miniature teaset painted in blue, the jug marked inside the footrim 14 and the saucer 10. Circa 1770. Height of teapot, 3 inches; height of jug, 2 inches.

Painting in colours was probably not begun until the late 1760's, and then much of it was in imitation of imported Chinese porcelain of the time. Some of it, competently decorated with neat sprays of flowers and diaper borders in the *famille rose* style, once assisted the argument of those who were convinced that both copies and originals were produced at the East Anglian factory. The work of one painter is recognisable from a liking for including tulips prominently in bouquets, but he or she is anonymous and can only be referred to as 'The Tulip Painter'.

A few figures were made at the factory. This had long been suspected, and the finding of fragments of both figures and moulds on the factory site early in the present century provided confirmation.

In recent years some of them have been identified, and the list includes at present some dancing cupids, a dancing man and woman (Fig. 293), animals and swans. Examples are rare, and no doubt more await discovery.

The Lowestoft factory did not employ a distinctive mark for its products, but some or all of the painters wrote a numeral neatly just inside the foot-rim of table wares.

Below, *Fig. 291: Sauceboat with painted and printed decoration in underglaze blue. Circa 1780. Length, 7 inches.* **Right,** *Fig. 292: Cup and saucer printed in blue. Circa 1780. Diameter, 4 inches. (City Museum and Art Gallery, Plymouth.)*

While the practice is not confined to employees of this concern, it is often a help in making an attribution. Both the Worcester open crescent and script *W* and the Meissen crossed swords were used occasionally.

Fig. 293: Figure of a dancing girl. Circa 1790. Height, 7¼ inches.
(Sotheby's).

THE Caughley manufactory was at Ironbridge, Shropshire, and a pottery already existing there was converted and enlarged to produce porcelain. This took place soon after 1770 and the man responsible was Thomas Turner, son-in-law of the owner of the pottery, Ambrose Gallimore. According to Llewellynn Jewitt, writing in 1878, 'it seems pretty certain that he [*Turner*] was, at an early period, connected with the Worcester china works, and it is an established fact that he was an excellent chemist, and had thoroughly studied the various processes relating to porcelain manufacture'.

By 1775 the concern was apparently on its feet and a local correspondent noted:

'The Porcelain Manufactory erected near Bridgnorth, in this County, is now completed, and the proprietors have received and completed orders to a very large amount. Lately we saw some of their productions, which in colour and fineness are truly elegant and beautiful and have the bright and lovely white of the so much extolled Oriental.'

Perhaps owing to the proximity of Worcester, a matter of about forty miles along the river Severn, and certainly because Turner had worked there, the wares of the two factories bear a close resemblance. Not only were Worcester shapes and decoration imitated, but the finish of the footrim, with the apparent shrinkage of glaze in the recess, also occurs on many Caughley pieces. Further, the Worcester crescent mark was blatantly duplicated; either as it stood, or with the addition of a serif to convert it into a capital 'C'.

A further link with Worcester came when the engraver Robert Hancock left there, and announced that he had become associated in some capacity with the Caughley works. An advertisement in *Aris's Birmingham Gazette* on 3 July 1775 stated:

SALOPIAN China Warehouse, Bridgnorth. R. Hancock begs leave to acquaint the public and particularly dealers in china ware, that having disposed of his share in the Worcester work, he is now engaged in the Salopian China Manufactory, on such terms as enable him to serve the trade at the most moderate rates. He has already an ample assortment of the blue and white, and will with all possible expedition proceed in the enamelled or burnt in china. The sole province of dealing in this manufactory, except in the London trade, being assigned over by Mr. T. Turner and Co. Hancock, country dealers [sic.: a printer's error here] will find it turn to their account to be supplied by him in the same manner as they were by Mr. Turner from Worcester. — Wanted a diligent clerk at the above warehouse. Likewise a person who has been used to china printing. — Letters directed to R. Hancock, at the Salopian China Warehouse, Bridgnorth, shall be duly attended to.

Some engraved copperplates bearing Hancock's signature were found by Jewitt at the Coalport factory, which acquired Caughley in about 1799, and others have come to light more recently. There is,

however, no certainty that he worked exclusively for the factory. It was said a century ago that when he departed from Worcester 'he went to the Potteries to conduct a printing establishment'.

In 1783 Turner opened a London depot at 5 Portugal Street, Lincolns Inn Fields, which was listed in directories of that year as being in the occupation of 'William Hussey, chinaman'. The premises had been built in 1713-14 as a theatre, and in 1728 the first performance of John Gay's 'Beggar's Opera' took place there. It was

Fig. 294: Butterboat painted in blue and marked S. Circa 1780. Length, 4 inches.

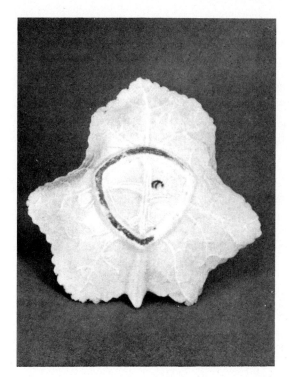

presented by John Rich, builder of the edifice, and as a result of its success it ran for sixty-two nights; a wit suggesting it had made 'Gay rich and Rich gay'. In 1732 the theatre changed hands and became in turn a concert and exhibition hall, a barracks, an auction room and finally a warehouse.

The Caughley works supplied Robert

Left, Fig. 295: Mug decorated in blue with 'Chantilly sprig' pattern and marked with a crescent. Circa 1780. Height, 3⅜ inches. (City Museum and Art Gallery, Plymouth.) **Above,** *Figs. 296 and 297: Top and underside of a pickle tray painted in blue with 'Chantilly sprig' pattern and marked with a crescent. Length 3½ inches.*

Chamberlain with ware, when he and his son left the Worcester firm and set up on their own account in the city in 1789. A letter written by them to Turner in that year stated: 'Unpacked three casks yesterday, and were much disappointed to find so small a quantity of blue ware'. Presumably the majority of the consignment was unpainted china which would take time to decorate, and the letter continued:

> Can only say we are every day disobliging our customers and injuring ourselves for want of them—in reality, we find greater difficulty in getting the goods than in selling them.

Turner is supposed to have travelled to France in 1780 in order to study French methods of porcelain manufacture, and to have brought back with him some French workmen. He was perhaps responsible for introducing on this side of the Channel the pattern known as 'Chantilly sprig': a group of flowers, delicately painted and centred on a pink or *oeillet*. It had become popular at several Continental factories, where it appears sometimes in underglaze blue. A variant of it is occasionally seen on Caughley wares (Figs. 295-7). The Belgian factory at Tournai was also a source of patterns, among which were pieces with basket-moulded borders.

A small quantity of Caughley ware with coloured decoration has been recognised, but it is undistinguished in appearance. It has been suggested that some of the painting was executed outside the factory, and Thomas Baxter, who had a studio in Goldsmith Street, Gough Square, London, may perhaps have been responsible for the work. It is thought that he did all or most of the bright gilding seen on some Caughley blue wares.

Thomas Turner retired from potting in about 1799, when he was fifty years of age, and sold the manufactory to the owner of a nearby establishment, John Rose. The latter continued to run both concerns, sending the ware made at Caughley to be glazed and painted at his other works, Coalport, on the other side of the Severn.

Plate 47 *Lowestoft: teapot painted with a Chinese design,* circa *1770, height 5¼ inches; two-handled bowl and cover with knob in the shape of a bird,* circa *1760, height 9 inches. (City Museum and Art Gallery, Plymouth.)*

Caughley or Salopian china often closely resembles Worcester, as mentioned above, and similarly contains a proportion of soapstone in its composition. When held against the light it has an orange or brown translucency compared with the pale green usual in Worcester, but on its own this is not an infallible basis for attribution. More characteristic of Caughley, especially in the case of wares of later date, is the inky tone of the blue printing, which is easy to recognise.

In addition to the initial *C* and the crescent, the letter *S* (for Salopian) was used sometimes as a mark. The name Salopian, thus or all in capital letters, was occasionally impressed on plates and dishes.

Marks in the form of numerals disguised with random strokes so that they have an Oriental appearance were once thought to have been used at Caughley, but it is now known that they occur only on wares made at the Worcester factory.

Above, *Fig. 299: Jug moulded with a mask on the spout and printed in underglaze blue with a version of the 'Willow' pattern. Circa 1790. Height, 5½ inches. (Stephen Simpson Collection: City Museum and Art Gallery, Plymouth.)* **Below,** *Fig. 300: Sauceboat with printed decoration in underglaze blue and marked* S. *Circa 1790. Length, 7 inches.*

21 Plymouth and Bristol

Below, *Fig. 301: Jug decorated with a Chinese design in underglaze blue. 'Wreathing' is visible in the lower part of the body, and the base is distorted (on left). Marked under the base with the sign for Tin in blue (see Fig. 302). Height, 8 inches. (Mrs. G. C. S. Coode.)*

THE various types of English porcelain so far described and illustrated have one feature in common: all are of so-called 'soft paste', as explained earlier (page 195). The city and port of Plymouth, Devon, was the seat of the first manufactory of true or 'hard paste' porcelain in this country, and the credit for its introduction belongs to a Quaker chemist, William Cookworthy, who was born at Kingsbridge, about 20 miles from Plymouth, in 1705.

After the death of his father, the thirteen-year-old boy was sent to London and apprenticed to two of his co-religionists, Silvanus and Timothy Bevan, of Plough Court, London, where they traded as apothecaries. Silvanus Bevan, incidentally, married in 1715 the daughter of Daniel Quare, the clockmaker, and achieved some renown as an amateur ivory-carver. His study of William Penn, who had attended the wedding, was in 1770 'said to be a good likeness' and formed the basis for Wedgwood's jasperware portrait plaque of the founder of Pennsylvania.

At the end of his apprenticeship, allowing he served the usual period of seven years, in 1726, Cookworthy went to Plymouth and set up in business as a wholesale chemist and druggist. His work entailed travelling in Devon and Cornwall, and in a letter he wrote on 30th May 1745 there are references to his journeyings. The letter, which was addressed to a Cornish surgeon in Penryn, contained an important reference to china-making, which read:

> I had lately with me the person who hath discovered the china-earth. He had several samples of the chinaware with him, which, were, I think, equal to the Asiatic. 'Twas found in the back of Virginia, where he was in Quest of

mines; and having read du Halde [*author of a history and description of China published in Paris in* 1735], discovered both the petunse and kaulin [*petunse: petuntse, china-stone - kaulin: kaolin, china-clay*]. 'Tis the latter earth, he says, is the essential thing towards the success of the manufacture.

It is thought that the man who had travelled from America was Andrew Duché, and that during his stay in England he arranged to supply some of the earth to the newly-founded Bow manufactory, just outside London.

A further paragraph in the above letter makes it clear that Cookworthy was actively experimenting:

I have at last hearkened to thy advice, and begun to commit to black and white what I know in chemistry—I mean so far as I have not been obliged to other folks. Having finished my observations on furnaces, I intend to continue it as I have leisure, as it may be of use after my death.

In due course, the stone and clay were found, and a later memorandum in Cookworthy's handwriting, tantalizingly undated but perhaps written in the early 1760's, states:

It is now twenty years since I discovered that the ingredients used by the Chinese in the composition of their porcelain, were to be got, in immense quantities, in the county of Cornwall . . . I first discovered it [*the stone*] in the parish of Germoe, in a hill called Tregonning Hill; the whole country in depth is of this stone. It reaches from east and west, from Breage to Germoe, and north and south, from Tregonning Hill to the sea. . . . I have lately discovered that, in the neighbourhood of the parish of St. Stephen's, in Cornwall, there are immense quantities both of the Petsunse stone and the Kaulin, and which, I believe, may be more commodiously and advantageously wrought than those of Tregonning Hill, as, by the experiments I have made on them, they produce a much whiter body, and do not shrink so much, by far, in baking, nor take stains so readily from the fire. Tregonning Hill is about a mile from Godolphin House, between Helston and Penzance. St. Stephen's lies between Truro, St. Austell, and St. Columb . . . .

The land at St. Stephen's was owned by Thomas Pitt, Lord Camelford, nephew of William Pitt, Lord Chatham: the latter was Prime Minister of England and, in due course, so was his son. As with so many stories of discovery there is another version, and Lord Camelford wrote in 1790 that it was a friend of Cookworthy who had found both clay and stone on the estate.

Whoever did make the actual discovery, and it is usually credited to Cookworthy, he was certainly the man who put the materials to practical use. On 17th March 1768 he patented his invention, stating that 'the materials of which the body of the said porcelainn is composed are a stone and earth, or clay'. He continued by describing the appearance and properties of the two constituents, and how they were prepared for use. The china stone, he explained 'gives the ware its whiteness and infusibility, as the stone doth its transparency and mellowness'. When the prepared ingredients were mixed to a suitable consistency and made into the required shapes, they were given a light or 'biscuit' 1st firing to harden them. Then they were dipped in the glaze, which was made from ground and sieved stone with lime and fern-ashes, 'in such quantity as may make it properly fusible and transparent when it has received a due degree of fire in the

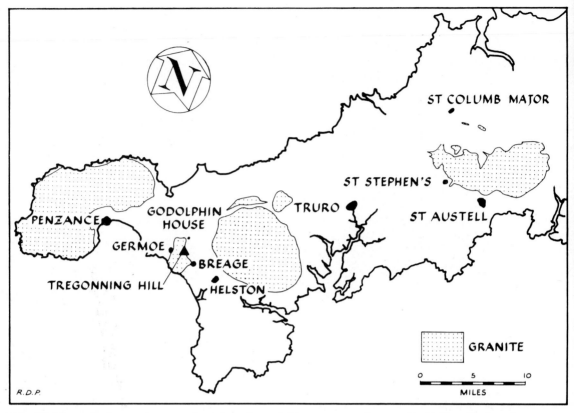

Fig. 305: Cornwall, showing the areas where china clay and china-stone were discovered by William Cookworthy.

second baking'.

Blue decoration was applied between the biscuit and final baking stages; hence the term 'underglaze blue', because the colour was beneath the glaze. Other colours would not withstand the heat needed to melt the glaze, so they were employed after the final baking, and then required a further light firing to make them permanent. Gilding also was an additional overglaze process, with a further heating to fix the gold.

As was the case with most other English factories, the first productions were painted in blue in rivalry with imported ware from China. The earliest known Plymouth piece is a mug decorated in this manner on which are the arms of Plymouth and the inscription *March* 14 1768 *C.F.* It is in the British Museum, and a family tradition was that Cookworthy himself ornamented it; the initials standing for *Cookworthy Fecit.*

Amongst the shareholders in the venture, all of whom were Quakers, was a Bristol banker, Richard Champion, who was concerned not only in making money from it but was interested in the actual manufacture of porcelain. Also from Bristol, and financially involved were John and Joseph Harford, Joseph Fry and Thomas Frank; the last-named a member of a family prominent in the flourishing potting trade in the city (see page 62). It is thought to have been Champion's keenness, perhaps with the help of his fellow-residents, that induced Cookworthy to remove the manufactory from Plymouth to Bristol.

Exactly when this event took place is uncertain, but some time in 1770 seems probable. A drawing, published in 1873, shows a tall kiln and is dated in Champion's hand *October* 16 1770 with the note: *the*

Last Burning of Enamel Nov. 27. 1770.
Made in that year is the little sauceboat
shown in Figs. 309 and 310, the red-painted
inscription leaving no doubt that the piece
was made and painted prior to the removal
to Bristol. A further link with the date in
question is an advertisement that appeared
in the *Worcester Journal* on 22nd. February
1770, which read:

CHINA WARE PAINTERS WANTED
For the Plymouth New Invented Patent
Porcelain Manufactory.
A number of sober ingenious Artists,
capable of painting in Enamel or Blue,
may hear of constant Employment by
sending their Proposals to Thomas
Frank, in Castle Street, Bristol.

Cookworthy himself went to Bristol to
manage the establishment, which occupied
premises at Castle Green. By November
1772 production had become sufficiently
well organised for an advertisement to be
placed in *Felix Farley's Bristol Journal*.
It stated that 'the figures, Vases, Jars and
Beakers, are very elegant, and the useful
Ware exceedingly good'. Adding:

It may not be Improper to remark, that
this Porcelain is wholly free from the
Imperfections in Wearing, which the
English China usually has, and that its
Composition is equal in fineness to the
East Indian, and will wear as well.—
The Enamell'd Ware, which is rendered
nearly as cheap as the English Blue and
White, comes very near, and in some
Pieces can equal the Dresden, which
this Work more particularly imitates.

The aping of foreign work became more
attainable with the employment of more
hands, and at one period the staff included
as many as twenty-four painters.

It is known that in June 1773 the public
were offered

Complete tea sets in the Dresden taste
highly ornamented, £7 0s. 0d. to
£12 12s. 0d. and upwards. Tea Sets,
43 pieces of various prices as low as
£2 2s. 0d. Cups and Saucers from
3s. 6d. to 5s. 6d. per half-dozen, and all
other sorts of useful Ware proportion-
ately cheap.

A forty-three-piece teaset of the time, from

Fig. 306: (Left and right) *boy and girl, each holding a dog, height 7 inches;* (centre) *bird raised on a rococo base, height 4¾ inches.* (*Fenton House, London: The National Trust.*)

Bristol or any other manufactory, normally included:

Teapot
Milk jug
Bowl
Plate
Caddy
Teapot stand
Small tray to hold spoons
12 teacups
12 coffee cups
12 saucers.

There would not appear to have been any hard-and-fast rule as to the precise composition of sets, and no doubt the pieces other than cups and saucers varied according to the factory and the choice of the customer.

In 1774 Cookworthy, then aged 69, retired and assigned the patent to Richard Champion. The latter immediately set about obtaining an extension of the period of the patent, which was due to expire in 1782 and allowed him too short a period in which to recoup his outlay. It was necessary to promote a Bill in Parliament to achieve the object, and this was opposed by the Staffordshire potters under the leadership of Josiah Wedgwood. In the end, in 1775, Champion was granted an extension of fourteen years, but this applied solely to the use of china-stone and china clay for making porcelain. The two basic ingredients might now be employed by any person for other purposes, for example in the manufacture of pottery, and they were duly embodied in improved Staffordshire wares (see *Chapter* 10, page 157).

In spite of his success over the patent,

Plate 48 *Vase and cover; the latter is a modern replacement. Height, 15¾ inches. (City Museum and Art Gallery, Plymouth.)*

Plate 49 *Figures, circa 1770-75:* (top row) *boy playing pipe and tabor, height 5½ inches; girl playing lute, height 6 inches; Cupid holding a basket, height 4½ inches;* (bottom row) *goat, height 4 inches; sheep, height 2½ inches; figure emblematic of Winter, height 5½ inches. (County Museum, Truro.)*

Fig. 308: Set of figures representing the Seasons: (left to right) Winter, Summer, Autumn, Spring. Average height, 10½ inches. (Fenton House, London: The National Trust.)

Champion experienced increasing difficulties. The expenses in promoting the Bill and fighting the potters had been great, and the ware itself was costly to make with high expenditure on materials, fuel and pieces spoiled in the kiln. There was little or no possibility of making it sufficiently cheaply to compete with soft paste porcelain or with most of the imported Chinese hard paste, so Champion set out to attract those who might buy Dresden or Sèvres. The Continental standard was a high one, and it could not be equalled or approached without heavy outlay.

In November 1780, Josiah Wedgwood reported to Bentley:

Amongst other things Mr. Champion of Bristol has taken me up near two days. He is come amongst us to dispose of his secret—His patent, etc. and, who could have believed it? has chosen me for his friend and confidante. I shall not deceive him for I really feel much for his situation. A wife and eight children (to say nothing of himself) to provide for and out of what I fear will not be thought of much value here— The secret of China making. He tells me he has sunk fifteen thousand pounds in this gulf, and his idea is now to sell the whole art, mystery and patent for six . . . .

Wedgwood was true to his word and gave Champion a list of possible buyers. In 1781 a group of Staffordshire potters purchased the patent together with the services of Champion as adviser and manager, but three years later he gave up all connection with ceramics and emigrated to a farm near Charleston, South Carolina.

Ill-luck dogged him over the Atlantic, for in 1790 his wife died and a year later, at the age of 48, he was afflicted with what was termed 'a bilious fever' which caused his death.

*   *   *

THE difference in appearance between hard and soft paste porcelain can in time be recognised by the eye alone; the requirements being a combination of experience and determination. With Plymouth and Bristol the glaze is only very rarely completely smooth and glassy, and normally is composed of a myriad of minute bubbles resulting in a surface that is finely pitted and very slightly matt or one that is glossy and uneven. Both Cookworthy and Champion were unable to conquer completely the brown smoke-staining that discolours much of the ware, and the instability of the ingredients together with the required heat distorted a sizeable proportion of the total output.

It is rarely possible to differentiate between wares produced at Plymouth and Bristol, as not only was marking haphazard but the moulds were transferred from the one site to the other. Underglaze blue painting in the Chinese style is recognisable by its blackish-blue or greyish tone, which is distinctive. The draughtsmanship is good, as is that on other pieces

Above left, Fig. 309: Sauceboat of rococo pattern painted in colours. Length, 5½ inches. (City Museum and Art Gallery, Plymouth.) **Above,** *Fig. 310: Inscribed base of sauceboat in Fig. 309.* **Right,** *Fig. 311: Biscuit plaque modelled with flowers and leaves centred on a bust of Benjamin Franklin, American statesman and scientist (1706-1790). Height, 8¾ inches. (From an engraving; the plaque is now in the British Museum.)*

decorated in blue and red in the Japanese Imari style.

Coloured enamels tended not to sink into the glaze, as on soft paste, but remained above the surface. A brownish-crimson was very popular, and this was used not only for general decoration but to pick out the rococo scrollwork on the bases of figures. Gold was employed, especially to embellish tablewares. The faces of figures were sometimes finished to give the effect of a deathly pallor, which may have been the idiosyncracy of one particular painter.

Output was divided between tablewares and figures and groups, the former concentrating on upright pieces rather than broad flat ones. Plates and bowls proved

Left, *Fig. 312: Cup and saucer printed and painted with birds in a tree. Marked* New Hall *within two rings. (City Museum and Art Gallery, Plymouth.)*

Right, *Fig. 313: Bristol mug initialled* J E M. *Height, 4¾ inches. (Christie's.)*

most difficult to make successfully, and were very prone to emerge from the kiln badly warped. The handles of cups and jugs tended to go awry, and many pieces made on the wheel show spiral markings ('wreathing') said to be due to unskilful potting (Fig. 301).

Figures differed little from those made at other factories, with sets of Seasons and shepherds and shepherdesses vieing in popularity with classical gods and goddesses and sets of the Continents. A connection between the modelling at Derby and that at Bristol has been noted, and the ubiquitous 'Mr. Tebo', or Thibaud, (page 272) left his mark under the bases of Plymouth figures and other pieces. Some figures and groups are close copies of those produced earlier at Longton Hall, and it has been suggested that Champion somehow acquired the moulds after the closure of the Staffordshire factory. Alternatively he can have used actual Longton examples in order to make his own, but in either case the circumstances remain unknown and the pieces represent one of the numerous unsolved mysteries of English china-making.

Champion's rarest pieces are a number of plaques made of biscuit (unglazed) por-celain, usually devoid of decoration but in a few instances partly painted, which were for presentation to friends and potential patrons (Fig. 311). They are most delicately modelled, and it was reported that each cost as much as £5 to make; no large sum to-day, but a considerable amount at the time.

For those of his wares that were marked Cookworthy used the alchemist's sign for tin: a numeral 4 with the front upright curled forward (Fig. 302). It was painted in blue, red or gold, and while certainly employed at Plymouth was not discontinued after the move to Bristol. At the latter place either a cross in blue or a copy of the Dresden crossed swords was used, but much of the output was unmarked. In the latter category are figures and groups, and these can often be confused with Continental hard paste examples.

THE six Staffordshire potters who purchased Champion's unexpired patent in
1781, first began porcelain-manufacture
in their home county at Tunstall, near
Stoke-on-Trent. A year later, a fresh start
was made nearby at Shelton, where premises were taken. The building was later
known as the New Hall, and this name has
been given to the ware produced there.

Instead of continuing to make the costly
types of articles that gave Bristol its
renown, the New Hall proprietors concentrated their attention on a range of

*Fig. 314: Milk jug painted in colours.
New Hall, circa 1800. Height, 4 inches.*

simple tablewares, almost all in the form of tea and coffee sets. While the body is very similar to that used earlier, the glaze is different in appearance; it is softer and thicker and it has been suggested that it was applied after the pieces had been fired at full heat. The glazed ware was then re-fired, but at a lower temperature.

The shapes used at New Hall were the current neo-classic ones seen in other makes of porcelain, in pottery and in silver. Decoration was usually slight with the draughtsmanship of varying quality. The unsophisticated nature of the patterns has endeared the ware to those who eschew the virtuosity to be found in Chelsea and Worcester, and this once-neglected factory can now boast a following of keen collectors. As a result much information about its products has been brought to light during the past few years.

Printed decoration was used at New Hall, and much of it was roughly painted over in bright colours (Fig. 315). The making of hard paste porcelain ceased in about 1810, and the factory then adopted the bone china formula general throughout the Potteries. Marks were seldom used, but some pieces bear numerals preceded by a script 'N' to indicate the pattern number. After 1812 the name *New Hall* within concentric circles was sometimes transfer-printed. The factory closed in 1835.

Fig. 315: Plate with a moulded border, the centre printed and painted with a view of Bear Place, Berkshire. Marked New Hall *within two rings. Circa 1810. Diameter, 8¼ inches. (City Museum and Art Gallery, Plymouth.)*

22 19th Century Porcelain: Part 1

Plate 50 *Tureen, stand, and dish from a dessert service. Unmarked. Circa 1810. (Bearne's, Torquay, Devon.)*

Left, Plate 51: *Vase. Unmarked.* Circa *1810. Height, 15 inches. (F. T. W. Collection.)*

Fig. 316: *Pen tray painted with birds in colours within gilt borders. Mark, see Fig. 329. Derby,* circa *1810. Length, 10 inches. (County Museum, Truro.)*

THE 19th century opened with the old-established factories of Worcester and Derby in close rivalry, and with an increasing number of newly-founded ones seeking to gain for themselves a share of the growing market. The days when anything whatsoever made of porcelain was a novelty, and which sold whatever its finish, were over, and the high standards attained in both potting and painting by the best makers were yardsticks reached by more and more entrants to the industry.

The Derby factory carried on from 1796 under the ownership of Michael Kean and the widow of William Duesbury II. They continued to make wares of the types that had proved popular in early days, and some of the biscuit of the time was of superior quality. From the turn of the century, the standard was often lower, with a growing use of shiny gilding and the occasional employment of lace as an embellishment of

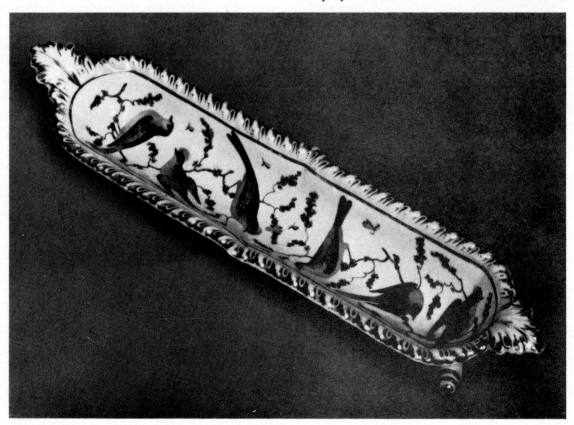

figures. This decoration was made by dipping real lace into slip, placing it where required and in the heat of the kiln the fabric vanished to leave the fragile clay coating.

In 1811 the concern was purchased by the firm's clerk, Robert Bloor, and from then until he retired insane in 1826 and onwards to 1848 when the establishment was finally closed, the old standards were slowly lowered in the face of economic necessity. Imitation took the place of originality, and the few new designs introduced were not sufficiently good or plentiful to halt the decline.

The long-standing traditions of the firm founded in the 1750's, in the heyday of exciting experiment, were carried on by one of their apprentices, William Billing-sley. He went to Derby in 1774 and became an accomplished decorator of porcelain (see page 248), so that his name is even today applied to well-painted floral groups that may or may not have been his work. As a result of his general interest in the subject of porcelain-making he acquired a knowledge of the various ingredients and processes, and gained the reputation of being an 'arcanist': one who possesses the secrets of manufacture. He was the nearest equivalent produced by England of the

Fig. 317: Pair of groups known as 'The Welsh Tailor' and 'The Welsh Tailor's Wife'. Mark BLOOR DERBY *and a crown. Circa 1830. Height, 5¾ inches. (Saltram, Devon: The National Trust.)*

many men who had earlier wandered across Europe offering such services and information to whoever would pay for them.

In 1795, while employed at Derby, Billingsley made the acquaintance of John Coke, a local young man of property, who had returned recently from a Continental tour that had included a visit to Meissen. It inspired him with a desire to make porcelain of his own, and following correspondence between the two men, dealing with the possible cost and profits of such a venture, a partnership was formed. A factory was built at Pinxton, about fifteen miles to the north-east of Derby, and manufacture was commenced.

Billingsley, like all other arcanists, was a restless man, and stayed at Pinxton only a few years. During that time he introduced an excellent porcelain body that served him in good stead during his subsequent travels, and gained for the little factory a reputation for pieces of good quality. A contemporary local writer refers to the 'manufactory of elegant, useful and ornamental china', but on the whole the enterprise went unremarked.

Coke carried on the works with a fresh partner, a Lincoln attorney, Henry Bankes, but this arrangement did not endure for much more than a year. The *London*

Fig. 318: Cup and saucer. Mark, P63. Pinxton, circa 1800. Diameter of saucer, 5¼ inches.

Gazette announced the dissolution of partnership as from 1st January 1803, and John Coke was again solely responsible for the concern. Finally, he was able to dispose of it in 1806 to a china-painter, John Cutts, but there is little or no evidence of what wares were made during his ownership. It has been suggested that he ran the pottery solely as a decorating establishment, using the remaining white stock on the premises and augmenting it with purchases made elsewhere. After a chequered career of seventeen years, the works was closed early in 1815, subsequently being converted into dwellings and demolished in 1937.

The white porcelain body devised by Billingsley could be potted thinly, had a good translucency and a clear glaze, and was a soft paste containing bone ash. Another type made at Pinxton, especially after 1801, resembled Derby in both appearance and characteristics, and a likeness of both varieties to Derby is to be seen in the shapes used and their decoration. Of the latter, Billingsley wrote to Coke in 1795:

> . . . I am certain that it is far more advantagious to finish the Ware than Dispose of it in the White.

Pinxton followed popular contemporary styles and was not responsible for any innovations (Fig. 318). Decorative patterns were similar to those at Derby not only because of the close proximity of the factories, but also because some ex-Derby men joined Billingsley and carried on working in the manner of their teaching. Marks were used intermittently, and the most frequently found is a script capital 'P' followed by a pattern number.

After leaving Pinxton in April 1799, Billingsley went a few miles away to Mansfield, where he set up as a decorator and is known to have employed at least one assistant; a gilder, named Tatlow (Fig. 319). Then, between 1802 and 1803 the arcanist was in Lincolnshire, at a small place named Torksey, situated midway between Gainsborough and the city of Lincoln. Here it has been suggested that he was concerned in manufacturing porcelain, but there is no real evidence that he did so. It is probable that he only decorated goods bought in the white from other sources.

Billingsley next appeared as an employee of the Worcester manufactory, and with his son-in-law, Samuel Walker, was responsible for the installation of a kiln for firing painting. He also experimented

Above left, *Fig. 321: Plate painted in colours with fruit within a gilt border. Coalport, unmarked, circa 1810. Diameter, 9¼ inches.* (*Christie's.*) **Above,** *Fig. 322: Pastille burner painted with flowers in colours on a blue and gold ground. Spode or Derby, circa 1820. Height, 4½ inches.* (*City Museum and Art Gallery, Plymouth.*) **Right,** *Fig. 323: Plate from a service made for King William IV on his accession in 1831. Marked Royal Porcelain Works, Flight, Barr, and Barr, Worcester, and Coventry Street, London.* (*From a woodcut.*)

with porcelain bodies during the five years, 1808 to 1813, that he remained there. What effect Billingsley had on production at Worcester cannot be assessed, but the factory was among the foremost at the time in producing the high-quality wares then so much in demand. Extremely careful painting was usually framed in heavy gilding on a coloured ground, resulting in a rich effect that can cloy by reason of its perfection.

At the same time, the Chamberlain factory at Worcester was producing very similar work. Both makers received orders for large dinner services that fashionably vied for extravagance in appearance and cost. One for the East India Company in 1818 comprised more than a thousand pieces at £2,170 15s. 0d., the '1456 Coats of Arms, painted proper, at 15s.' forming £1,092 of the total.

Before departing from Worcester in 1813, Billingsley changed his name to 'Beeley'. In company with Walker, he suddenly left the city despite being bound not to divulge any of the Worcester 'secrets' and with a liability to pay a £1,000 fine for so doing. The two men went to Nantgarw, Glamor-gan, where they enlisted financial help from persons in the locality and then proceeded to make use of their recently-acquired knowledge. Flight, Barr and Barr, went so far as to threaten proceedings against both men, but apart from writing to state their 'firm resolution of instantly giving our attorney Instructions to commence an Action' nothing would appear to have been done.

Efforts to make and market a profitable ware at Nantgarw proved fruitless, and in 1814 the concern was removed forty miles away to the prosperous Swansea pottery. Three years later Billingsley and Walker returned to Nantgarw and resumed operations, but by 1819 their capital was exhausted, and the two men left in the next year for Coalport. Thus the factory had a short and unsettled career, but in spite of this it produced some very beautiful porcelain.

Billingsley's Nantgarw soft paste was a difficult body to fire and a high proportion of damaged, warped and unusable pieces was taken from the kiln. The perfect specimens are highly translucent with a brilliant smooth glaze, and have been the subject of careful study. Much of the painting was done on the premises, but some of the output was sold undecorated to dealers who had it painted to their taste. Tea and dessert services were the principal productions, but spill vases, inkstands and pen trays were among other items made.

The marks used were varied, and include SWANSEA impressed or in script writing.

Most common is NANT GARW above the letters C W; the latter standing for 'China Works'. The marking was impressed before glazing, and the thick glaze sometimes fills the shallow lettering and makes it difficult to see. As both Nantgarw and Swansea porcelains have been esteemed for a considerable period and their values are high, collectors are advised to be on their guard against imitations.

The factory of John Rose at Caughley was closed in 1814, and he concentrated on his works at nearby Coalport. During 1822 and 1823 Rose bought the moulds and stock of the Swansea concern, acquiring also the services of Billingsley and Walker. As a result, a distinct likeness to Nantgarw porcelain can be observed in

much Coalport dating from after their arrival there.

At one time it was usual to attribute to the factory all the unmarked flower-encrusted ware surviving from the decade 1820-30 when it was enormously popular. Recent research has proved, however, that much of it was made elsewhere, and the careful attention given to the successful products of competitors was as prevalent in the 19th century as it had been in the 18th. In the case of Coalport this extended to the use of a mark naming the product as 'Coalport Felt Spar Porcelain'; the firm going as close as it possibly could in rivalling Josiah Spode's 'Felspar'. Marks used include a monogram of *C* and *D*, *C Dale*, and sometimes, the alternative name for the factory written in full: *Coalbrookdale*.

EITHER Josiah Spode (1733-97), or his son of the same name (1754-1827), is credited with establishing English bone-china and causing it to be accepted and manufactured widely. As early as 1649 the white powder remaining from burned bones had been mentioned in a German publication as a constituent of opaque white glass. A century later Thomas Frye was using it at Bow, and a few other factories duly adopted it. By about 1800 the virtues of the material were widely recognised, and although it produced a ware lacking some of the qualities of hard paste it was less costly to make and more durable than soft paste.

Fig. 324: Three vases modelled with 'pearl' borders, painted in colours and gilt. Worcester, Flight, Barr and Barr, circa 1815. Height of small vases, 3⅝ inches.

With the aid of bone ash, the potters were able to produce a good, white porcelain that was not wasteful in manufacture. Paradoxically, current taste ran to heavy and elaborate decoration, so that in many instances little or no actual china was visible after painting. So far as present-day collectors are concerned, the standardisation of formula results in considerable difficulty in attributing pieces to one factory or another. Unless they are marked it becomes almost impossible to be certain of the precise origin of most specimens made after about 1800.

Josiah Spode I served his apprenticeship from 1749 with Thomas Whieldon (see page 114), and in 1770 commenced working on his own at Stoke-on-Trent. He made pottery at first, but probably soon turned his attention to porcelain, and following the expiry of Richard Champion's patent was enabled to experiment freely with china-stone and china clay. His son succeeded to a flourishing business and, in his turn, was able to introduce new types of ware. Certainly at least two important varieties ('Stone China' and 'Felspar Porcelain') were introduced during his lifetime, and it is not unlikely that he was responsible for much of the work in developing the bone china formula.

Early 19th century Spode wares were carefully painted in bright colours, or else printed in stipple. The latter succeeded the earlier type of engraved transfer-printing, and replaced the lines by small dots which gave a very delicate result. Instead of printing the stipple-engraved designs on paper, they were printed on thin slabs (or 'bats') of glue. It had been found that much finer effects could be obtained in this way, and a large proportion of the better-quality printed decoration in the first half of the century was the result of bat-printing.

Fashions in subjects for painted decoration changed from time to time, but the most sustained was for variations of old Japanese designs; which are to be found on Derby and Worcester as well as on Spode. They were carried out largely in dark blue and red with gilding and, often, other colours added in small quantities. The general effect is usually garish, but the taste of the time, led by the Prince Regent, later King George IV, demanded extravagance and display. Other painted work embraced a wide variety of subjects, with flowers predominating. In all instances the workmanship was impeccable to the point of appearing mechanical, and the finer pieces of the time, both by Spode and

Fig. 325: Two-handled vase painted in colours with country children in a landscape and on the reverse with a panel of flowers. Chamberlain's Worcester, circa 1830. Height, 18¾ inches. (Christie's.)

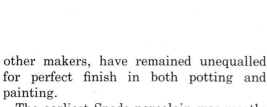

other makers, have remained unequalled for perfect finish in both potting and painting.

The earliest Spode porcelain was mostly sold without a mark, but from about 1790 the name of the firm together with a pattern number was written under bases. 'Spode Felspar Porcelain' within a wreath of flowers was printed on ware containing a proportion of feldspar in its composition between about 1815 and 1827.

Rivalling Spode in diversity of output was Mintons, also situated at Stoke-on-Trent.   Porcelain manufacture did not begin in quantity until about 1825, and was mainly confined to tablewares. Examples dating back to about 1800 are recorded, and differ little from the productions of other factories.   Brightly coloured formal patterns, vignettes of country landscapes, and conventionalised floral scrolls vied in popularity with bouquets of flowers.   More

distinctive is the work of an anonymous artist who made a speciality of figures of young Chinamen, which are a reminder of the *chinoiserie* of the contemporaneous Royal Pavilion at Brighton.

After 1825 Mintons rapidly extended their range of goods to include the more ornate styles of which Spode had been the principal supplier to date.   Much of the fussily-decorated wares that had always been attributed to Coalport are now known to have been made by Mintons, but as each factory copied the actual porcelain composition of the other, as well as shapes and decoration, no certain attributions can be made in the case of unmarked pieces.

A large proportion of the Mintons output left the factory unmarked, but some bears an imitation of the mark used on Sèvres porcelain from 1753: two crossed script 'L's', the initial of the King of France, Louis XV.   The Mintons version includes a capital *M*, and sometimes a pattern number (Fig. 330).

Wedgwood's then directed by Josiah II, son of the original Josiah Wedgwood, made bone china for about ten years from 1812. Most of the output comprised tablewares, and one of the painters employed was John Cutts, who specialised in landscapes and had formerly been at Pinxton. Wedgwood porcelain was marked with the name in capital letters printed in red, blue black or gold.

Below left, *Fig. 328: 'The Rhinoceros Vase', painted with scenes from* Don Quixote. *Rockingham, 1826. Height, 45 inches. Formerly at Wentworth Woodhouse and now at the Municipal Museum and Art Gallery, Rotherham, Yorkshire.*

Well finished wares in most of the prevailing styles were made also by John Davenport and his two sons at Longport, a few miles to the north-west of Stoke-on-Trent. They made pottery and, for a time, glass (an unusual combination of products from the one source), and began porcelain manufacture early in the nineteenth century. The body varied in quality from time to time, and while sometimes it almost rivalled that of Nantgarw, on other occasions it was greyish in tone or showed a strong tendency to discolour to a shade of brown.

As the Derby works fell into decline their well-trained staff went to more flourishing factories, and the work of their painters is to be seen on Davenport and other wares. Marks used at Longport include an impressed anchor which should not be confused with the *raised* anchor of Chelsea; the latter not only stands up from the surface, but is superimposed on a small oval pad. The name Davenport sometimes appears on its own, with an anchor, or over the word Longport.

Among the Derby-taught painters who left their original employment and worked elsewhere were members of the Steele family, Thomas Steele and his sons, Edwin, Horatio and Thomas. The eldest of the boys, Edwin, was a skilful flower-painter, and journeyed to Yorkshire to join the factory at Swinton, near Rotherham, built on the estate of the Marquis of Rockingham.

The manufactory had started as a pottery founded in the mid-eighteenth century, and was eventually acquired by members of the Brameld family (see page 171). In

(Left to right) *Fig. 329: Mark in red on the Derby pen tray in Fig. 316. Fig. 330: Mark used by Mintons between 1805 and 1816, usually painted in blue over the glaze. Fig. 331: Rockingham mark in use between 1826 and 1830.*

about 1820 they began to make bone porcelain, but within a few years got into difficulties and were declared bankrupt. To avoid the local unemployment that would ensue if the concern closed, the Bramelds' landlord, Earl Fitzwilliam, agreed to advance the sum of £10,000. In gratitude, the establishment was named the 'Rockingham Works' and it was allowed to use the griffin of the Earl's crest as a mark (Fig. 331).

As elsewhere in England, highly ornate and flamboyantly colourful pieces were made, but although their style may not be generally admired it must be agreed that they were well potted and are usually of a flawless porcelain. Tea, coffee and dessert services would seem to have been a speciality, and in 1830 the firm supplied King William IV with a particularly magnificent dessert service of 200 pieces at an alleged charge of £5,000. The bulk of it remains at Buckingham Palace, where it is occasionally used at banquets.

A few years earlier, in 1826 and perhaps to exhibit their skill to their noble patron, the factory produced the famous (or notorious) 'Rhinoceros Vase'. It was for a century and a quarter at the Fitzwilliam seat, Wentworth Woodhouse, but since 1949 has been on view to the public at the Clifton Park Museum, Rotherham (Fig. 328). A near-duplicate, made slightly later, has been in the Victoria and Albert Museum since 1859.

Both vases are fine examples of potting, but their design and decoration have produced varied reactions. Jewitt in 1878 referred to the 1826 specimen as 'of surpassing beauty', whereas W. B. Honey 55 years later wrote of the Victoria and Albert one, which is painted by Edwin Steele, as 'not without a vulgar abundance and excess that reveal an unmistakable vitality, if little taste'.

Figures, both coloured and biscuit, were made at Rockingham, and pastille-burners in the form of miniature cottages, houses and castles were also produced. The first decades of the nineteenth century saw a big demand for small-sized figures of poodles, which had their clipped fur rendered realistically by a sprinkling of shredded clay. By long-standing tradition many of them have been attributed to Rockingham, but there is no evidence whatsoever that they were made there and without doubt they originated in Staffordshire.

Although aided by further financial assistance from Earl Fitzwilliam, the firm continued to experience difficulties. In 1841 their landlord, the Earl's son who had succeeded to the title in 1833, made it clear that he was unwilling to allow further credit. The sum of £4,500 was outstanding for rent, and in May 1843 'the valuable Stock of China . . . . including some Beautifully finished Cabinet specimens' was sold by auction.

23 19th Century Porcelain: Part 2

Right, *Fig. 332:* Narcissus, *modelled in parian porcelain, after the sculpture by John Gibson, R.A. Copeland and Garrett, 1846. Height, 11⅞ inches. (Victoria and Albert Museum.)*

THE period of years between about 1845 and 1870 might be aptly named, so far as ceramics were concerned, 'The Age of Parian'. Parian china was a type of porcelain which, as Jewitt wrote, was a 'development of the old and ever-famous Derby biscuit ware'. In the same paragraph, in his *Ceramic Art of Great Britain* (1878), he stated that it was made at the suggestion of John Gibson, the English sculptor who spent the major part of his life in Rome.

While on a visit to his native land in 1844 Gibson had been consulted by Sir Robert Peel, then Prime Minister, about the state of sculpture in the British Isles and about sending promising students to study in Rome. It must have been on this occasion that he formed one of a group of men who gave optimistic opinions on the new material, which was called at the time 'Stone China' and 'Statuary Porcelain'. There is no doubt that the ware had been devised and tested before Gibson came on the scene, and although Jewitt was incorrect in stating that the sculptor inspired its actual invention, he certainly did all in his power to encourage it once he became aware of its existence.

Although it was first made not so much more than a century ago, the same argument and obscurity overshadow the origin of Parian as other and older innovations. It was claimed by both Copeland & Garrett, Minton and by T. & R. Boote, all of Staffordshire. The first-named were successors to Spode of Stoke-on-Trent, and the firm is credited with three men of whom all have been said to have invented Parian: John Mountford, an employee, Spencer Garrett, one of the partners, and Thomas Battam, its art director.

Mountford stated that he made his discovery in 1845, whereas Thomas Boote claimed to have ante-dated it by four years. At any rate, by 1846 it was being produced on a commercial scale, and after an initial hesitancy the public eagerly purchased it.

The purpose of the material was to imitate real marble as closely as possible, and while Copeland's eventually (*circa* 1849) called theirs *Parian*, Wedgwood's gave their version of it the name *Carrara*; both

363

being named after types of Italian marble used by sculptors. Articles made from the various kinds of Parian vary in tint from white to pale ivory, and all have in common a smooth, and what has been called a 'seductive', surface.

Its success was due to the patronage it received from the Art Union; a body founded in 1836 to 'advance art by the improvement of public taste and to advance civilisation by the improvement of art'. Subscribers, who in 1847 contributed the sum of £17,871, were given lottery tickets entitling the winners to suitably artistic prizes. The lucky members were given money with which to buy whatever they chose from selected exhibitions, and the objects were then displayed before being taken to the homes of their owners. The Union additionally commissioned original works, and made a start with engravings. In 1845 the Committee announced that

> they have determined to reduce some fine statue to a convenient size and to issue a certain number of copies in stone china, as manufactured by Messrs. Copeland and Garrett.

One of John Gibson's works in marble, *Narcissus*, of which the sculptor had given a version to the Royal Academy as a Diploma work in 1838, was chosen for reproduction. Others followed in subsequent years, and in 1855 no fewer than 878 copies of *Clytie*, from the marble in the British Museum, were presented to those who had been loyal subscribers for ten years without having won a prize.

Below left, *Fig. 333: Vase in the form of a right hand holding a vase. Worcester,* circa *1865. Height, 6 inches.* **Below,** *Fig. 334: Begging spaniel in parian porcelain. Unmarked,* circa *1850. Height, 2¼ inches.*

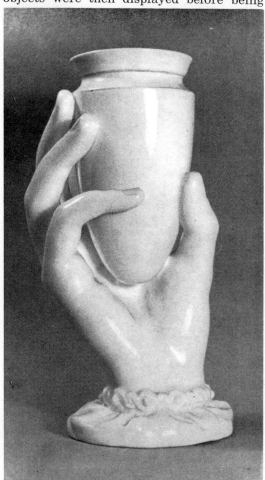

Plate 52 '*Vatican Dove Vase*', *a flower bowl modelled with four doves and encrusted with flowers. Minton,* circa *1835. Height, 6¼ inches. (Saltram, Devon: The National Trust.)*

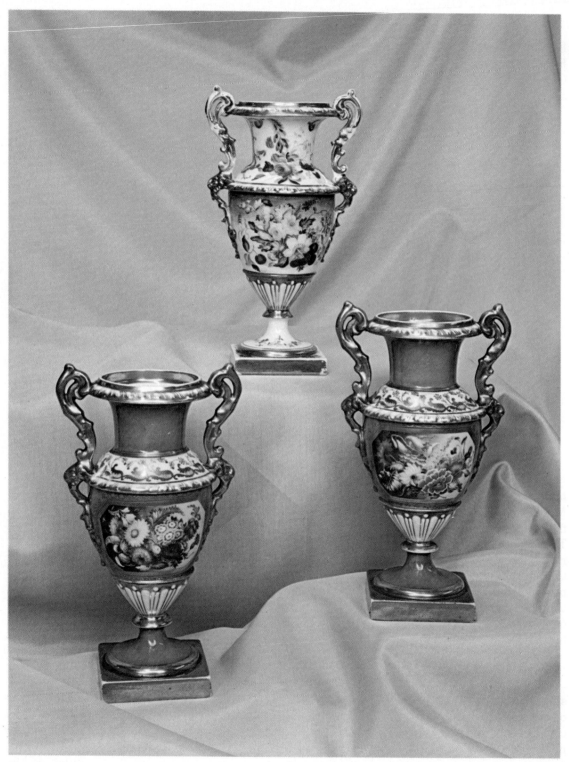

Plate 53 *Three vases with floral decoration. Unmarked, circa 1835. Heights, 7 and 6¾ inches. (City Museum and Art Gallery, Plymouth.)*

In 1851 nearly a dozen firms showed Parian wares on their stands at the Great Exhibition, and the Jury in their report on Ceramic Manufactures mentioned it at some length. They said, very fairly, that:

It has already led to the great multiplication of copies of both antique and modern groups and statues, as well as to new designs of a similar kind. But whilst fully acknowledging the importance to the ceramic art of this material, we do not feel called upon to found upon it any recommendation for a Council Medal. In the first place, the amount of novelty in the material is not easily defined, it being a modification of that which has long been known, and applied to the same department of art, under the name of Biscuit. However important this modification may be, it is hardly entitled to rank as an entirely new invention, especially as the improved result is attainable by several varieties of composition. . . .
In addition to this consideration, the Jury find that they could not recommend an award of the Council Medal for the invention of parian without deciding on the disputed claim of priority between very eminent firms, who severally advance that claim with equal confidence.

Copeland's, who listed their exhibit as 'porcelain statuary', included works by many of the noted sculptors of the day. Models of four of Queen Victoria's children, from life-size statues executed by Mary Thornycroft, portrayed each of them as representing one of the Seasons. Casting them in their roles must have strained protocol somewhat severely, and the fact that Prince Alfred as *Autumn* held a bunch of grapes caused a critic to write loftily, but doubtless sincerely:

To connect childhood with intoxicating wine is repugnant to our feelings.
Minton's showed not only a variety of statuettes and busts, also mainly the work of contemporary sculptors, but other articles as well. All were catalogued under the heading of 'Parian', and they ranged from a set of chessmen designed by John Bell to a complete chimneypiece. There were also

Fig. 335: Herbert Minton (1793–1858), a miniature on porcelain by John Simpson. Height, about 2½ inches. (Museum and Art Gallery, Hanley.)

candlesticks, pairs of wall-brackets, and vases, amongst the latter a pair named the 'Parnassus Vases'. They were formed of parian in combination with ordinary porcelain, 'the china in mazarine [*blue*] and gold, and the bas-relief, Apollo and the Muses, in Parian'.

The 1851 Exhibition saw parian also used in combination with metal. R. W. Winfield, of Birmingham, displayed an elaborate gas chandelier suspended from a bracket. The metalwork, which was described as 'of the style of Francis I', bore figures of children holding garlands and the whole was surmounted by a lady with clasped hands at whom Cupid was taking careful aim. The object was reproduced in a woodcut in the *Art-Journal Illustrated Catalogue*, where any comment that might be born in the minds of disloyal readers was firmly stifled with the words:

The gas lamp and bracket is one which, we understand, has been purchased by the Queen, a fact that supersedes the

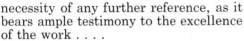

necessity of any further reference, as it bears ample testimony to the excellence of the work . . . .

The firm of Grainger, of Worcester, also exhibited some of the new ware, but apparently only two pieces of it:

Cast of a female hand, 14 years of age, in Parian;

cast of a female hand, 80 years of age.

Some years later, the original Worcester factory had a great success with posy vases modelled in the form of human hands. Many firms made them, but the Worcester examples are to be distinguished by their good finish and the maker's mark beneath the base (Fig. 333). They can sometimes be found in pairs, left and right hands. There is certainly a link between the two exhibits of 1851 and the vases, although whoever was responsible for designing the latter remains anonymous. While they are criticised sometimes for epitomising the necrolatry often traceable in the second half of the century, they have today no lack of admirers and collectors.

In 1868, when they were being made and

Above left, Fig. 336: Vase listed in the Minton design books as 'Dresden Match Pot' and finished as this example or flower-encrusted. Similar pieces were made at Worcester. Circa 1835. Height, 5 inches. Above, Fig. 337: Table thermometer, of which a version without the flowers was also made. Minton, circa 1835. Height, 7¼ inches. (City Museum and Art Gallery, Plymouth.) Right, Fig. 338: Figure of a poodle. Minton, circa 1835. Length, 4¾ inches. (City Museum and Art Gallery, Plymouth.)

at the height of their popularity, Charles Lock Eastlake, nephew of his namesake Sir C. L. Eastlake and a writer on art subjects, published his book entitled *Hints on Household Taste*. In it he castigated many of the objects then available for the average home, and in a chapter entitled 'Crockery' gave his weighty opinion on these sentimental trifles in the following words:

No doubt some of my readers may have noticed in the shop-windows a little flower-vase of 'biscuit' or Parian ware, in the shape of a human hand modelled, *au naturel*, holding a narrow cup. A more commonplace and silly notion of a vase can scarcely be imagined, and yet so delighted were the public with this new conceit that it sold everywhere by hundreds. In one establishment alone twelve men were constantly employed in producing relays of this article. I suppose by this time everybody had discovered that his neighbour has bought it, and all pronounce it commonplace.

*   *   *

ALTHOUGH Parian in one form or another probably attracted the most attention during the mid-19th century, wares of traditional type continued to be made throughout the period. The two leading firms, Minton's and Copeland's, vied with each other in the magnificence of their displays at the Great Exhibition, and each occupied about a page-and-a-half of the catalogue. As all nations were represented at the Exhibition rivalry was

intense, and each manufacturer tried to outdo the other in providing a suitably splendid array. More often than not, this resulted in the showing of goods that reflected more on the technical skill than on the good taste of the exhibitor.

Thus, the pieces made for the 1851 Exhibition and the numerous successors to it are seldom truly representative of what might have been found in shops and homes at the time. They serve to show, however, the high quality of craftsmanship available, and were responsible for raising and maintaining standards in many branches of manufacture.

The catalogue of the Great Exhibition carefully lists the various pieces shown, and although it is not always possible to make positive identifications from some of the entries it is not difficult to discern what many of them looked like. Woodcuts

and engravings of the time also assist, and the publication of factory records is enabling attributions to be made with increasing certainty. Additional impetus has been given by the Victoria and Albert Museum, where displays of furniture, china, glass and silver of the Victorian era have evoked considerable interest.

A proportion of the Minton stand was occupied by vases and other articles in the Sèvres style. Most of them were painted with panels of flowers reserved on coloured grounds, typical examples being the following:

Vases, a pair, bleu de roi, and a pair Sèvres green: the grounds, with painted flowers, and raised festoons, gilt.

Pair of vases, turquoise and painted wreaths of flowers, with festoons of oak, laurel, &c., gilt.

Pair of beaded vases, with a turquoise ground, painted pink, Cupids in compartments, and gilt.

The copying of the products of the French factory was partly due to the current fashion for old Sèvres porcelain, which was then beginning to realise high prices. Partly, also, the factory had regained some of its former eminence under the direction of Alexandre Brongniart, and this focused an international interest on its wares, both past and present. Following the political troubles of France that led to the disorders of 1848, numbers of skilled craftsmen left the country for England. They included Arnoux, who had studied at Sèvres and became Art Director at

Above, Fig. 339: Cups made by Copeland and Garrett and exhibited in 1851. (From woodcuts.)

Mintons, and a number of painters. All these men must undoubtedly have assisted in re-creating Sèvres styles in their new homeland, and had a considerable influence on ceramic design.

The Coalport factory did not rely on Frenchmen for its Sèvres imitations, which were frequently so good that one of them, bearing a forged mark, was illustrated in colour as a genuine piece in a book on French porcelain published in 1905. The principal painter employed was John Randall, who had been trained by his uncle. The latter had acquired a convincing Sèvres-style from his practice in re-decorating 18th century Sèvres ware bearing restrained painting which retarded its sale. He added panels of Watteau figures, birds or flowers and surrounded them with rich coloured and gilt borders in the taste of the time.

Flowers, either painted or modelled in the round, had featured on many of the vases made in England from the beginnings of porcelain manufacture. From about 1830 they were modelled to entwine all kinds of

articles, and vases, inkstands, thermometers (Fig. 337) and, more appropriately, pot-pourri jars were covered profusely with them. On the products of the better factories they were carefully made and coloured, but on cheaper wares they have little realism, small decorative value and are only ugly dust-traps.

Teawares continued to be made in all qualities. In contrast to those of 18th century date, the pots were much larger in size and after fashionably being of oval shape in about 1800-20 they returned to a globular form. At the same time, *circa* 1835, they began to be raised on short legs, and were given moulded ornament similar to that found on silver examples of the time. Cups also changed, and by the time Victoria ascended the throne they were being made

Right, *Fig. 343: Vase painted with a scene showing Anna Maria Hall being crowned Rose Queen of Salency. Mrs. Hall (née Fielding) (1800–81) was a novelist and the wife of S. C. Hall, who edited the* Art Journal *from 1839 to 1880. Chamberlain's Worcester, circa 1840–45. Height, 18⅜ inches. (Victoria and Albert Museum.)*

Below, *Fig. 342: Small tray with a pierced border, the centre panel painted in magenta and reserved on a green and gold ground, after an 18th century Sèvres example. Perhaps Coalport, circa 1850. 4¼ inches square.*

374

shallower and wider in shape; a thoroughly misconceived alteration which allowed the tea to chill quickly and destroyed a virtue of 'the cup that cheers'. A further change in taste caused many cups to be painted on the inside, rather than outside as hitherto, and their handles were often of such complex pattern as to make them difficult to hold. By 1851 (Fig. 339) more practical shapes had returned to favour.

Figures and groups in ordinary porcelain, as opposed to parian, were not plentiful in number between 1830 and 1850. Many were adaptations of 19th century specimens, but among the original models were some of prominent actors and actresses. They included the comedian John Liston as 'Paul Pry' and in other roles, and the singer-actress-manageress Madame Vestris (Elizabeth Mathews, née Bartolozzi, grand-daughter of the famous engraver) in 'Buy a Broom'.

Even more popular at the time were small-sized figures of dogs, with affection divided between greyhounds and poodles. The latter were depicted in many poses, from seated and begging to standing and holding a bone or a basket of flowers. While some were made at Mintons, the

Fig. 345: Vase painted with flowers in colours by C. F. Hürten, who was born in Cologne and worked at Sèvres before coming to England. Copeland, circa *1860. Height, 54 inches.*
(Victoria and Albert Museum.)

majority of them can seldom be attributed to a particular factory.

The range of animals was extended in the case of Worcester. There, the Chamberlain establishment made not only a variety of dogs but also cats and mice. Each was usually modelled on a coloured cushion, and bears the name of the factory neatly written under the base. From the same source came a set of five figures of Tyroleans in their native costume: models of the Rainer family of four men and a girl who were popular Austrian entertainers. They were first made in about 1830, and other figures of the same date, and from Worcester, include milk-maids wearing yokes from which hang milk-pails.

In 1840 the original firm, then Flight, Barr & Barr, came into the ownership of the one-time breakaway Chamberlain's, and as Chamberlain & Co., they exhibited in 1851. Their display was not a large one and included 'china slabs' and vases painted with local views, and such trivialities as 'China bracelets and brooches; China mortice door-furniture'. In the same year, affairs having obviously reached a low ebb, two new partners took charge: W. H. Kerr and R. W. Binns. The former managed the commercial side of the business, and the latter assumed the title of Art Director.

Two years later, the 1853 Dublin Exhibition gave the newly-invigorated concern an opportunity to show its prowess, and the 'Shakespeare Service' was displayed. It was a dessert set for twenty-four persons, incorporating in its modelling a number of figures from the plays designed by an Irish sculptor, William Boynton Kirk. From this start the firm began to prosper and quickly regained a prominent position.

At the same time as the many concerns in the Potteries and elsewhere were actively producing quantities of everyday ware that suited the tastes of their customers and sold well, there was a movement afoot to improve design. The Society of Arts (now The Royal Society of Arts) had from 1843 enjoyed the privilege of having the Prince Consort, Queen Victoria's husband, as its President, and he quickly made apparent his keen interest in the objects of the body. The Society's secretary was a friend of Henry Cole, then employed in the Public Record Office, whose outlook and energy differed little from those of the Prince. When the Society offered prizes for 'a tea service and beer jugs for common use', Cole, using the pseudonym Felix Summerly was one of the winners.

Early in 1847 Summerly Art Manufactures was launched, and Cole invited

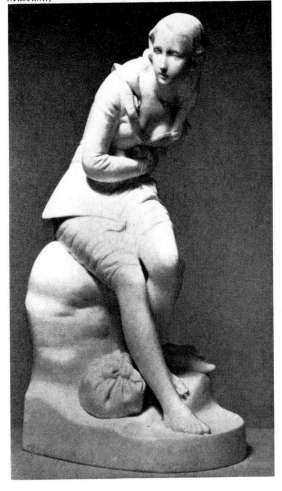

selected artists and sculptors to submit designs for pottery, porcelain, silver and glass. If judged artistically praiseworthy they were passed on to manufacturers, who paid Cole a royalty in return for the publicity he gave the scheme. As he had become secretary of the Society of Arts he was in an excellent position to carry out his part of the bargain, and saw to it that, among other benefits, examples of the chosen goods were prominent in the annual display organised by the Society.

The Summerly goods included a pottery teaset and various items made of ordinary porcelain as well as of Parian. Of the latter a figure of 'Dorothea', from *Don Quixote*, shown ineffectually disguised as a boy by wearing an eye-catching low-cut jacket, proved highly popular with buyers (Fig. 346), and was alleged to have been the only one of the articles to show a profit to the maker. As was much of the other pottery and porcelain, it was made by Mintons, with whose director, Herbert Minton, Cole had been friendly for some years.

The project did not endure long. The various manufacturers, who had the costly task of translating ideas into fact, grew tired of promise and required profit that was too seldom forthcoming. In addition, Henry Cole became closely involved in the organisation of the Great Exhibition, and in 1849 Summerly's Art Manufactures came to an end.

24 19th Century Porcelain: Part 3

THE Great Exhibition of 1851, held in Hyde Park, London, succeeded the small but successful Society of Arts exhibitions of modern manufactures which took place from 1847. The same two men were the moving spirits behind both: the Prince Consort and Henry Cole. The 1851 display was on a vastly bigger scale than anything seen before, and while modelled on the French Quinquennial Exhibition of 1849 it differed from it by inviting exhibitors from all the nations of the world.

Cole went to Paris to see what he could learn there, and on his return reported his findings to the Prince. He recorded a conversation he had had at Buckingham Palace in June 1849 in the following words:

> I asked the Prince if he had considered the Exhibition should be a National or an International Exhibition. The French had discussed if their own Exhibition should be International, and had preferred that it should be National only. The Prince reflected for a minute, and then said, 'It must embrace foreign productions,' to use his words, and added emphatically, 'International, certainly.'

Once the scope of the project was decided it was necessary to pick a suitable site, and after rejecting Leicester Square as being too small agreement was reached on Hyde Park. The entire scheme was then

Below, *Fig. 347: Part of the rim of a plate from the dessert service made for Queen Victoria in 1861, the painting on a turquoise ground by Thomas Bott. Worcester. (Dyson Perrins Museum, Worcester.)*

Above, *Fig. 348: Vase in the form of a mermaid holding aloft a nautilus shell. 'Raphaelesque Ware', Worcester, circa 1870. Height, 15 inches. (Dyson Perrins Museum, Worcester.)*

Opposite, *Fig. 349: Vase, one of a pair, showing the making of pottery, the figures simulating carved ivory on an imitation lacquer ground. Designed by James Hadley, Worcester, circa 1872. Height, 10¼ inches. (Victoria and Albert Museum.)*

lifted from the shoulders of the Society of Arts and the burden elevated to the care of a Royal Commission under the chairmanship of Prince Albert. Active opposition and innumerable obstacles were encountered and overcome, and on the 1st of May 1851 the *Great Exhibition of the Works of Industry of All Nations*, as it was named, was opened by Queen Victoria. She noted in her Journal:

> This day is one of the greatest and most glorious days of our lives, with which to my pride and joy, the name of my dearly beloved Albert is for ever associated! . . . God bless my dearest Albert, and my dear Country, which has shown itself so great to-day.

The exhibition was open to the public for a total of 144 days (it was closed on Sundays) until the 11th October, and after being visited on the 13th and 14th of the month by exhibitors and their friends closed finally and with due ceremony on the 15th. During that time the number of visitors was 6,039,195, with a peak attendance on 7th October, when the admission charge, as on 79 other days, was one shilling. The enterprise left the Commissioners with a profit of about £186,000.

Using the money in hand, plus a loan which was repaid, the Commissioners bought 87 acres of land in South Kensington. On part of it, in due course, arose the museums that stand there, and not the least important of them is the Victoria and Albert, which was opened in its present form in 1909. The museum was started in 1851, when the Board of Trade was allowed by the Treasury the sum of £5,000 'for the purchase of such examples of manufacture, shown in the Exhibition, as it might seem desirable to acquire for purposes of study'.

Together with articles loaned by the Queen and her subjects, the purchases were displayed at Marlborough House, Pall Mall. With the dispersal of the big collection of works of art formed by Ralph Bernal, of which the auction sale occupied 32 days during 1855, an opportunity arose to greatly

increase the size of what was then called
the Museum of Ornamental Art, and many
purchases were made. From its opening
in 1853 until 1873, the museum was under
the control of Henry Cole, who was
knighted in 1875.

Since then, large and small gifts and
bequests have enabled the Victoria and
Albert Museum to attain a position of
eminence. In ceramics its most fruitful
year was 1885, when Lady Charlotte
Schreiber gave her fine and extensive
collection of English pottery and porcelain;
a collection which, together with enamels,
glass and other objects, numbers nearly
2,000 items. A further large acquisition
was in 1901, when the important collection
built up since about 1835 was transferred
from the Museum of Practical Geology, in
Jermyn Street, to South Kensington. Subsequently, gifts, bequests and purchases
have made the array of English wares the
most comprehensive to be seen anywhere.

The interest in design and craftsmanship
aroused by the Exhibition quickly spread
throughout the country, and led to the
founding of colleges of art as well as
museums. In turn, these began to affect the

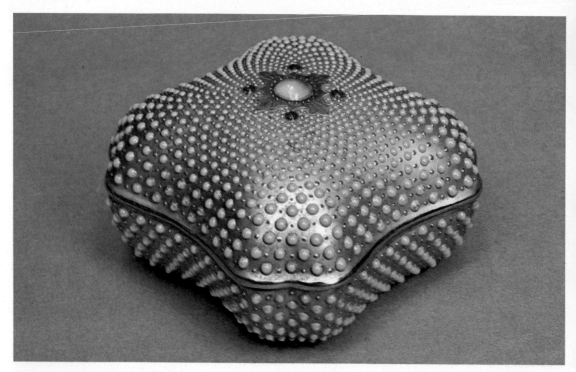

Plate 55 *Box and cover with 'jewelled' ornament. Marked COALPORT A.D. 1750. Circa 1880. 3 inches square. (City Museum and Art Gallery, Plymouth.)*

Plate 56 *Cup and saucer with printed and painted decoration commemorating the Jubilee of Queen Victoria, 1887. Diameter of saucer, 5⅜ inches. (City Museum and Art Gallery, Plymouth.)*

Fig. 352: Bowl from a dessert service made for the Prince of Wales in 1866. Copeland. (From a woodcut.)

manufacture of all kinds of objects, including those of porcelain. The availability of specimens made in different countries and in many periods encouraged makers to imitate and improve upon the work of past centuries, and evidence of this is seen in much of the ceramic output of the second half of the century.

* * *

ONE of the first effects of studying old works of art is seen in wares made by Kerr and Binns at Worcester. There, Thomas Bott, who joined the firm in 1853, carefully reproduced in porcelain the enamelled copper for which Limoges had been renowned in the Renaissance. It gained the artist and the factory high praise, and it was reported that:

In 1854 Mr. Binns obtained permission to exhibit specimens of his new invention to his royal highness [*Prince Albert*], whose commendations were most emphatically and unhesitatingly expressed, and he at once purchased all the examples which had been shown him, saying they were the best things he had seen. Her Majesty subsequently ordered some specimens of this work, which was all on dark blue ground; and latterly an order for a magnificent dessert service, in the same style of work, on a turquoise ground, has been ordered by her Majesty (Fig. 347).

Items from the Royal collection and from others were loaned to Worcester, and the Prince is supposed to have advised, sagely:

> Let your artists study the works of the Old Masters, and, when they have become imbued with their spirit, let them design for themselves.

The advice was taken occasionally at Worcester and elsewhere, but often such 'designing' took the form of distorting the original.

Thus, the so-called 'Raphaelesque Ware' was modelled in low relief in the manner of 18th century Doccia porcelain, which was then thought to have originated at Capodimonte, with subjects copied from 15th and 16th century tin-glazed earthenware. The latter, Italian majolica, was known at the time as Raphael ware, and its name was borrowed for the newly-introduced version (Fig. 348). The mixture of styles and periods was applied with undoubted sincerity, but the result was laboured and the various factors seldom blend satisfactorily.

From the making of parian in imitation of Paros marble, it was a short and perhaps inevitable step to devising a body closely resembling ivory. It was first done at about the date that the firm suffered another, but more enduring, change of name, and became the Worcester Royal Porcelain Company. This took place in 1862, and the various marks used from then onwards incorporate in them a crown.

The ivory porcelain became popular after it had been exhibited in 1871 in the newly-fashionable Japanese style. The sequel to the opening of the ports of Hiogo and Osaka following international negotiations at gun-point in 1865, was a flow of goods to Europe. They were received with wonder at the technical accomplishment of their makers, and with a variety of emotions at their design and ornamentation. The enthusiasm of French artists and critics, which pre-dated 1865, was soon emulated in London, and from Degas and Manet

Above, *Fig. 353: Flower vase, copying a Sèvres* jardinière à éventail, *decorated in* pâte-sur-pâte *by Marc-Louis Solon. Minton, circa 1890. Height, 6¼ inches. (Victoria and Albert Museum.)* **Right, above,** *Fig. 354: Part of a dessert service painted with flowers in colours within a turquoise-blue border. Minton, 1863, pattern A6306. (Sotheby's.)* **Right, below,** *Fig. 355: Teapot decorated with a 'Japan' pattern in red, blue and gold. Derby, circa 1880. Height, 3 inches. (City Museum and Art Gallery, Plymouth.)*

crossed the Channel to be adopted by the discriminating. Notably, by the American-born painter, James McNeill Whistler.

The principal modeller employed at Worcester on the Japanese-style wares was James Hadley, and while occasionally he simulated carved ivory, he also made imitations of lacquer (Fig. 349). The result of this was often a complex double copying, because the lacquer itself was imitating the surface of wood or metal. The close likeness of the porcelain to ivory and lacquer was admired at the time,

although a writer in the *Art Journal* in 1872 noted:

> It should perhaps be stressed that these Japanese wares were not imitative in the sense that they were copies of original pieces . . . [*Binns*] has seen and appreciated the value of Japanese art and . . . he has improved where he has borrowed, taking suggestion rather than models.

Another example of the ware is the vase shown in Fig. 351. The 'carved ivory' brush pot or spill vase is modelled with a mountainous landscape, rather more Chinese in origin than Japanese, represented as being mounted on a stand formed as tree trunks in bronze. The whole is surmounted by a European-looking pierced gallery that brings the piece back from somewhere in the Far East to mid-19th century England.

Pierced work proved highly attractive to many buyers at the time, who admired it when it covered the entire surface of vases, tea sets and other pieces, all of which resemble carved honeycombs. While they testify to the skill and patience of the craftsmen responsible for their execution, it is to be regretted that so much time was not put to better use and that porcelain

Above, *Fig. 356: Vases in Sèvres style. Coalport, circa 1875. (From a woodcut.)* **Right,** *Fig. 357: Teapot, a man on one side and a woman on the other, inscribed underneath the base:* 'Fearful consequences through the law of natural selection and evolution in living up to one's teapot', *paraphrasing an epigram by Oscar Wilde. Worcester, circa 1880. Height, 6 inches. (Dyson Perrins Museum.)*

was treated so unsuitably. Several factories made wares of this kind, among them Grainger & Co., of Worcester, founded in 1800, which was absorbed by the Royal Porcelain Company, of the same city, in 1889.

Other manufactories were also active in bringing forward new processes and styles. At Mintons Marc-Louis Solon, who had been employed at Sèvres but came to England with some of his compatriots, was responsible for introducing and specialising in the *pâte-sur-pâte* process. It had been developed in France from studying a Chinese vase 'which showed a design of flowers and foliage of white paste heavily embossed on a white ground'.

Instead of 'sprigging' in the manner employed by Josiah Wedgwood with his jasperware cameos, Solon built up his decoration by painting it in successive coatings of slip: clay thinned with water. This meant that each example was unique, and the purchase price accordingly high. The work was finished in the same manner as sculpture, and in 1901 Solon wrote:

> By means of sharp iron tools the substance is scraped, smoothed, incised, forms are softly modelled, details neatly defined, outlines made rigorously precise.

Finally, the piece was fired, glazed and re-fired, although the decorator himself regretted that some specimens were not left in the biscuit state. The ware was given a high gloss over the delicately contrived white embellishments, which are often cupids or mythological gods and godesses, on a dark-coloured ground (Fig. 353).

Solon remained with Mintons from 1870 until he retired in 1904, and was renowned not only for his work in *pâte-sur-pâte* but for his serious interest in old English pottery; his collection was sold by auction at Hanley in November 1912. While at Mintons he trained some apprentices, of

Left, *Fig. 358: Bust of Llewellynn Jewitt (1816–1886), ceramic historian, in parian porcelain. Goss, circa 1870.*

Right, *Fig. 359: Bust of Robert Southey (1774–1843) inscribed at the back 'From the drawing by Hancock, 1796'. (The drawing by Robert Hancock is now in the National Portrait Gallery, London.) Marked* W. H. GOSS, *printed and impressed.* Circa *1880. Height, 7 inches.*

whom a few left the firm to work in his style elsewhere.

While considerable publicity was, and still is, given to Solon's pieces, Mintons continued to produce good quality porcelain of traditional types. Among them were vases and other pieces in imitation of 18th century Sèvres, which continued to be no less fashionable than it had been in previous decades. Jewitt, whose judgment of contemporaneous productions was both enthusiastic and uniformly favourable, wrote in 1878 that:

> Whatever emanates from their factory, indeed, may safely be pronounced to be perfect and unsurpassed, both in design, in manipulation, in body, in glaze, and in colouring.

Sèvres was imitated also at Derby, where following the closing of the old Bloor factory a new one was opened in King Street by a group of the original employees. They used a version of the old 'crown and baton' mark (see page 361, Fig. 329, left) with the initials of the owners, Stevenson and Hancock, and then of the latter (Sampson Hancock), at either side. Another company was established in Osmaston Road in 1876, and in 1890 was allowed to call itself the Royal Crown Derby Porcelain Company. Finally, in 1935 the latter firm acquired the King Street concern.

The factory reproduced some of the eighteenth century models, and according to John Haslem, who wrote in 1876:

> .. some have, at sales of old Derby China, realised considerable prices, under the impression that they were genuine 'old Derby'.

According to another and later writer, they made some sets of original figures in the 1880's, were noted for the richness of their gilding, and for their 'fish and game plates, of which wealthy Americans are the largest purchasers'.

Although all the factories of importance supplied the public with imitations of 18th

century Sèvres, the most consistent and successful was the Coalport establishment in Shropshire (see page 360). One of the earliest to cater for the demand for this sterile application of craftsmanship, they consistently produced good copies of the French wares. From time to time, they also imitated Chelsea gold anchor and earlier pieces, and were not always careful to affix their mark to them.

From 1875 onwards the firm sometimes marked its products with the legend *COALPORT A.D. 1750*. It has led many people to believe that the date denotes the year when the piece bearing it was made. Since 1939, however, the practice, which has deceived many thousands of innocent owners into thinking they possessed antiques of rarity and value, has been dropped.

Among the numerous smaller factories active in the second half of the century was that of William Henry Goss, at Stoke-on-Trent. It was opened in 1858, and made both parian (Fig. 358), and ivory-tinted porcelain. Portrait busts were modelled by W. W. Gallimore who, prior to working for Goss lost his right arm in an accident with a gun. Jewitt noted:

> His modelling has, therefore, ever since then, been entirely done by his left hand, and strange as it may seem is far better than when he had both.

A comment that probably expressed the truth, but might surely have been phrased with greater delicacy.

W. H. Goss also made a variety of small articles, including:

> floral jewellery and dress ornaments, in which brooches, hair-pins, scent-diffusers, crosses and other beautiful articles are made: jewelled porcelain, in which vases, scent-bottles, tazzae, and other ornaments are produced; and vessels to be filled with perfumes, including illuminated scent-vases, pomade-boxes, rice-powder jars, pastil and scent ribbon burners, &c., these latter being made largely for the great Paris and London perfume-houses.

Experiments made at Worcester with

Above, *Fig. 360: Centrepiece of a dessert service made for the Prince of Wales. Belleek, Ireland,* circa *1868.*
(*From a woodcut.*)

clay found in county Fermanagh, Ireland, led to the starting there, at Belleek, of a china works in 1863. Within a decade the hands employed numbered two hundred, and the output was on a corresponding scale. Figures and groups of parian porcelain were made, but the best-known pieces were tablewares modelled with seashells, coral and other marine growths. The distinguishing features of the ware are its thin potting and nacreous glaze.

At the time this was described rapturously as being 'so irridescent as to have almost an unearthly appearance of liquid beauty'. C. L. Eastlake thought otherwise, and at about the same date wrote:

> The thick highly lustrous glaze which covers almost all modern crockery is much to be deplored. The worst instance of its use may be noticed in what is called 'Irish porcelain'—a detestable ware of recent invention, which glistens like wet barley sugar.

The centrepiece of a dessert service, made in about 1870 for the Prince of Wales, shown in Fig. 360 is a typical example. The jardinière (below) dates from about 25 years later, and bears the printed mark which includes the country of origin. The latter denoting that it was produced after 1891.

Fig. 361: Jardinière modelled with flowers and birds. Marked BELLEEK CO. FERMANAGH IRELAND. *Circa 1895. Height, 8 inches.*

INDEX

Numerals in ordinary type refer to page numbers; *italic* numerals refer to monotone illustrations, and numerals in **bold** type to colour plates. Certain general terms are indexed under their first mention.